179

WAYS TO
SAVE
A NOVEL

MATTERS OF
VITAL CONCERN TO
FICTION WRITERS

PETER SELGIN

WD
WRITER'S DIGEST
BOOKS

WritersDigest.*com*
Cincinnati, Ohio

For more resources for writers, visit www.writersdigest.com/books.

To receive a free weekly e-mail newsletter delivering tips and updates about writing and about Writer's Digest products, register directly at http://newsletters.fwpublications.com.

14 13 12 11 10   5 4 3 2 1

Distributed in Canada by Fraser Direct, 100 Armstrong Avenue, Georgetown, Ontario, Canada L7G 5S4, Tel: (905) 877-4411. Distributed in the U.K. and Europe by David & Charles, Brunel House, Newton Abbot, Devon, TQ12 4PU, England, Tel: (+44) 1626-323200, Fax: (+44) 1626-323319, E-mail: postmaster@davidandcharles.co.uk. Distributed in Australia by Capricorn Link, P.O. Box 704, Windsor, NSW 2756 Australia, Tel: (02) 4577-3555.

Library of Congress Cataloging-in-Publication Data

Selgin, Peter.

179 ways to save a novel : matters of vital concern to fiction writers / by Peter Selgin. -- 1st ed.

   p. cm.

Includes index.

ISBN 978-1-58297-607-5 (alk. paper)

1. Fiction--Technique. 2. Fiction--Authorship. I. Title.

PN3365.S45 2010

  808.3--dc22

2009053137

Edited by Scott Francis
Designed by Claudean Wheeler
Cover illustration by MG & co/ iStockphoto
Production coordinated by Mark Griffin

Dedication

"To Walter Cummins.
And to my students, especially
those who argue with me."

ABOUT THE AUTHOR

Peter Selgin is the author of *Drowning Lessons*, the Flannery O'Connor Award-winning story collection, and *Life Goes to the Movies*, a novel. His work has appeared in dozens of publications, including *Ploughshares* and *Best American Essays*. He is also the author of *By Cunning & Craft: Sound Advice and Practical Wisdom for Fiction Writers*. He edits *Alimentum: The Literature of Food* and leads an annual writing workshop in Italy. Visit the author's website: www.peterselgin.com

Table of Contents

Matters of Symbol, Myth, & Metaphor

Matters of Style

Matters of Soul

Other Matters

Introduction

Why learn from our own *mistakes when we can learn from those of others?* That, essentially, is the premise of this book. No artist should ever be ashamed to make mistakes. The only thing to be ashamed of is not learning from them.

Here, then, are 179 meditations inspired by works-in-progress—interesting works that have one thing in common: There's something *wrong* with them. These meditations collate and condense the advice of over a thousand critiques that I've given in my years as an editor and a teacher of works by well-published writers as well as beginners. Through their mistakes we all stand to learn.

The meditations are grouped under six headings: Substance; Structure; Symbol, Myth & Metaphor; Style; Soul; and Other Matters. You may enjoy dipping into the book at random when in need of nonspecific advice, inspiration, or criticism. In that case I hope reading it will feel something like sitting down at your favorite tapas bar and letting the waiter serve you at his whim and pleasure.

Or read the book straight through, since both sections and individual meditations are also arranged to play off and enhance each other.

However you encounter them, these meditations aren't intended to add up to a how-to book. Their purpose is to challenge, to inspire, to provoke—and occasionally to tickle or annoy—but mainly to awaken a deeper awareness of the fiction writer's many challenges and thorny choices.

Finally, this book isn't just for writers. It's for readers of novels and stories who want to deepen their understanding and appreciation of the fiction writer's craft and art.

Matters of
Substance

An Artist Chooses

I read them all the time, as an editor and as a teacher. Stories of characters whose lives never move beyond their status quo, where scenes vanish before my eyes, where the point of view is either nonexistent or as slippery as a greased tadpole, fictional stories that should be memoirs, and memoirs that should be stories—not to mention stories so fundamentally clichéd they might best not have been written in the first place.

Nearly all of an artist's challenges come down to choices. Until an artist limits her choices, nothing close to art will happen.

"*Everything*," said Antonin Artaud, "is the enemy of art."

The antidote to "everything" is making, and standing by, one's choices.

1 } INVESTING IN IMAGINATION: HOW TO DIVE OFF A CLIFF

In making choices, we take risks; we invest heavily and whole-heartedly in our own imagination, and hope and pray that our investment pays off.

And we should make our choices fearlessly. To make art is to take a running dive off a high cliff.

But fearlessness in the absence of technique is a recipe for disappointment if not for disaster. Any one of our brave choices may determine whether we end up with a masterpiece or an "experiment."

Not that experimentation is bad. As John Cheever told *The Paris Review,* "Fiction *is* experimentation; when it ceases to be that, it ceases to be fiction. One never puts down a sentence without the feeling that it has never been put down before in such a way, and that perhaps even the substance of the sentence has never been felt.

Every sentence is an innovation." When our experiments succeed, they cease being experiments and become works of art.

2 } ON CHOOSING WELL: PLAUSIBLE, UNIQUE, ORGANIC, AUTHENTIC, SIFTED, & SORTED

Spinoza said, "All happiness or unhappiness solely depends upon the quality of the objects to which we are attached by love."

As writers our happiness—or grief—depends largely on choosing the *right things to write about.*

Any idea, situation, or character can serve as raw material. But for that material to work as fiction it has to pass certain tests.

For a start, our situations should be *plausible*: not necessarily by the standards of our everyday lives, or even of life anywhere in the known universe, but in the context of the world that each story generates for itself, from its first words. "One morning Gregor Samsa awoke from a restless dream to find himself transformed into a giant beetle." In the world generated by these words—the opening of Kafka's *The Metamorphosis*—men awaken from restless dreams to find themselves turned into monstrous insects. In this one sentence, Kafka establishes his world—one that parallels (however strangely) our own, and in which such events are plausible.

A story—of any length, including a novel—must present us with *unique events,* and not mere routines. Had Gregor Samsa been a giant beetle his whole life, there would be no story, no "metamorphosis." The story's first sentence prevents this: We enter the story at the moment when the transformation has taken place. That event *makes* it a story.

Next, a story should be *authentic*. It should be made of stuff that—if not entirely original—hasn't been appropriated from other forms of narrative art, from other stories or from movies or television. Or, if it has, it should be sufficiently reprocessed through the author's unique sensibilities so the resulting work has its own authenticity.[1]

A story should generate its own actions and emotions *organically*. Any supplied artificially result in *sentimentality* or *melodrama* and subvert or destroy authenticity (see Meditations # 28–37). Similarly, characters constructed as heroes or villains or other preordained "types" will undermine a story's authority.

Finally, our material should be *sifted and sorted* to serve the story being told. Any detail or fact that doesn't serve our stories or their themes will likely detract from their effectiveness.

Characters: Heroes, Villains, & Victims

3 } THE LIGHTS ARE ON, BUT NOBODY'S HOME: FICTION'S ONLY SUBJECT

Good fiction—as Henry Ford might have put it[2]—can have any subject, so long as that subject is *people*.

A student submits the first pages of a six-hundred-plus-page novel on which he has spent the past five years. The novel is based on a highly complex computer game at which the author is expert, and the "action" consists of the two main characters, Quest and Mortimer, facing off from adjacent computer terminals, locked in a battle of cyber-wits.

The entire six-hundred-plus-page opus is, in a word, static.

---

1 Thus no less a writer than Shakespeare is said to have derived at least the cruder elements of his *Hamlet* (1599) from *The Spanish Tragedy* (1582–1592), by Thomas Kyd.

2 "People can have the Model T in any colour, so long as it's black."—Henry Ford.

In this case, the author's passion for computer games has blinkered him to the fact that not everyone is engaged in that world, and those who are would rather *play* computer games than read a novel about them. The author's blind love for his subject made it impossible for him to see its inadequacy as a subject for fiction.

Another student writes a different kind of war story, one in which the characters are engaged in literal combat.

> The entire Second Mechanized Corps climbed into their cockpits, strapped themselves tight and flipped ignition switches. The wide range of Archons, from the light, fifteen-ton Corsair Renaissance Archon to the thirty-ton Berserker Artillery Archon, made their way to the docking bays of the Albatross Titan Military Dropships. Deployment crews attached the Archons to the deployment clamps of the Albatrosses, checking the drop mechanism and retro-boosters. ...The pilots gave the thumbs-up to the crewmen and hung tight to their controls as front hatches sealed themselves shut.

This war takes place several hundred years in the future and is therefore wholly fictional, but that doesn't matter. It could be World War II or the Civil War or the War of the Roses; its battles and skirmishes could be rendered as vividly as any in Tolstoy; it could be the most detailed and authentic document yet produced on the subject of war.

But as fiction it would lie dead on the page. There are no *people* in it: not people of flesh and blood and bones; not people with thoughts and feelings; not people of wit or cunning or cowardice, who suffer or worry or laugh or cower or cry.

Fiction succeeds only when it confronts us with—or better yet, *immerses us in*—the experiences of seemingly real human beings.

Beginning writers don't always understand this. They think because they give their characters names and dialogue that they've created characters. They write stories about war instead of stories about men *at* war.

The first thing to realize when choosing a subject for fiction is this: that, really, you *have* no choice. You have to write about people.

4 } CENSURING CHARLIE: AUTHOR AS HANGING JUDGE & JURY

Now that we've decided—as we must—that our subect will be people, we must decide which people to write about.

Unless we are writing satire, the characters whose situations we choose to narrate should be characters we feel some sympathy or empathy for. At least we should try to empathize with them, and leave judgments to our readers.

One of my students writes a story about Charlie, the worst kind of womanizer. We know he's terrible because the author tells us so:

> Charlie Maxwell loved women, oh he loved them so: he loved their long legs and their firm breasts and their behinds: he especially loved their behinds, the pear-shaped kind, especially. Good ol' Charlie: he could never get enough of a pear-shaped behind, or what the French, who know about these things, call a *derriere poire.* . . .

When we set out to judge—to ridicule, pillory, condemn, sneer at, or otherwise impugn our characters—we fail at our objective. Instead of making our characters look bad, we make *ourselves* suspect.

Now, it may well be that Charlie Maxwell loves women, and that in particular he loves their nether regions, specifically those that put him in mind of certain fleshy fruits. It's not the content of this passage that's judgmental, but its tone. That *oh he loved them so* drips sarcasm. Would Charlie himself think those five words?

You may object that it's not Charlie saying or thinking these things about himself, but the narrator. But either the tone of the passage is that of an objective omniscient narrator (and it is anything but objective), or it expresses, via *close third person* (or what James Woods calls "free indirect style"), the character's own thoughts—which, as we've established, isn't credible.

That leaves one possibility: that the author has injected her own viewpoint. What we get here in place of *actions* is the author's judgment of Charlie's behavior, as conveyed by the tone of the omniscient, though hardly objective, narrator.

To test my conclusion, I asked the author to read the above passage out loud. When she did, she accented the "oh" and the "so"—the very words that convey the most irony, confirming my suspicions. After she had finished, I remarked that she didn't seem to like Charlie very much.

"That's just the point," my student replied.

"You meant to get him good, did you?"

"I did," she said, proudly.

"Well," I said, "you may have given it to Charlie, but in the process you've bitten the nose off your story."

"What do you mean?"

"I mean you've flattened it as fiction and turned it into a polemic against such 'types' as Charlie Maxwell. Through your tone you say to us, 'Look at this Charlie guy. Isn't he a jerk?' And we look and see a man on whom you've pasted a big sign saying JERK, as opposed to a man whose actions render him a jerk. We're more aware of the sign than of the man and his actions."

My student responded, "But that's how I *feel* about this person."

"Then maybe you shouldn't write about him."

"Are you saying I should only write about characters that I like?"

"I'm saying you should only write about characters whose viewpoints you're willing to try on for size, that you're willing to understand at least to where you begin to see what motivates them. If there's no willingness to understand, then you stand to learn nothing about this character that you don't already think you know. And your reader isn't bound to learn much either, other than your opinion, which is obvious within less than a paragraph."

Though an omniscient narrator may—should, *must*—have feelings about the people whose situations he narrates, and though those feelings may come wrapped in irony or sarcasm, still, they should allow room for sympathy, or at least for some degree of understanding. If, on the other hand, the author (and his omniscient narrator) has already determined that a character is not only flawed but reprehensible, then we get, not a portrait, but a poster bearing the word MISOGYNIST (or BIGOT or AIRHEAD or NUTCASE) in big, fat letters.

In passing judgment on our characters, no matter how gently, subtly, or slyly, we rob the reader of the chance to form her own set of judgments. And the reader may not want to judge our characters; she may simply want to experience them as they go about their lives. And who are we, after all, to pass judgments on Emma Bovary, Don Quixote, Huck Finn, or Ahab?

Whether as writers or as readers, to encounter characters in fiction is to take a step toward understanding them, however little they remind us of ourselves.

5 | LOVEABLE LOSERS: MORT THE SCHLEMIEL

Judgments needn't be harsh or condemnatory. Just as often, beginning writers go out of their way to depict their characters as sympathetic—or merely pathetic. They do so usually not through tone (which in amateur works typically veers toward sarcasm, as if that were the only seasoning in the tonal spice rack), but through authorial manipulation of a character's actions, i.e., by tampering with the evidence.

Then there are those stories where the deck is stacked against a character to render him doltish, lacking common sense or sound judgment: in a word, a *schlemiel*.

Take Mort, a lonely geek who can't get himself a girl—or a life, for that matter. A Professor of Behavioral Science at a large Midwestern coeducational university, Mort knows no women who are eligible and attractive, or find him so. One evening, having dined alone as always, Mort wanders the streets of the town until he drifts into a homosexual bar—not just any homosexual bar, but a notorious (author's word) gay nightclub, where he endures one cruelly embarrassing situation after another.

This scene, so indicative of Mort's entire existence, down to his Izod shirt with the iron-burn, has been trumped up by his creator to make us feel sorry for and laugh at him. That Mort lacks social skills I have no trouble believing. I'm even willing to buy that he goes into a gay club—not by accident, but by choice, out of loneliness. But having a "notorious gay nightclub" materialize in his path just so that he may drift into it—that's stacking the deck.

To writers who find themselves with a Mort or two on their hands, I say, cut your character some slack.

Because novels[3] are long and make substantial demands on a reader's investment of time and attention, it's especially important for them to offer at least one character—a hero or a heroine—that readers can identify with.

And when the deck is clearly stacked against a protagonist, when an author's own prejudices toward his creation mar, twist, or otherwise distort our view, then as readers, unless we happen to share those prejudices and read for the pleasure of having them substantiated, we are understandably reluctant to make that investment.

---

3 Unlike the short story, the novel—because it requires the reader's investment of time and attention—usually requires at least one character that readers can identify with—a hero or heroine. A short story carries no such obligation. In *The Lonely Voice,* Frank O'Connor goes as far as to state that the short story "has never had a hero." We look upon the characters in short fiction as we do worms and other insects in a terrarium, as objects not of identification, but of curiosity.

6 } SADISTIC LOVERS & INNOCENT MASOCHISTS

The abusive relationship story is a staple of all Intro to Creative Writing classes. I've seen hundreds of them. The doe-eyed protagonist invariably obeys her charismatic abuser's every abusive whim. She follows him everywhere. In a word, she's spellbound. Until—too late—the spell wears off.

What the authors of such stories often fail to understand is that, for their stories to work, the reader must share at least some of the protagonist's feelings toward the object of her obsession. Instead, her lover (we'll call him Jack) is a transparent creep, albeit good-looking, "with a thick wrestler's neck and sinuous back muscles, and a loop of black hair twisting rebelliously over his forehead." But Jack's good looks and animal magnetism can't help us understand Jill's staying with someone who abuses her mentally and physically.

Surely Jack must have some redeeming qualities, or at least some powers of seduction beyond his good looks. It would help, for instance, if his dialogue consisted of more than Neanderthal grunts ("Yeah," "Huh,") alternating with Spock-speak ("I have to hurt you; it is part of the process.").

When we're given no grounds whatsoever for Jill's attraction to him, we find ourselves wondering why she's such a masochist. What in her past might account for her pursuit of the cruel Jacks of this world? Who is Jill, and why does she hope against hope?

Perhaps—between acts of abuse and seduction—Jack teaches her the names of flowers in his wild garden, or he shows off his collection of antique egg scales.

Lacking a dimensional antagonist, the reader's attention is drawn to question the victim. And so it pays to allow your antagonists some redeeming qualities.

7 } AGAINST ARCHVILLAINS: LET OUR CHARACTERS (AND NARRATORS) BE HUMAN

But even if they are downright villains, our characters should be *human*. Otherwise they come off like the Wicked Witch of the West, or high-ranking members of SMERSH, rubbing warty hands or petting fluffy cats while delivering lines like, "Well, [Dorothy, Mr. Bond], how good of you to drop in on us this way!"

Archvillains—like violence and melodrama—work better on film than on paper.[4] Clever art direction, musical scores, close-ups, and skillful acting supply the dimensions lacking in the characters as written. We who must convey character solely with little black marks on paper can't count on such assistance.[5]

How to make characters human?

By giving them more than one dimension. By recognizing that, except in very rare cases,[6] there's no such thing as pure evil or pure good.

8 } WOE IS MY HERO/HEROINE: PROTAGONIST VICTIMS

Stories about victims that ask us to sympathize and even pity them, even in the most exotic settings, tend to bore.

My standard advice is to change the focus. Focus on the character *least* likely to arouse the reader's automatic sympathies, and who will therefore—if rendered with an effort at understanding—be most interesting.

---

4 In evidence I offer *Goldfinger,* the movie, vs. *Goldfinger,* the novel.

5 In defense of Ernst Blofeld, Rosa Kleb, and other Bondian archvillains, they *do* have roles to play, and good ones, too, in *genre* fiction. But not in works of serious literature.

6 And in those cases we're *not* dealing with recognizable humans, but with monsters.

This is what Flannery O'Connor does in her most famous short story, "A Good Man is Hard to Find," about a family who, while vacationing in Florida, encounter a band of escaped killers. Within the story's final pages the author deftly shifts the focus away from the vacationing "innocent" family, to the head killer, known only as "the Misfit," who somehow wins the reader's sympathy even as, one by one, he brutally executes the innocent family members. In a bizarre twist, antagonist becomes protagonist: not a hero, but someone not easily labeled or defined. The reader's assumptions—about right and wrong, about good and evil—are turned upside down, and the story resonates long after the last page is turned.

In beginner stories, though, the "heavies"—the drunken father, the abusive lover, the tyrannical spouse or boss—are seldom objects of sympathy, interest, or even curiosity. They function primarily as clubs for beating the stories' protagonists, and are just about as interesting.

Protagonists that function primarily as punching bags are equally uninteresting.

9} SKEWERING SAINTS: MALICIOUS NARRATORS

A special case of villainy: the malicious narrator, a character choice that almost invariably reflects an author's agenda and precludes authenticity and understanding.

Example: In a story about a homeless drug addict named Teresa (can the allusion to Mother Teresa be unintentional?) we confront an unidentified narrator who is initially quite brutal in his judgments of Terry, whom he refers to as a "junkie whore" and "a religious fanatic." We are thus carefully and all-too-obviously primed for the eventual reversal when the narrator discovers that she may truly be a saint.

The problem with this strategy is that, rather than presenting us with a clear lens through which to observe Teresa in her world, the narrator's jaundiced account draws our attention away from the story's real subject, Teresa. The narrator's surly disposition isn't the point of the story; the point is Teresa's struggle—and the narrator's catharsis, as he finally recognizes what Teresa has been through, and how a homeless woman has indeed displayed some saintly virtues.

By stacking the deck to render her narrator's catharsis more "poignant," the author ruined her story by rendering it inauthentic.

10 } UNRELIABLE NARRATORS: PSYCHOPATHS & OTHER MAD PROTAGONISTS

Just as actors can't resist portraying serial killers and other psychopaths, writers can't resist writing about them.

That's understandable. We're fascinated by evil, and especially by the inner workings of an evil mind. Part of the fascination reflects our inability to comprehend how such minds work. But another part lies with the fact that we *can* understand: If we look carefully enough, we can recognize the potential for evil and madness, however deeply suppressed, in ourselves. Every child who crushes an ant or sets a caterpillar's nest on fire senses this potential. If we're drawn to read and write about evil and mad characters, it may be as a way of purging our own mad and evil impulses.

But writing about mad characters has its hazards.

A writer may demonstrate great authenticity in entering into the off-kilter mind of a potentially homicidal character. But that authenticity may *do the story in*. Part of what makes the experience feel authentic is the sense that the mind of the character and that of the author are one, with both minds, apparently, off-kilter.

This makes for what's called an *unreliable narrator,* a narrator whose grasp of the story being narrated is anything but sure. The story that he tells is substantially different from the story that we *get.*

But when the narrator is a psychopath, his unreliability may extend beyond the *interpretation* of facts to the facts themselves. That is, we can't trust *anything* he says. When directly or by implication a character/narrator tells us, in so many words, "I am not to be trusted," the frankness is appreciated. But when, some pages later, the same narrator says, "I pulled the trigger," we're left with nothing to hold onto. It's like that old Zen trick. One side of the piece of paper says, "The statement on the other side of this piece of paper is false." We turn the paper over to read: "The statement on the other side of this piece of paper is true." This makes for a wonderful conundrum, and it certainly qualifies as fiction. But does it make *satisfying* fiction?

Famous works have in fact had authors as unstable as their narrators, and vice-versa. I think of Dostoevsky's *Notes From Underground;* the novels of Céline; Jean Genet's hallucinatory/masturbatory masterpiece, *Our Lady of the Flowers;* the narrators of Burroughs's *Naked Lunch* and Charlotte Perkins Gilman's "The Yellow Wallpaper"; Malcolm Lowry's swacked Consul in *Under the Volcano.* In each of these works, the minds portrayed are addled by confinement, drugs, or liquor.

Yes, psychotic heroes can affect us deeply. Remember Travis Bickle, the "hero" of Martin Scorsese's *Taxi Driver?* Bickle is a psychotic Dante, giving us a tour of the underworld as viewed through the steam-fogged windows of a New York City taxicab. Bickle is certainly an unreliable narrator. But in movies, the camera's objectivity can balance the character's paranoia and other psychic warps. And in the case of Bickle, we sense that there's method to his madness: We are gaining true insight into the ways of a wicked world. When Travis describes the "scum" who nightly populate and pollute the back seat of his cab, we never doubt the sincerity or even the accuracy of his acutely skewed observations. We may not share Travis's paranoia, but we do share his disgust.

Similarly, Dostoyevsky's underground man Zverkov has more to offer us than a toothache and bile. He symbolizes our own powerlessness in confronting the weight of *determinism*, the philosophical theory that a person's actions have already been mapped out for him. Zverkov's madness has both a method and a moral.

And yet, personally, I tend to find such minds hard to invest in, to the extent that a novel requires. I tend to doubt that they have *enough* to teach me about life, beyond the simple fact that it has driven them mad. And can you blame readers for not wanting to spend time with people who are "just plain crazy"?

There have been and will always be exceptions, stories and novels that owe their magnificence to an author's willingness and ability to inhabit, through a first person narrator, the mind of a character more than slightly off his rocker.

On the other hand, psychotic narrators have long been a staple of the short story, from the quivering narrator of Poe's *The Tell-Tale Heart,* to the far more self-possessed but equally unhinged protagonist of Adam Haslett's *Notes to My Biographer.*[7] But as with all exceptions, these tend to prove the rule.

11} COLORFUL ECCENTRICS

Sometimes authors rely too heavily on the eccentricities of their characters and settings.

---

7 Other examples of successful novels with unreliable narrators: Nabokov's *Pale Fire,* Thomas Bernard's *The Loser,* and, most recently, Rivka Galchen's *Atmospheric Disturbances,* narrated by a psychiatrist who may suffer from Capgras syndrome (a bizarre mental condition whose victims believe that their lovers or friends have been replaced by imposters).

A story about a woman living in a trailer park is rich in atmosphere, with such descriptive details as the "loose skinny dog" that sniffs around the narrator's trailer, and the narrator's "apricot lipstick" and "musky, sweet smell."

But the protagonist's eccentricities take over to the point where they no longer complicate or complement her character, but overwhelm it. Eliza burns logs in her living room; she brushes her teeth with Comet and "cures" her diabetes by mainlining Gila monster spit, and she writes letters to dead American presidents. We start to feel that she's not just eccentric, but pathological (see Meditation # 10).

Great characters in fiction often tend to be eccentric to some degree—whether protagonists (Gatsby, Miss Jean Brodie, Gully Jimson) or antagonists (Ahab in *Moby-Dick;* Rochester in *Jane Eyre).* Thanks to their eccentricities, fictional characters act on the impulses that "normal" people typically suppress.

There's a fine line between eccentricity and madness, between unconventional or impulsive behavior and pathology. When a central character's actions appear to be pathological, motivated not by circumstance or character but by disease or even by author manipulation, the resulting story is bound to be less satisfying.

12} WHAT'S IN A NAME: ANONYMOUS PROTAGONIST

When I come across an unnamed protagonist in a story, especially a first-person narrator, I become skeptical. Intuition tells me that, were I to ask the author, "What's your character's name?" I'd be met with a blank stare, indicating that the character doesn't fully exist for this author.

Sometimes authors withhold their characters' names in a misguided attempt to imbue them with universal qualities, to make them *everyman* or *everywoman.* But the absence of a name isn't a quality; it's a negative space, a vacuum. And, as with all vacuums in literature, what tends to rush in to fill it? Cliché.

There is also the danger that an unnamed first-person narrator will be confused with the author—a mistake made not just by readers, but by writers, too, when they assume that their own personalities will fill in the blank.

Until a clear distinction is made between author and character, an umbilical cord remains, binding them.

The first step toward cutting that umbilical cord is to name your narrators.

13} THE DOPE ON JUNKIES: CHARACTERS IN SENSATIONAL CIRCUMSTANCES

Since the late 1940s, when Nelson Algren broke the taboo with his National Book Award winning novel *The Man With the Golden Arm,* the subject of drug addiction has been treated extensively in literature and movies. Some who've treated it (including Algren) never used heroin themselves, but knew junkies and traveled in their circles. Others, like Alexander Trocchi (*Cain's Book*) and William S. Burroughs *(Junkie, Naked Lunch),* were poets *and* junkies.

One student's story approaches this theme from a familiar angle—the addict's struggle to kick his habit, suffering from withdrawal, itching for a fix.

Familiarity puts a heavy burden on author and story. It demands an extra measure of poetry and authenticity to rise above previous treatments, or at least to avoid cliché.

When handling sensational material like drug addiction, authors need to be extra careful to avoid cheap shots. Inflating the drug dealer's cruelty is a heavy-handed ploy to win sympathy for the junkie (see Meditations # 5 and 8). And anyway, it's been done: Algren did it sixty years ago.

A kindly dealer would be less predictable and might better serve the theme: heroin's deadly grip on one man's life, a grip no dealer, kind or cruel, can loosen.

When dealing with characters in horrific situations we have to deal with the reality, horrific as it is. Paint it vividly, but not garishly—since the situation itself is already lurid.

14} FICTION'S LOFTIEST GOAL: HUMANIZING HITLER

Fiction's loftiest goal is to put us into the minds and hearts of characters who are not at all like ourselves, so that we may see that they aren't as unlike us as we thought.

"Show me the insurance salesman who suffers!" James Jones admonished a class of writing students, who apparently didn't think insurance men were capable of suffering. But everyone suffers, everyone with a nervous system. Even psycho- and sociopaths suffer. Hannibal Lecter suffers, his pathology the result of childhood trauma, of seeing his sister Mischa killed and cannibalized by war criminals.

To be human is to suffer. And to the extent that we suffer, we *are* human.

I've often thought the ultimate test of the novelist's skill would be to make Hitler human: not to make him good, but simply to make him comprehensible, recognizable as one of our own species, as the history books do not.

In his novel *The Castle in the Forest,* Norman Mailer tried to do just that, depicting young Hitler as the bed-wetting son of a violent man who bullies his family and impregnates his own daughter. Needless to say, the book drew sharp criticism. Mailer—who once dared to write about Jesus from Jesus' point of view—was accused of trying to "explain" away the extermination of the Jews, of trying to make the incomprehensible comprehensible.

But a superior writer should be willing to embrace humanity in all its forms, with an attempt to understand as his first, not his last, goal.

We *need* to understand our characters. As writers we are or ought to be driven by a desire for understanding that is stronger than our desire for love, approval, a laugh, or revenge. But the way we understand our characters isn't to figure them out the way a doctor figures out what's wrong with a patient, or the way a cryptographer deciphers a code. The way to understand them is to *become* them, to inhabit them, to walk in their shoes and eat and breathe and think with them as they think. Understanding them from without is little better than a judgment.

When we stand in judgment of our characters, we stand outside them, above and beyond them. We may judge them to be saints or sinners, or even devils. But our job as authors is not that of judge or jury, but to present the evidence. It's for readers to judge our characters.

That said, the better we do our job of writing, the greater the likelihood of acquittal or a hung jury.

Situations: General vs. Routine

Once we accept that our ultimate subject is people, we should give serious thought to the situations we put them in. Choose the right situation, and the story may just write itself. Choose unwisely, and you devote most of your energy to avoiding clichés, extracting suspense from routine, and detaching fiction from memoir—while still failing, finally, to convey your characters' experiences convincingly, vividly, and with urgency.

Amateur fiction often suffers from an inability to distinguish *events* from routine. Under routine circumstances, people don't change. Changes in an individual's nature are brought about only by extraordinary circumstances.

Working from the baseline of routine, like a seismograph the fiction writer takes the measure of her subject's responses to upheavals large and small. How her characters adapt to extraordinary circumstances will determine their fate. Ideally, a story should congeal around a single unique event (or a series of them). Such singular events cast life's routines into the background, where they belong.

15 } HO-HUM SYNDROME: A ROUTINE TRIP TO PLANET B1620-25

No matter how exotic our characters' daily routines may be, readers are not all that interested.

Take a story set in the future. Matt Starhopper travels on the first day of each month to a space station located on B1620-25, the farthest known planet at the core of the globular M4 cluster. Along the way he confronts the usual interplanetary flotsam and jetsam: green, gooey space aliens, treacherous asteroid fields, and gravitational follies—all rendered with a master's eye for detail, an astronomer's love of planetary lore, and an imagination to rival Jules Verne's.

Yet the faithful reader feels her attention flagging. Her eyelids droop, she yawns and turns on *Jeopardy!* What went wrong?

In a word: Routine.

Consciously or not, our reader understands that Matt Starhopper has taken this same voyage two dozen times before, and will take it dozens of times more. She's tracking not a *specific* but a *general* voyage. She presses gamely onward in the hope of encountering those two words that signal the start of a true fictional journey: *"One day…"*

It's that "one day" that pricks the reader's ears, that says, "Something extraordinary is about to happen."

The actual words "one day" need not appear, but they should be implied.

16} LIFE FROM DEATH: A NURSING HOME STORY

During the Passover Seder the youngest child traditionally asks, "Why is this day different from every other day?" Writers might well ask the same question of the situations they put their characters in.

Emily, a young woman, visits her slowly dying, barely coherent father in a Bronx nursing home, a routine she has followed daily for three years. *Why is this day different from every other day?*

Several things that occur in the course of the story depart, in potentially significant ways, from Emily's routine:

1. En route to the nursing home she visits the house where she grew up.

2. She remembers her dead sister, Rose.

3. She has a conversation with a boy who works at the bakery where she buys her father's favorite pastries.

4. Her father reveals a secret (true or imagined) about her mother's death.

5. Emily meets the bakery boy for lunch at the hospital.

None of these occurrences, however, rises to the level of an *event* that lifts the story out of the status quo. The author might consider making *one* of these events the story's dramatic centerpiece, and either eliminating the others or making them subordinate. This would provide dramatic tension and give the story its focus—eliminating the sense of bathos that washes over the story's inventory of sad routines. A dying man is, after all, a dying man. And

Emily's visits, we know, are obligatory. Hence we ask: What is the story *really* about? *Why is this day...?*

Maybe the story is not actually about the dying father at all, but about a young woman's encounter with the pastry shop employee, a boy with little or no experience of life or death and whose blunt attitude she finds refreshing—until their encounter ends with some misunderstanding, revelation, or epiphany, or all of those things.

Whatever happens, the status quo story of the dying father should be shoved into the background where it belongs. The story should be not about death, but about life juxtaposed against death.

Whether your characters journey daily to a nursing home or to distant planets, what matters to the reader is the singular event that distinguishes one day from all the others.[8]

17 } BLURRY NARRATORS: DIVING BELLS & DRUNKEN CONSULS

As always, there are exceptions.

One can present readers with a fundamentally "static situation" that serves as a framing device through which we experience dramatic incidents or events of the past.

Jean Dominique-Bauby's *The Diving Bell and the Butterfly* is an extraordinary memoir by the former editor-in-chief of *Elle* magazine, who suffered from locked-in-syndrome—a rare condition caused by damage to his brain stem after a stroke. Bauby's memoir wasn't written but rather *blinked out*, letter-by-letter, chapter-by-chapter, using only his left eye—the one body part he could still move. To call his situation *static* is an understatement:

---

8 For a discussion of word choices that contribute to the sense of generalization or routine, see Meditation # 132.

The man was literally imprisoned in his paralyzed body. He died in 1997, two years after being struck down.

Yet the story Bauby tells couldn't be more dramatic. That the narrator is unable to move is what makes his story so moving. All the trials, triumphs, loves, and joys of his past are framed by a present in which he is immobile. The static present serves as a foil for the active past. It puts that past into high relief.

But a narrator needn't be paralyzed to offer a static yet illuminating view into her existence. A steady supply of mescal, tequila, and any other liquor at hand did the trick for both Malcolm Lowry and for the protagonist of his masterpiece, *Under the Volcano.* Lowry plunges—surreally, and at times psychedelically—into his drunken consul's stream of consciousness. (For all its sublime artistry, however, many have found Lowry's masterpiece unreadable.)

To construct a story out of such static material is certainly risky, but not impossible.

Inauthentic Writing:
Cliché & Convenience

18 } STOLEN TALES: A CLICHÉ ROSE IN SPANISH HARLEM

A writer's job is to *write* stories—not to steal or borrow them and, with a coat of fresh paint, pawn them off as original.

That should be obvious, but it's not always completely clear. Our own private thoughts, dreams, intuitions, and fantasies are inevitably colored by what Jung called the *collective unconscious*—

the vast, reservoir-like body of shared human experiences, of myths, symbols, and legends.

Take this story set in Spanish Harlem, where Emilio Bermudez, a rookie fresh from the police academy, stakes out a bodega with his partner Joe. While on duty Emilio falls hard for Dulce, the lovely sister of the drug-dealing bodega owner.

Need I fill in the rest? In the climactic drug bust, Joe sees Dulce reach for a "weapon" and fires. The bullet goes straight through her heart. Dulce had been reaching innocently for the love note Emilio had sent her, and she dies in Emilio's arms.

If these characters and their situation seem familiar, they are. We've all seen similar stories a hundred times.

Most sensational subjects have been treated to death. Result: a minefield of clichés. And, as Martin Amis tells us, "All good writing is a war against cliché." The story's problems might be partially redeemed by crisp dialogue, vivid descriptions, and an impeccable edgy style—but the plain fact is, they *shouldn't* be solved. This clichéd rose is wilted down to its thorns.

Steer clear of tired plots and you, your characters, and your readers will avoid all kinds of heartache.

19} THE LURE OF THE SENSATIONAL: ONE FLEW OUT OF THE CUCKOO'S NEST

For beginning and even experienced writers, the temptation to choose intrinsically dramatic subjects is hard to resist. Drug deals and busts gone wrong, kidnapping, abortion, car crashes, murder, madness, rape, war—with such sensational raw material to work with, how can writers go wrong?

They can and they do.

A student of mine, Henry, turns in a story set in a mental hospital. He has described the hospital and its setting in painstaking detail, vividly rendering the ward's "colorful" gallery of assorted patients.

Henry doesn't realize that in choosing this situation he has bumbled into a minefield of clichés; he will need to avoid all the stereotypes of loony-bin lore coined by Ken Kesey in *One Flew Over the Cuckoo's Nest,* and recycled in a myriad of TV shows and books.

Soon enough, we encounter a tyranical head psychiatrist— a male Nurse Ratched—and his intractable patient, a hapless schizophrenic named Ben (read: Billy Bibbit) whose brother, Warren, happens to be a resident shrink on the ward and the narrator of the story. Only after Ben hangs himself does heretofore passive Warren emerge from his catatonia to seek revenge, storming the tyrant nurse's office and pumping him full of melodramatic lead.

I read Henry's story with a mixture of sadness and horror— horror at seeing so much talent and effort wasted on a fundamentally flawed choice of subject matter. Not that you *can't* set a story on a mental ward, or that you can't tell stories about mental patients and the abuses they suffer at the hands of their keepers. But if you do so, you need to realize what you're up against.

And what you're up against is cliché.

20} PUT SCHIELE ON A LADDER: ARTSY CLICHÉS

Every milieu has its clichés, its stock characters and stereotypes.

Another stereotype is that of the starving artist. Just once, I'd like to read about a successful artist—a Thomas Kincaid or a Peter Max—grinding out schlock art while raking in millions. Or just a talented, hard-working painter, supplementing his small income from gallery sales through teaching, grants, and fellowships.

This, after all, is the reality for *most* professional fine artists.

Instead we get Giorgio, the Italian gigolo-slash-genius, in his Soho loft, seducing and/or being seduced by his models.[9] Or a consumptive artist in his frigid garret, tearing up his master-pieces to feed to the wood stove while the landlord pounds on his bolted door. Or the genius at work in the French countryside, lashed by the mistral winds, gripping his easel while chewing the paint from his brushes. These clichés owe much to (respectively) *La Boheme* and *Lust for Life* (the movie version of Irving Stone's novel about van Gogh, starring a clench-toothed, fiery-eyed Kirk Douglas).

A former painter myself, I have limited tolerance for these clichés. Even poor Vincent, that most depraved and deprived of artists, fails to live up to the image. The letters he wrote to his brother Theo and others show how sane this "madman" was. True, he often went hungry, and he suffered from incapacitating seizures. But the cartoon of the foaming madman does him no justice.

But the real problem with clichés is that they deprive us of genuine details, which, though less sensational, are both more convincing and more interesting. A deeper look into the life of any artist will reveal facts that have it over all clichés.

Take a look, for a moment, at the life of Egon Schiele, another "depraved" artist. The biographical facts of Schiele's life are much more interesting than the chestnuts. In his late teens he was already a student in the Vienna Academy. At nineteen he moved into his own studio in Kurzbauergasse. At twenty he had his first paintings exhibited at the International Art Show in Vienna. Soon afterwards he moved in with his model, a woman named Wally Neuzil who was not yet sixteen, and was charged with breach of moral code. He began sketching nudes around 1910. Most were

---

9 As anyone who has gone to art school will tell you, nothing is less sexy than a figure-drawing session.

done not at an easel, but on a ladder, with an "eagle's eye" view of his subjects.

The truth is the best weapon we have for authenticity and against cliché: whether it's the literal truth or the truth of imagination doesn't matter.

Put your fictional artists on ladders and readers will not only get more convincing, authentic descriptions, but more moving ones.

21} HOW NOT TO BORE: IMITATION STORIES & PRACTICING SINCERITY

When we produce stories that are derivative, we're not being honest with ourselves. We're borrowing someone else's aesthetics and selling them as our own.

In choosing intrinsically sensational subjects writers think they're getting a free—or a cheap—ride. But as with all things in life, you tend to get what you pay for. The best way to avoid cliché is to practice sincerity. "Sincerity," wrote Borges, "isn't a moral choice, but an aesthetic one."

If we've come by sensational material honestly, through our own personal experience or imagination, we may rightly claim it as our own. Otherwise, we'd best steer clear. Our stories should be stories that only we can tell, as only *we* can tell it.

22} BORE ME STIFF, I DARE YOU: A FAVORITE EXERCISE

I ask my students to write two pieces, one at a time, each about a minute long. Piece #1 should rivet the reader; Piece #2 should bore the reader stiff. Each student reads both pieces out loud. They have one minute either to bore the class silly or to draw us to the edges of our seats. A show of hands afterwards decides which of the two pieces is the more interesting.

Here are opening paragraphs from one student's two pieces. I leave it to you to guess which is which.

> 1. Percy Battenberg strained against the force of the yacht's wheel, struggling to keep *Contessa* on course for Yarmouth. The squall had come up quickly and the forty-four-foot sloop careened off the thick, fast-moving, and relentlessly towering swells. Over and over again the wind pushed her up a wave's backside where she paused at the crest as though to enjoy the view, her three tons momentarily weightless, before pitching violently forward and surfing out of control down the wave's face, burying her bow into the next swell and beginning the process again.

> 2. Having gotten off the plane, I proceeded down a series of fluorescent-lit, gray-carpeted passageways into the terminal. Airports have always intimidated me. Since I had no idea how to get to baggage claim, I followed some fellow passengers from my flight—an elderly couple—who seemed to know what they were doing. I really had to go to the bathroom, and knowing the trip into the city was probably going to take a while was tempted to duck into the first restroom I saw, but I didn't want to risk losing my elderly guides and not finding my way to baggage claim. But then, I thought, if I go to the bathroom *after* baggage claim, I'll have to carry all my bags into the stall. That could get a little tight, and airport bathrooms aren't always clean. Damn, I should have gone back there, on the plane, and to hell with the seat belt sign.

If you guessed that Piece #1 was supposed to be riveting, while Piece #2 was meant to bore us silly, you're right. But as measured by a hand vote after each piece was read out loud, the results were contradictory.

To the majority of students (and to their teacher), Piece #1 was trite from the start. Beyond the dropping of a name, there are no characters in it, no human beings to relate to, just a squall of nautical terms, with the sloop as protagonist. After the first paragraph I had to force myself to keep listening.

Piece #2 presents us with a recognizably human character in a situation that most of us can relate to; it kept me and others engaged. Riveting? Hardly. But relatively authentic.

Whenever I've done this experiment, in almost every instance the result is the same: *The "riveting" piece bores, while the "boring" piece holds interest.* There are several reasons for this. In their effort to grip us, beginning writers tend to rush: They equate their own adrenaline with that of the reader. Conversely, when trying to bore, the same writers *take their time;* they don't hesitate to lavish 250 words on the subject of a wall of white paint drying. And—to their consternation—the result mesmerizes. At any rate it holds our attention.

But far worse than rushing, in trying to interest us, most writers abandon sincerity, and with it authenticity. They choose sensational subjects on the basis of little personal knowledge and no genuine emotional investment. They do so on the assumption that their *own* stories aren't interesting enough, that what they have to offer us as writers isn't suitably "sensational." In fact, every human being is in some way unique, and this uniqueness in itself makes us each "sensational," in our own ways.

In pretending to be anyone other than themselves, writers sacrifice the very thing we most crave from them: authenticity.

23} RESCUING STORIES FROM CIRCUMSTANTIAL CLICHÉ

As the moth is attracted to flame, less-than-vigilant writers are attracted to the bright light of intrinsically dramatic situations, where the drama is preassembled, ready to use—*convenient.*

We're drawn to clichés because they're convenient. And convenience for writers—convenient plots, convenient characters, convenient coincidences, convenient settings or situations or strings of words—almost always spells doom.

A writer sets her story in an abortion clinic. What are the expectations raised by such a setting? To the extent that those expectations are met head-on, her story fails. It descends into cliché and denies the reader an authentic experience.

One expects (for instance) that a young woman will face an excruciating choice under great pressure. She may or may not be accompanied by the man or boy who put her in this position; he may be callous or callow, or he may be sensitive and confused. The drama may occur on the way to Planned Parenthood, or on the way home, but the implied setting is still the clinic itself.

What will the author do to rescue that drama from our expectations, from cliché?

In "Hills Like White Elephants," Hemingway rescues his abortion story by doing away with the setting. Instead of locating his story in the abortion clinic, he sets it in the station where the man and woman await the train that will take her to the city and (as we infer, since abortion is never mentioned) to the clinic. Hemingway's story of an abortion was powerful then because no one had previously dared to raise the subject. It remains powerful today because Papa avoided the obvious, and in so doing rescued his story from a cliché before the cliché had even been coined.

In "Miserere," one of seven mercilessly authentic stories gathered in *Bear and His Daughter* by Robert Stone, a widowed librarian salvages aborted fetuses from clinic dumpsters in order to have them blessed for burial.

Stone avoids the obligatory abortion clinic setting, as well as the distraught patient and her callous and/or contrite boyfriend. Stone steers clear of such well-trodden territory to give us a story that reawakens our senses to a subject that has in and of itself become a cliché.

24 } SOMEBODY UP THERE LIKES CLICHÉS: AN IMITATION BOXING STORY

F. Scott Fitzgerald said, "All good writing is swimming underwater and holding your breath."

Either your chosen subject plunges you into the imagination's deeper waters, or your story will probably drift into one of two shallow waterways:

(a) the autobiographical estuary, in which you write strictly about characters and events from your own life,

or

(b) the brackish bay of stereotype and cliché.

A student's story about a boxer drifts into the second waterway, recycling familiar material from old boxing movies: *On the Waterfront, Requiem for a Heavyweight, Rocky I, II, III, etc.* That the boxer-protagonist happens to be female doesn't rescue the story, especially now that female boxing stories have already entered the Kingdom of Cliché.

The way to rescue this and other clichés may lie in exploring those parts of the story that don't belong firmly to the cliché. When she's *not* boxing, what is our female pugilist doing? Does she have friends, family, children? Maybe she's boxing to put her son or daughter (or herself) through college, or to support her stroke-victim father? Or maybe she's doing what she's doing to regain her confidence and strength after losing her husband, or after a serious illness?

By investing our characters with concerns and struggles that point away from the hackneyed and sensational and toward the earthier dramas of "ordinary" existence, by taking the most trite elements of our stories out of the foreground and putting them in the background, we begin to lift them out of cliché.

Melodrama & Violence

25 } I'LL SAVE YOU, NELL: MELODRAMA (NOT) TO THE RESCUE

Convenient choices are prone not only to cliché, but to *melodrama*.

We call a story or a scene melodramatic when its protagonists are too obviously heroes or victims, while its antagonists are obviously villains. Another acid test for melodrama is the tendency to resort to violence, either emotional (catatonic seizures, gasps, screams, floods of tears, verbal confrontations) or physical (fisticuffs, or worse, depending on the caliber of melodrama and available firearms).

Most television shows, especially courtroom, police, and medical dramas, tend to be melodramatic. But what works in front of a camera usually fails on the page, where nuance has to be supplied by the reader.

But for all their technical bravado and talent, television and movies are hard-pressed to deliver what fiction delivers so well: a character's thoughts, feelings, and perceptions—i.e., *subjective* content. A close-up of an actor's eyes may suggest a lot, but it can *only* suggest; it can't put us directly in a character's mind. Only fiction can do that.

And good fiction does it extremely well.

Given this ability to inhabit our characters, to experience their subjective responses as our own, a little drama goes a long way, while too much careens into melodrama.

Gratuitous violence is synonymous with melodrama. So is the gratuitous gesture, as when a character who has just come into a fortune tosses fistfuls of greenbacks like confetti into the air—a cliché that probably has never once happened in real life. (When it does happen, I want to be there.)

Any over-the-top action results in melodrama.

A male lover, freshly dumped by his girl, throws himself into the nearest river. Melodrama. Or, being told by the same girl that she loves him, he boards a crowded subway and kisses everyone in sight, including a blind man and the conductor. Melodrama. The specific circumstances *might* explain such behavior (and casting a young Jimmy Stewart would help). But the likelihood is slim.

26} FISTICUFFS AND SHIPWRECKS

Melodrama is to authentic drama what crab sticks are to the real thing: an inferior substitute.

When people punch each other out in stories, suspect imitation. In real life people seldom use their fists. It's dangerous, and illegal. A solid fist to the bridge of a nose could result in death, and appropriate charges.

In one story, an estranged father and son meet in a bar after a long separation. Chad, the son, still enraged by his father's abandonment, swoops over the table and punches him in the face. The author didn't share with us the *genuine* drama, Chad's pent-up rage that hides a deep longing for his father.

The scene would be more convincing, and more moving, if the son's urge to strike his father were *felt* but not acted upon: if it remained, like a U-boat, lurking somewhere below the surface of the scene.

Sometimes the mere piling on of sensational events results in melodrama. In a story set during the renaissance, a young girl disguised as a boy stows away aboard a merchant sailing ship. The plot is clearly designed to appeal to the young. (One key to writing successful YA—Young Adult—fiction is *never* to condescend to your audience. Write *for yourself*, for the younger person in you.)[10]

In this story, not only does the heroine succeed against all odds with her outrageous plan, she ends up surviving a shipwreck—all in four pages. The result feels melodramatically absurd, like a movie played on fast-forward.

Another result of cramming too much drama into too few pages is a paucity of *authenticating detail*,[11] the sort of small, precise, carefully chosen and calibrated descriptions that help suspend a reader's disbelief and make it possible for her to enjoy a story no matter how unlikely or outrageous.

I find such sketched-in action cartoonish: The story calls to mind a cartoon ship caught in a cardboard tempest, with little Isabella clinging to her generic floating hatch door or barrel. Had the author taken more time, there would be four pages for the storm alone, and a dozen more to develop authentic relationships between the stowaway and the crew members. When the reader gets stranded with them on the cartoon desert island, he'd at least have some authentic characters to cling to.

By *slowing down* and taking the time and trouble to imbue our stories with authentic, rich, specific moments and details, we achieve real drama and avoid its floozy cousins, sentimentality and melodrama.

---

10 It's no accident that much of the best YA fiction also appeals to adults. It is for young people only in so far as its subject and characters are ones that young people are inclined to identify with.

11 Not long ago a field guide to birds of the northeastern United States misidentified a species of bird as indigent to Massachussetts. Asked to account for the error, the author claimed that such a bird was mentioned in an Updike novel set in that state, and—since Updike was known to be fastidious in his details—he took the bird to be factual. Updike reminded this reader that he was a fiction writer. "I'm *precise*," he said, "but I'm not always accurate." This nicely illustrates what I mean by *authenticating detail*.

27 } SOAP & HISTRIONICS: DRAMA VS. MELODRAMA

Melodrama results partly from an author's unwillingness to find the true emotional resolution of a story's conflict. It's the narrative equivalent of all-out war, as opposed to seeking a diplomatic solution.

In real life people do throw water in their spouses' faces, and shout accusations at each other; they even commit murder out of passion or for vengeance. Such things can happen in your fiction, too. But when violent confrontations *become* the story, when they are the rule and not the exception, then violence usurps drama.

The result is melodrama, what soap operas are made of. And soap operas are *not* dramatic; they are intrinsically nondramatic, since their perpetuity depends on nothing ever being dramatically resolved. The characters never *change*.[12]

In soap operas we get wish fulfillment and negative fantasy in place of real resolutions: Husband finds gardener in bed with wife; abused son catches drill-sergeant father cross-dressing; set-upon secretary slaps her chauvinist-pig boss in the face. Do these scenarios sound familiar? They are the stuff of melodrama.

In a soap opera, the rivalry between brother and sister is evoked through bald confrontations and accusations, or equally bald confessions and apologies. When a relationship is "dramatized," nearly all of the dialogue is head-on and histrionic, vomiting up plot and backstory. Accusations and apologies are served up along with great gobs of personal history.

A more dramatic, less histrionic approach would convey the status quo between brother and sister up front, through exposition, leaving subsequent scenes free to explore behavior and character. What the protagonist and antagonist do when they're together, how they treat each other, how they say things and which

---

12 See Meditations # 16–18.

things *don't* get said—these things reveal their personalities and relationships. We read the story to see how these siblings will cope (or not) with each other under *specific* circumstances (e.g., they have to pick a coffin for their mother's funeral).

When authors explode drama rather than describe it, their material deteriorates into soap opera and blows up in everyone's face.

Deaths: Unearned

28} POOR MARTHA, WE HARDLY KNEW YE: DEATH AS DRAMA

Melodrama can be deadly—not just to our stories, but for our characters themselves.

In a story about an elderly spinster named Martha, we are presented with a series of nonevents leading up to her sudden "natural" death (she dies in her sleep). Martha's death is meant to touch us deeply, and even to move us to tears. For some readers it might succeed.

But editors can be stony about such things. They don't like to be manipulated. To prepare readers for the death of a major character takes a lot of development—more than a short story can deliver, usually—so the death feels inevitable and justified, and not like a ploy to force sympathy for an underdeveloped protagonist. [13]

---

13 Distinguishing plot from story, E.M. Forster gives this example: "The King died and then the Queen died is a story. The King died, and then the Queen died of grief is a plot." Though it serves to illustrate the concept of plot, the Queen's death by grief is a sentimentally motivated action and therefore melodramatic. In real life who dies purely of a broken heart? Not even Theo van Gogh, brother of the famous painter—who died, legend has it, "of grief" six months after his brother's suicide. In fact the brothers were as united by syphilis as by fraternal devotion. Both carried the disease; it's probably what drove Vincent mad. And though grief may have hastened Theo's death, the *Treponema pallidum* spirochete is what finally killed him.

In this example, however, we barely know poor Martha before her creator bumps her off. And sad though it may be, a character's natural death—or, for that matter, her accidental death—reveals little if anything about her. The emotional journey of a story in which the protagonist dies should be established by the protagonist herself, through acts other than dying. Give Martha some conflict: Put her in a situation that tests her spinsterhood or places it in high relief. Have her go on a date, or have a friend try and set her up, something that breaks the routine of her days.

In the story as written, Martha (a retired teacher) watches a high school football game. She eats popcorn and has a chat with a former student. This could be poignant, especially if we learn that the student had been a favorite of hers, or her least favorite, and that he has gone on to great success in the world of finance (or politics or art), while her own life dwindles to a spinster's vigil. As written, however, the chat exists only to highlight Martha's everyday loneliness.

Even in a photorealistic, slice-of-life story whose method consists of putting a character through her grim paces, each scene must be vivid and real, meaning that it takes place in a changing, not a static, world.

We need to care about Martha not just because she dies, but because she's someone we have connected to and felt something for.[14]

29 } SUICIDE: IN FICTION AS IN LIFE, A LAST RESORT

No act in life is more intrinsically dramatic than suicide. In suicide, protagonist and antagonist are one; all of the emotions implied by that duality are bottled up in a single being and expressed by a singular action.

---

14 For one of the best death scenes in literature read *Stoner*, by John Williams.

Shakespeare knew this: He hinged the plot of *Hamlet,* the greatest of all dramas, not on the question of vengeance, but on an even more vexing question: *To be or not to be?* But as with all explosive material, suicide must be handled with great care.

For example, a teenage girl watches, helplessly, uncomprehendingly, as the father she adores plunges into despair and resorts, finally, to suicide. Such a story obviously has great dramatic potential. And it happens that its author knows how to create character and mood and to write good dialogue.

Nevertheless, I have trouble with the father's suicide. On one hand, I find it predictable; on the other I find it unconvincing. Suicide being the exception rather than the rule (otherwise there'd be bodies strewn everywhere), the onus is on the author to make the act seem *not merely plausible, but inevitable.*

In fiction as in life, suicide should be the last resort, taken only when all other options have been exhausted. Otherwise, even assuming that the action is justified and believable, we lose sympathy for the protagonist and define him mainly in terms of that one action.

Personally, I think the girl's father would hold out longer. As despondent as he is over his wife's death, and as uncomfortable as he is with retirement, unless he's clinically depressed he might find some occupation. And assuming he's bound to do himself in, a bottle of over-the-counter sleeping pills probably wouldn't suffice, especially if his daughter finds him and rushes him to the hospital, as she does in this story.

In the interest of turning the story's focus away from its sensational centerpiece, we might hear more about the daughter's own life, and make her the focus of the action. She is finding herself while he loses himself, and she must struggle to make peace with a man she adored who ultimately abandons her in the worst of all possible ways.

Sentimentality &
Other Sticky Stuff

30} EMOTIONS UNEARNED: TEARS, VOMIT, & OTHER SENTIMENTAL BODILY FLUIDS

If melodrama is action in excess of circumstances, or unearned action, then sentimentality is emotion in excess of circumstances, or unearned emotion. Melodrama and sentimentality both bubble away in their symbiotic soup. One can't exist without the other.

In weak fiction, characters cry a lot. Tears routinely pour, drizzle, stream, or cascade down faces in quantities sufficient to supply the rinse cycle of an automatic dishwasher. Or they may fall singly ("As little Sheila slid, with a gasp, to the floor, a single tear slipped from the corner of her eye"). Either way, the tears are gratuitous. Which is to say, sentimental.

We tend to think of violence in terms of violent *action*. But there's such a thing as emotional violence. When tears stream down people's faces, as in mediocre stories, they are no less a manifestation of gratuitous emotional violence than a "bloodcurdling scream." In bad fiction, all bodily fluids are fodder for sentimentality.

Case in point: a story about a woman visiting her developmentally disabled kid brother in prison, where he has been condemned to Death Row for a murder he didn't commit.[15] Even before she has pulled out of her driveway, Gloria "puke[s] three times." She does so, presumably, because visiting her brother in jail upsets her so—though she has made this voyage a dozen times before.

---

15 To have this mentally challenged character actually *be* guilty of murder would break a cardinal rule of sentimentality, which requires adherence to the expectations created by the prior versions of a similar story.

When she arrives at the prison gate, the guard "crinkle[s] his nose at the faint eau de vomit." Here the author has sacrificed sincerity for sentimentality: In all likelihood Gloria (the narrator) doesn't really smell her own puke, nor can she know why the guard, standing several feet away in his wooden kiosk, "crinkles his nose." The guard's response doesn't belong genuinely either to the guard or to Gloria. It has been contrived by the author and foisted upon her readers, in the hope that they'll be gullible enough to buy it.

And some readers will buy it. The best-seller shelves are brimming with sentimental fluids, overflowing with unearned actions and emotions.

By all means write such a book, but know that you've done so for the sake of commerce, and not art. Then laugh all the way to the bank.

31} THE BATHETIC BEDROOM: SEX (OR THE LACK THEREOF) & SENTIMENTALITY

Sex is certainly part of "real" life. And, unlike murder and suicide, it's a commonplace occurrence, as common as every woman, man, or child you see on the street. But for the act of sex, they wouldn't be there.

However commonplace, in fiction (as in life) even sex should be treated with caution and with respect for both psychological and physiological truth, and not exploited for sentimental value in the name of shock or poignancy. This exploitation typically takes the form of gratuitous sex, with clothes flying off of bodies that have barely met, and whose superficial souls, assuming they have any, are as easily stripped away. In that case, we call the result *pornographic.*

But sex can be sentimentalized by other, less graphic means. It can even be sentimentalized out of existence.

A student submits a story in which an upper-middle-class family, living in a tame Connecticut suburb, takes in a homeless boy from New York's urban jungle. Even less credibly, the parents put twelve-year-old Ricky in the same room with their pubescent daughter.

A sensational premise, full of "dramatic" potential. But *the more sensational the choice of raw material, the greater the burden of plausibility.* The author must convince his audience that the world in which such things happen is "real" and exists somewhere proximate to the world you and I live in. Every time an author introduces an inauthentic or incredible detail into a story, however trivial, the reader loses faith in the "reality" of the story. We slip through the cracks and find ourselves standing outside of the story, *in judgment of it,* rather than inside it, *living it.*

So, in the above story, when I learn that Ricky and Jennifer share a bedroom, having been told that in his former life Ricky was a child prostitute, what am I to make of their innocent nocturnal cuddling? How "innocent" can it possibly be?

You say: "Well, to have them have sex would be even more sensational, more gratuitous. Wouldn't it?"

What makes a fictional element gratuitous is a lack of motivation, an insufficient grounding in "reality"—either *our* reality, yours and mine, or its own reality, established in the first paragraph or sentence of the story (see Meditation # 2). Here, what is gratuitous (and sentimental) is the innocence of that "innocent" cuddling, the lack of sexual experience or sexual heat, excised—presumably—to permit what the author deemed a more touching scene of interracial asexual harmony, however spurious.

In writing fiction, we have to deal with realities, either the realities of our world or those of an invented world. We can invent the facts, but we can't—or anyway we shouldn't—ignore them.

32 } SENTIMENTALITY SELLS: BEING NICHOLAS SPARKS

Telling students not to write sentimentally can be a thankless undertaking, like telling a child not to believe in the Tooth Fairy or Santa Claus.

How often have I had to endure the argument that Nicholas Sparks is the world's greatest writer, and the proof lies in his having sold X-million books, and therefore I should take all my arguments to the contrary and ... (I'll let you guess what my students think I should do with my arguments.)

I have nothing personal against Mr. Sparks. In fact I think him supremely gifted at what he does. And what he does is write books that sell and sell and sell. But they are commercial, not artistic, achievements. They are to great fiction what Cheez Doodles are to cheese. Guess which product sells in greater quantities?

Here is a sample from *The Notebook* of Sparks-style dialogue:

> She leaned into him. "Tell me, Noah, what do you remember most from the summer we spent together?"
>
> "All of it."
>
> "Anything in particular?"
>
> "No," he said.
>
> "You don't remember?"
>
> He answered after a moment, quietly, seriously:
>
> "No, it's not that. It's not what you're thinking. I was serious when I said 'all of it.' I can remember every moment we were together, and in each of them there was something wonderful. . . . Poets often describe love as an emotion that we can't control, one that overwhelms logic and common sense. That's what it was like for me. I didn't plan on falling in love with you, and I doubt if you planned on falling in love with me. But once we met, it was clear that neither of us could control what was happening to us. We fell in love despite our differences, and once we did, something rare and beautiful was created."

Discounting the fact that people *never* talk to each other this way, the thoughts expressed here are pure, unadulterated, industrial-strength mush, designed to suck tears from gullible eyes. Sparks can write: As a stylist he knows a thing or two. But slash the sentiment from this scene and what's left? Nothing. No scene. No characters.

Offered here, as a corrective, some love-chat in Ivan Gold's less sentimental hands:

> "You're so very good," she said.
> "I've never done that before."
> "Done what?"
> I came off her, rolled away, and took her hand.
> "The . . . how shall I say . . . reverse flip?"
> "Oh. Did you like it?"
> "It was priceless."
> "One can't move very much."
> "This is true. You like to move?"
> "Yes."
> "I'd noticed."
> "You find it unpleasant?"
> "No, babe, not unpleasant. A little overexciting, maybe."
> "The water is boiling away."
> "So it is. You want some coffee?"[16]

The success of most fiction bestsellers owes at least something to sentimentality: sentimental plots (Nicholas Sparks's *The Notebook; The Bridges of Madison County,* by Robert J. Waller; Alice Sebold's *The Lovely Bones*); or a sentimental prose style (Toni Morrison); or both *(The Road,* by Cormac McCarthy).

Call me a snob, but I don't care how well a book sells; I care only how good it is. And unless it's well written, a book can't be good, not as far as I'm concerned.

Not that bestsellers can't be good. Stephen King at his best is a superb writer. Jodi Picoult's novels are popular and well done. In

---

16 From his novel *Sick Friends.*

his time Dashiell Hammett was a bestseller and a damned good writer, and so was James M. Cain. So was Dickens. So was Jules Verne. So is Susan Isaacs. Alice Hoffman. Anita Shreve. Amy Tan. Wally Lamb. Carl Hiaasen. Patricia Highsmith. Ken Follet. Len Deighton. *Peyton Place* and *Gone With the Wind* have more virtues than vices. To the list of writers who are both good *and* successful there's no end.

(You may now stop calling me a snob.)

Authenticity in Realms of the Absurd

33} PLANTING ABSURD SEEDS IN REALISTIC SOIL

Readers of fiction don't want cartoons—and for sure they don't want to have to work for them.

That's why, when writing about absurd or incredible situations, those situations must be grounded in a world that *makes* them credible, so readers will be willing to invest in them.

Imagine a novel about a group of ten-year-olds hijacking an airliner. Neat idea, huh? So are Wile E. Coyote's ideas, and they never come off. Sociologically, legally, psychologically, physically, the novel's premise is absurd.

Remember the scene in *Catch-22* where Milo Minderbinder—mess officer, genius entrepreneur, and President and CEO of M & M Enterprises—contracts with the Germans to bomb his own air squadron for them, at cost plus 6 percent? The absurd premise works because it grows organically out of the absurd environment of Heller's novel as a whole. Yes, Heller is writing about World War

II, but it's not the World War II that we read about in history books. It's an analogous World War II taking place on a fictional island in a parallel universe, one in which such things are not only possible but happen all the time. Within *Catch-22's* first pages this parallel universe is firmly established, and the rules of Heller's sly game are spelled out. The author has contracted to deliver us absurdity, and absurdity is what we get.

Other works that embrace the absurd, like Lewis's *Narnia* books and Tolkien's *The Lord of the Rings,* and the Harry Potter books, are works of pure fantasy set in an alternate (as opposed to parallel) universe, or in a mythical past. Emotionally, the worlds of such novels may relate to our world; physically, they have little in common. In the Harry Potter books, J.K. Rowling succeeds admirably in conflating her imagined world of magic and spells with the prosaic world we all know, defying its limitations to the delight of hundreds of millions of fans.

Other books stay within the real world while bordering on the absurd. In John Irving's *The World According to Garp*, the title character's mother—a hospital nurse in want of a child—impregnates herself through intercourse with a perpetually priapic but vegetative ex-ball-turret gunner. Jenny Fields later becomes a feminist author and icon and is eventually murdered at a political rally. Her son Garp dresses as a woman so he can attend her funeral, since no men are allowed. Throughout his novel, Irving brushes up against, but never quite crosses, the line into absurdity.

Inexperienced authors plant absurd seeds in their realistic soil without ever acknowledging or exploiting the discrepancy. What emerges is neither credible nor convincing. There may well be a parallel universe in which ten-year-olds hijack airliners, but as it stands, that story crosses the line into ludicrousness, and beyond.

34 } THREE PREGNANT BANK ROBBERS: MOTIVATING ABSURDITY

Imagine the story of three pregnant women robbing a bank.

Hard to believe?

That, no doubt, is why the author chose to write it. Her intent was to shock readers with the originality of her premise, her sensational raw material. But here again the question needs to be asked: Under what circumstances, in this or an alternative world, would three pregnant women *contemplate* robbing a bank, let alone actually rob one?

Unlike Heller, who gives us a world where officers bomb their own squadrons, or Kafka, who gives us one where men turn into giant beetles, or H.G. Wells, who gives us one where a man travels backward and forward through time, or Shirley Jackson, who gives us one where the "decent" folk of a community take part in an annual stoning ritual in which one of their number are killed, this writer merely plops her three pregnant heroines into *our* world, the same one you and I live in, and expects us to believe it when they do something which, by our world's standards, isn't believable.

For such a story to work in our world, the author would have to establish motives for such incredible behavior. She would have to put her three heroines in a position where they have no choice but to rob a bank. Abandoned by the fathers of their children, perhaps they have been bosom buddies since childhood; perhaps one of them was a bank teller whose supervisor knocked her up and then fired her. Perhaps all three women worked at the same bank and were impregnated by the same lothario. Now at least there is opportunity and motivation.

It's still a stretch to believe that, by endangering their own lives as well as the lives curled up in their wombs, these women hope to gain anything. However, if as readers we are presented with such compelling circumstances in the story's first paragraphs or pages, we might just buy the story that follows.

Actions, however far-fetched, can be rendered authentic provided that they are sufficiently motivated.

35 } AUTHENTICITY VS. REALISM: DREAMING ON PAPER

When I insist on authenticity, plausibility, credibility, am I advocating "realism"?

No. In fact, I don't believe that what we experience as everyday life can or should be put on paper. Fiction isn't "real"—any more than life is made of written words. Fiction is a trick, an illusion, closer to dreams and to magic than to "reality"— one person's reality being another's definition of madness. And in any work of art, the "reality" is in any case artificial, as Lionel Trilling tells us:

"When we speak of literal reality, we are aware that there is really no such thing—that everything that is *perceived* is in some sense *conceived*, or created. ... Nevertheless, bound as we are by society and convention, as well as by certain necessities of the mind, there still is a thing that we persist in calling 'literary reality,' and we recognize in works of art a greater or less approximation of it."

Einstein: "As far as the laws of mathematics refer to reality, they are not certain; and as far as they are certain, they do not refer to reality."

Substitute "principles of writing" for "laws of mathematics."

Great fiction creates its own worlds, and in so doing it changes the way we look at the so-called "real" world. Massive bureaucracies today are said to be "Kafkaesque"; authoritarian institutions or states are described as "Orwellian"; scenes of debauchery (as well as gross humor) are classified "Rabelaisian." When he wrote *The Great Gatsby,* Fitzgerald had no idea that he'd written a love letter to the "The Jazz Age."

What we are pleased to call "reality" is actually a jumble of handed-down impressions inherited from those who lived before us, artists who preserved their impressions, dreams, and visions vividly in images and words.

Writing fiction is dreaming on paper—not passive dreaming, but active, lucid dreaming, with the author at the controls.

There's logic in fiction, too. But it's the logic of dreams.

36} DREAM LOGIC: SWIMMING IN THE DESERT

This is why I'm always insisting that the word "reality" be bracketed by quotation marks: It's such a relative term—relative, that is, to the set of perceptions perceiving it.

In one person's "reality," it's entirely possible, in the middle of a desert, to have a swim team.

Miranda July demonstrates this in her story "The Swim Team," about a woman who captains a swim team in a landlocked, dry-as-dust part of the United States. The narrator explains how she gives swimming lessons without a pool, pond, lake, or stream:

> We met twice a week in my apartment. When they arrived, I had three bowls of warm tap water lined up on the floor, and then a fourth bowl in front of those, the coach's bowl. I added salt to the water because it's supposed to be healthy to snort warm salt water, and I figured they would be snorting accidentally. I showed them how to put their noses and mouths in the water and how to take a breath to the side. Then we added the legs, and then the arms. I admitted these were not perfect conditions for learning to swim, but, I pointed out, this was how Olympic swimmers trained when there wasn't a pool nearby.

Do we really believe that any Olympic swimmers train this way, in "real" life? Ms. July sells us not only on that small departure from factual truth, but on her conceit as a whole. How does she do it? *By laying firm claim to her own fictional world,* one in which people learn to swim in bowls of water on apartment floors.

How does she create that world? When does she create it?

On the first page, in the first paragraph:

> This is the story I wouldn't tell you when I was your girlfriend. You kept asking and asking, and your guesses were so lurid and specific. Was I a kept woman? Was Belvedere like Nevada, where prostitution is legal? Was I naked for the entire year? The reality began to seem barren. And in time I realized that if the truth felt empty, then I probably would not be your girlfriend much longer.

With that first sentence already we're disarmed. A story the author *wouldn't* tell us if she was our girlfriend? The mix of negations, conditionals, and hypothesis is designed to make the reader dizzy, and—like a good battering with a pillow—it simultaneously softens us up for just about anything. We're told that this battered, disoriented "you" has guessed that the story is "lurid" and "specific": and so it will prove to be. Was the teller a "kept" woman? Who knows? Who *cares?* Just please tell us the story, Miranda, *any* story: At this point, we'll take whatever we get.

The comparison of Belvedere to Nevada suggests, slyly, that "Belvedere" is likewise one of the United States—one we've never seen or heard of, just as we've never seen or heard of people learning to swim in however many bowls of salt water. See how the author takes us from our world and slips us into her fictional one? "The reality began to seem barren." As will the reader's own reality, once he surrenders to that of the author—as he will any minute now. *And in time I realized that if the truth felt empty, then I probably would not be your girlfriend much longer*: i.e., if he doesn't accept what's coming, the reader can kiss his hypothetical girlfriend goodbye.

From then on it's the author's way, or the highway. Readers can either bail or surrender.

That's how fictional worlds get built.

37 } FROM IMPOSSIBLE TO INEVITABLE: THE CONTINUUM OF CREDIBILITY

Ideally a story's "world" should be established within the first few sentences. Otherwise, readers can't be blamed for trying to graft the elements of the story onto their own world, and finding that the graft won't take.

We can think of credibility as a gradual continuum, with *impossible* at one end and *inevitable* at the other. Between these two extremes lie *possible* and *probable*.

The level to aim for in fiction is *inevitable*.

When you can make the actions of your characters seem to be the *only* possible actions, you have achieved the quality of inevitability. You may even have yourself a masterpiece.

Short of that, the goal to aim for is *probability*: not only that something could possibly happen, but that it very well *might*. Mere possibility does not justify fictional events or provide a satisfying reading experience.

And—unless you're dealing with fantasy, surrealism, magic realism, or downright absurdity—*im*possibility disqualifies itself.

Autobiography: Its Pleasures & Perils

38 } WHAT IS TRUTH? ASKED JESTING PILATE: EXPERIENCE, IMAGINATION, & MEMORY

Though both memoir and fiction both rely on the devices of fiction—dialogue, description, etc.—they are fundamentally different.

While fiction is powered mainly by imagination, memoir has memory humming under its hood. To the extent that the memoirist uses her imagination, she undermines her purpose, which is to tell the truth.

Conversely, to the extent that the fiction writer relies on memory, he weighs down his imagination and keeps it from taking flight.

So there are benefits and risks to introducing autobiographical content into fiction. The benefits are obvious: The material of our own lives is readily available, and it comes with a seal of authenticity. Our own experiences and feelings, the things that we ourselves have seen and done, are surely true.

The risks may be less obvious.

Our lives aren't always the stuff of fiction, or we may not know how to *select* from our lives the most useful material. Experience furnishes us with countless sensations, memories, events, episodes, anecdotes, and intrigues, but the vast majority of these are useless as far as fiction is concerned. They are more likely to clutter and muddy our fictional worlds than enhance them.

39 } AUTOBIOGRAPHY IN FICTION: A CONCISE SURVEY

Autobiography has always played a role in fiction. It has furnished us with some of our greatest masterpieces. It has also resulted in embarrassment and scandal.

Disguising fiction as biography or autobiography goes back to the birth of the English language novel, to *Robinson Crusoe*:

> I was born in the Year 1632, in the City of York, of a good Family, tho' not of that Country, my Father being a Foreigner of *Bremen*, who settled first at *Hull*: He got a good Estate by Merchandise, and leaving off his Trade, lived afterward at *York*, from whence he had married my Mother, whose Relations were named *Robinson*, a very good Family in that Country, and from whom I was called *Robinson Keutznaer*; but by the usual Corruption of Words in

> *England,* we are now called, nay we call our selves, and write our
> Name *Crusoe,* and so my Companions always call'd me.

We know, as readers knew then, that *Robinson Crusoe* is a novel rather than a work of nonfiction. Yet the word "novel" appears nowhere on the book's title page, which instead primes the reader with a sense of authenticity by presenting the story as an account of factual events—as an historic *document,* albeit a forged one.

Ninety-nine years after Defoe stranded his fictional Englishman on a desert island, Mary Shelley wrote *Frankenstein, or, The Modern Prometheus.* Shelley's novel opens with a Captain Walton sailing his ship north of the Arctic Circle, where he encounters first Frankenstein's monster and then Victor Frankenstein himself, whom he invites aboard his ship. The novel now switches from the Captain's narration to that of Dr. Frankenstein, and is devoted to his strange story.

This "Russian doll" structure of a story-within-a-story is contrived to lend an air of authenticity to a tale that would otherwise read as sheer fantasy.[17] As with *Robinson Crusoe,* the idea was to trick the reader into thinking that he is being presented with something not madeup, but real. This approach remained the modus operandi of fiction for the next hundred years.

The limits of autobiography were put to an extreme test when, between 1913 and 1927, Marcel Proust published his fictional memoir in seven imposing volumes (translated title: *In Search of Lost Time* or *Remembrance of Things Past*). One hundred and thirty years had passed since Jean-Jacques Rousseau published his *Confessions,* in which he shares with his readers some of the most embarrassing moments of his life—like the time he framed a young girl for a theft he committed—and over three hundred

---

17 Despite Shelley's best efforts to imbue her book with authenticity, a majority of reviewers rejected its fantastic premise. One review called it "a tissue of horrible and disgusting absurdity."

since Montaigne wrote his essays. Through those centuries, the passion for ruthlessly examining one's mind and heart (and other body parts) leached into fiction in such introspective first-person novels as Samuel Richardson's *Pamela, or Virtue Rewarded* (1740), Goethe's *The Sorrows of Young Werther* (1787), and Charlotte Brontë's *Jane Eyre* (1847), presented, respectively, as diaries, a series of letters, and reminiscences.

But Proust marked out his own unique territory, using his life as the basis for lengthy ruminations on art, friendship, love, and loss, while at the same time dishing up the sort of social comedy and tortured romance that Victorian readers expected from a "novel." Although he vehemently denied that he was writing autobiography, the parallels between *Remembrance* and Proust's actual life are too many, the correspondences too rich, the novel's substance too clearly a product not of imagination but of memory. It has been argued that, though Proust and his narrator share the same name and much of their biographies, the first is the literal Marcel Proust, while the other is Proust as he *dreams* himself—a reflection or a projection. Proust himself delivered this succinct apology for his method: "To write [the] essential book, a great writer does not need to invent it, since it already exists in each one of us, but merely to translate it. The duty and task of a writer are those of translator."

This seems a far cry from Defoe's method—but in fact there are more similarities than differences. Defoe didn't invent the story of Robinson Crusoe so much as he translated that of a real-life castaway named Selkirk, a Scottish sailor who survived over four years marooned on a South Pacific island. But while Defoe goes to great pains to hide his biographical source (while presenting us with a bogus autobiography), Proust's masterpiece conceals nothing. Its author's protests notwithstanding, *Remembrance of Things Past* is blatantly, obsessively autobiographical.

Since Proust there has been no shortage of autobiographical stories presented as fiction (the *roman á clef*). But until recently the tendency has been to disguise them as novels, as Thomas Wolfe did with *Look Homeward, Angel* and his other Eugene Gant novels, and as Henry Roth did in *Call It Sleep*. Until recently "memoirs" were thought of as minor works penned by chauffeurs, ex-*aides de camp,* and the often vengeful offspring of the rich, powerful, or famous. To be taken seriously as a writer, one had to be a novelist, which meant one had to write a *novel*. This remains the case, though less so, today, while in the interim literary prestige and sales figures have parted company.

A second motive for the novelistic subterfuge was the author's vestigial sense of privacy and decorum. For this reason, *A Moveable Feast*, Hemingway's forthright and frequently vicious memoir of his Paris days, saw print only posthumously.

40 } A NOVEL APPROACH TO MEMOIR: THE JAMES FREY SCANDAL

But Neither Defoe nor Proust—nor Hemingway—could have foreseen a day when fiction would come to us disguised not as a true "document," but as a no-holds-barred confession, a sensational one bearing the author's own name.

Yet that day has come, and with it scandal. Thanks to Oprah, by now everyone knows the story of James Frey's *A Million Little Pieces*. Frey's memoir of drug addiction proved to be a work of fiction pawned off as "true" confession. The book began its career as a novel; but when all the big publishers (including Random House, which ultimately published it) turned it down, Frey and his agent hit upon the clever scheme of repackaging it as nonfiction.

What's most curious about the Frey scandal is what it reveals about readers: They don't read very carefully. The book's first paragraph should have alerted them to the element of fiction:

> I wake to the drone of an airplane engine and the feeling of something warm dripping down my chin. I lift my hand to feel

> my face. My front four teeth are gone, I have a hole in my cheek, my nose is broken and my eyes are swollen nearly shut. I open them and I look around and I'm in the back of a plane and there's no one near me. I look at my clothes and my clothes are covered with a colorful mixture of spit, snot, urine, vomit and blood. I reach for the call button and I find it and I push it and I wait and thirty seconds later an Attendant arrives.

At the very least this is *heightened* autobiography; the author is laying it on thick. That the narrator's clothes are "covered" in vomit isn't quite enough; we must be treated to a rainbow of bodily fluids (see Meditation # 30). And assuming Frey *really* got punched in the mouth, and that four teeth were loosened, what are the odds of them all being "gone"? And this in a scuffle with *airport security*?

If anything is the stuff of fiction, this is. Yet Frey's readers (including Oprah) believed it—in part because they *wanted* to believe, as we all want to believe that other people's problems are far worse than our own.

As with all commodities, with books we like to get our money's worth. Our culture puts a premium on *information*, while treating imagination, more or less, as a dinner guest views the precocious crayon art of her host's child. Today many of us, while more than willing to shell out $22.95 for a memoir, however embellished (or for an unhelpful self-help book), are less willing to dig so deep into our pockets for a *novel*.

This is the real scandal exposed by Frey's hoax: that what we value in our literature is not its emotional truth—what any good work of fiction supplies—but imagination packaged as information, as a commodity with material value.

41 } BIGGER THAN LIFE: SHAMELESS SELF-CHRONICLERS

Can the two forms—fiction and autobiography—successfully merge?

Some of the greatest works of literature toe the line between fiction and memoir: Jack Kerouac's *On the Road,* Kazantzakis's *Zorba the Greek,* Henry Miller's *Tropic* books, Céline's *Journey to the End of the Night,* most of Joyce and all of Thomas Wolfe. In each of these cases, however, autobiography surmounts its limits to become poetry, history, even philosophy. Books like *Zorba* and *On the Road* serve as a sort of pagan bible or manual for the rootless wanderer in all of us. They aren't novels bogged down with autobiographical details, but works of deep poetic imagination and intensity that *happen* to follow the contours of autobiographical fact while charting fresh literary waters. A sample:

> I am living at the Villa Borghese. There is not a crumb of dirt anywhere, nor a chair misplaced. We are all alone here and we are dead.
>
> Last night Boris discovered that he was lousy. I had to shave his armpits and even then the itching did not stop. How can one get lousy in a beautiful place like this? But no matter. We might never have known each other so intimately, Boris and I, had it not been for the lice.
>
> Boris has just given me a summary of his views. He is a weather prophet. The weather will continue bad, he says. There will be more calamities, more death, more despair. Not the slightest indication of a change anywhere. The cancer of time is eating us away. Our heroes have killed themselves, or are killing themselves. The hero, then, is not Time, but Timelessness. We must get in step, a lock step, toward the prison of death. There is no escape. The weather will not change.

Here is autobiography charged with surrealism and dosed with madness, the madness of a man who can stand at the edge of hopelessness and see nothing but joy. "I have no money, no resources, no hopes," Henry Miller goes on to announce in *Tropic of Cancer.* "I am the happiest man alive." We believe him. We believe him because we feel that there is indeed a *man* and not just a writer talking to us here, that his exposed nerve endings throb in these words, that he speaks to us from deep down in the grumbling belly of his soul. Miller takes us, his readers, into not just his heart, but deeper, into his bowels. Some may be less than willing to go there.[18] Yet who will deny the power of Miller's prose—or of his pose, that of a man squaring up to his own doom, spitting in its face, and laughing?

Living up to his name, author Ivan Gold turned the lead of autobiography into bullion. His 1969 novel, *Sick Friends*, was written many years after critic Lionel Trilling predicted that he would be "one of the commanding writers of our time" (a prediction that, thanks in part to Gold's drinking, never came true). Gold tells the story of his alter ego, Jason Sams, and his love affair with an Armenian "girl." (In 1969 one could get away with this). A typical passage:

> She had a second drink, then a third. I was very loose, drinking more than she but holding it as well as usual, calculating the impression I was making and finding it good. It was a Dale Carnegie special. All the world loves a listener. It was not my usual role, but I could manage it, and though she was anecdotal, and though the ghosts of boredom and distraction hovered, as they always will, she was seldom really dull.

What a difference between this and Frey's hyperbolic foaming-at-the-mouth. Where Frey bastes us with bodily fluids, Gold dips us in Jason Sams's wit, intelligence, and honesty—an honesty that admits to many crimes and misdemeanors, including being delivered to the edge of boredom while listening to the love of his life. Sensationalism wasn't Gold's aim. And yet there's something sensational about experiencing any character's life in such microscopic detail. What Gold's novel delivers to us, in great Promethean bursts, is Socrates's examined life. You can't read *Sick*

---

18 Women especially are turned off by Miller—wrongly, I think, for they take his crude, blustering bravado at face value, while failing to see the vulnerable romanticist it masks.

Friends without *being* Jason Sams, or at any rate without knowing what it feels like to be him.

Such a novel could never have been written from anywhere but deep inside its protagonist. And the only way to get that deep into a character is to have the character be *you*—that is, to write autobiographically.

The most abbreviated survey of autobiographical American fiction would be incomplete without this voice:

> I was fifty years old and hadn't been to bed with a woman for four years. I had no women friends. I looked at them as I passed them on the streets or wherever I saw them, but I looked at them without yearning and with a sense of futility. I masturbated regularly, but the idea of having a relationship with a woman—even on non-sexual terms—was beyond my imagination.

This isn't author Charles Bukowski speaking to us; it's his alter ego, Henry Chinaski. There's something to be said for a narrator who, within the first three sentences, lets us in on his solitary sex habits. This may scare off more than a few readers, but even they can be grateful for being forewarned of what's to follow.

The principle virtue of Bukowski is his supreme and utter lack of, well, *bullshit*—not only his frankness, but also his style, so simple and direct that it never betrays itself as "writing." For Bukowski that would indeed be a betrayal, for he aimed to present us not with a writer but with a man who happens to write—just as he happens to drink, to have sex, to bet on horses, and to work (occasionally) for the U.S. Postal Service.[19]

---

19 The examples above, you'll note, are all by men. The impulse to shameless autobiography has claimed far fewer women. Lady Caroline Lamb's *Glenarvon* (1816) chronicles her affair with Lord Byron; Sylvia Plath's *The Bell Jar* relates a young woman's mental breakdown. When women write about themselves, as did Colette and Anaïs Nin, they tend to use more subterfuge and discretion. Nin does so even in her supposedly "private" diaries—where her "frank" descriptions are aimed mostly outward at others while she reserves the role of objective observer for herself.

Autobiography:
Clutter & Anecdote

I've devoted some time to autobiography because one finds so much of it in novice fiction. The examples above demonstrate that autobiography can lend authenticity—either in the form of a grace note or notes, or by supplying the whole cloth from which a work of fiction is cut.

42} GILDING LILY: AUTOBIOGRAPHICAL CLUTTER

However, presented with their own lives as material, most beginners will fail to separate the wheat from the chaff, if only because there's so much chaff and so little wheat.

In a story about a woman tormented by the solitude she experiences in her new setting, we learn several facts: Before coming to New Mexico she lived in "a city where even the secretaries have bachelor's degrees"; she earned her graduate degree in medieval history from Columbia University; after graduating she worked as a bartender; she practices astrology, reads Milton and Blake, and has a talent for wine-tasting; and until her sixteenth year (when she moved in with her senator uncle in D.C.), she lived with her grandparents on their Kansas farm, where she befriended a domestic goose named Gertrude.

Even after learning all these things about Lily, by the time her story ends we still feel we don't know her. We don't know why she left the East Coast, or how she ended up in the desert of New Mexico, or why—having come there—she feels so unhappy. What brought her to her present circumstances?

What usually gives autobiographical content away is that it serves no clear purpose in a story. Specific details like these, concerning a character's interests and her background, ought to furnish us with strong clues as to why a character has ended up where she is, *who* she is, and possibly even where she is heading. Such facts must be carefully selected, not snatched at random out of an autobiographical grab bag. Even assuming that all these facts have been chosen with some purpose, there may be too many of them. They tumble over each other like lobsters in a tank.

The great challenge in using autobiographical material lies in knowing what to use and what to throw out—or save for another story or novel. Since each of us has access to a virtually endless supply of experiences and anecdotes, as soon as we open the floodgates to autobiography our choices increase by an order of magnitude.

And since all art is about making choices and thereby imposing limits, autobiography makes the artist's job not easier, but *harder* (see Meditation # 1).

Of course, our own lives are all we have. Everything we write must be, to some extent, autobiographical.

There are two approaches to working autobiographically. One is to begin with the autobiographical incidents and events of our lives and, by focusing, inventing, and embellishing, turn them into fiction. Thus, shapeless reality takes on the shape of meaning, colored by theme.

The other approach is to begin with an idea and "grow" the story from it, like the culture in a petri dish, with the author's autobiographical experiences nourishing his themes as they emerge. We take from our lives exactly what we need for our stories, and no more. What isn't supplied by life is supplied by our imaginations.

But on the whole when it comes to fiction it's better to reverse the formula, with life supplying only what isn't supplied by the imagination.

43 } THE LINGUISTICS PROFESSOR: WORKING FROM ANECDOTE

Then there is the risk of anecdote, which happens when episodes or events are served half-baked from the autobiographical oven, slathered with detail but lacking thematic or emotional relevance.

The word *anecdote* is defined by Webster's Eleventh as "a usually short narrative of an interesting, amusing, or biographical incident." While a plot may be built around an incident or incidents, anecdotes are mere transcriptions of such incidents with no purpose beyond amusement. In a work of fiction, characters are revealed, deepened, and often (though not always) altered. An anecdote reveals and alters nothing.

Real life hands us countless situations and incidents: anecdotes. It's up to us to turn those found objects into *stories*, to shift them from "what happened to me on the way to [fill in the blank]" into something else entirely, something where the emphasis is no longer on the novelty of the incident, but on the characters to whom the incident occurs, and the meanings that they—and our readers—extract from it.

In Paul Bowles's horrendous story, "A Distant Episode," a linguistics professor traveling in southern Morocco is set upon by Reguibat tribesmen who cut out his tongue, enslave him, and turn him into a kind of performing clown, covering him with bits of shiny metal and making him dance and mumble incoherently for their amusement.

Reduced to this pithy description, it's easy to imagine how Bowles's story could have started its life as an anecdote, a bizarre tale related over glasses of mint tea in a Tangiers rug shop.

Yet as written Bowles's story is anything but anecdotal.

> The Professor ran beneath the arched gate, turned his face toward the red sky, and began to trot along the Piste d'In Salah, straight into the setting sun. Behind him, from the garage, the soldier took

a potshot at him for good luck. The bullet whistled dangerously near the Professor's head, and his yelling rose into an indignant lament as he waved his arms more wildly, and hopped high into the air at every few steps, in an access of terror.

When read in full, the story's shocking conclusion strikes us not as a gratuitous event, but as an inevitability born of the professor's Western chauvinism and other damning character flaws.

Anecdotes amuse us for precisely the same reason that they don't work in fiction: because they're arbitrary, accidental, without precedent, significance, or meaning. Until it undergoes the necessary transformation, an anecdote is the antithesis of fictional art, which at best comes with layers of meaning and a sense of inevitability.

Lovers, Parents, &
Disappearing Narrators

44} TOO CLOSE FOR CLARITY: CHARACTERS BASED ON LOVERS & PARENTS

Another hazard of working autobiographically: It robs the writer of one of his most valuable tools—perspective.

Take a story where the author is describing his own father. It's unlikely that he'll be able to convey his father's character with clarity, much less objectivity.

For most of us, to obtain the necessary level of objectivity, either we must separate ourselves from our subjects, or they must separate themselves from us—death, of course, being the ultimate divider.

As always there are exceptions. Alexander Trocchi[20] wrote beautifully about his father during his father's lifetime; so did Joyce. But interestingly, both authors did so from a great distance of miles: Joyce from Zurich (with his father still in Dublin), and Trocchi from a gravel scow in New York harbor (with his father in Glasgow). In both cases, the son's feelings were sufficiently mixed to allow for a ruthlessly unsentimental portrayal.

For the rest of us mortals, our lovers and parents are the hardest people in the world to have perspective on. While living they are too huge in our lives: Our feelings toward them are too complex, tangled in a web of guilt, shame, anger, obligation, pity, terror, and what have you, enmeshed in judgment and sentiment.

When a lover or a parent leaves us for good (or we leave them), it changes everything. The passage of time allows us to see and understand much more, and to be fairer as well as funnier in our evaluations—and also more rigorous.

To gain perspective on characters based on living people is much harder than doing so for imagined characters, and may demand the kind of distance provided only by time or death.

45} DISAPPEARING & INVISIBLE NARRATORS

A final problem posed by vestigial autobiography is the disappearing or invisible first-person narrator. Assuming this "I" to be herself, the autobiographical author abdicates her responsibility to create a character for her.

Fiction writers ought never to confuse "I" with the person holding the pen. The person holding the pen exists; the "I" on paper needs to be created from scratch, using words.

---

20 A Scottish novelist (1925–1984) whose novel, *Cain's Book,* is a forgotten masterpiece.

The problem occurs especially with travel and adventure stories, where the author assumes that exotic settings, ordeals, and rituals (capturing dolphins in the wild, trekking to the top of le Grand Piton, partaking in Koukeri fertility rites) negate the need for characters; the narrator's role is reduced to that of a tour guide.

What does a narrator need? The same things that evoke the personalities of any of our characters: actions, gestures, dialogue, description[21]—and *attitude*. A narrator's attitude may be sarcastic or ironic, or deadpan, or earnest, or bitter, or nostalgic, or wistful: It doesn't matter, as long as he has an attitude.

Our characters, including our narrators, exist only after we have made them out of words. As William Carlos Williams said of Rebecca West (taking her to task for calling Joyce's writing "gibberish"):

> She has not yet learned—though she professes to know the difference between art and life—the sentimental and the nonsentimental—that *writing is made of words* [italics mine].

In memoir, experiences and meanings are supplied by memory; in fiction, by imagination. Any conflation of fiction and memoir will likely produce something confusing, like a movie projected onto a painting.

Perhaps in your own autobiographical fiction you'll succeed in honoring both memory and imagination, as Proust did. But given the odds, you'd be wise to commit to one form or the other—fiction or memoir—and avoid insulting both.

---

21 In describing their own physical features, narrators typically resort to reflecting surfaces: hence the proliferation of mirrors in first-person stories.

END NOTES:
Matters of Substance

To sum up Matters of Substance: It's not enough to love our subjects. We need to weigh their suitability as subjects for fiction, and then figure out how to go about making use of them. This means understanding what truly compelling questions are raised by our material (characters and situations), and how far we should go toward answering them. As Chekhov said, "The writer's task is not to solve the problem, but to state the problem correctly."

Our first task, then, is to know what the problem is. And that means making the right substantive choices.

Q. HOW DO I GO ABOUT CREATING HEROES, VILLAINS, VICTIMS?

A. Don't. Instead of thinking in terms of gross labels, think in terms of motivations and actions. If a character wants to strangle an infant in its crib, odds are such an action or desire will plant him fairly squarely in the villain category; whereas the character who fends off such an attack will be seen as a hero, and the baby will assume the category of victim.

But these labels are judgments, to be applied by the reader, and not by you, the writer.

Q. HOW DO I MAKE CHARACTER DESCRIPTIONS VIVID?

A. By selecting and emphasizing *telling* details—specific details that separate one old man or little girl from a sea of old men and little girls. "A salt-and-pepper beard" or "blonde hair and green eyes" won't do: We've seen hundreds of old men with salt-and-pepper beards, ditto little girls with blonde hair and green eyes. But we haven't seen many old men with plum-sized boils on the backs of their necks, or little girls with eyebrows so arched and fine they look painted on with a Japanese sumi brush.

Q. HOW DO I MAKE MY DIALOGUE AUTHENTIC?

A. By recording not what you think characters would or should say, but what they *do* say, spontaneously, almost in spite of you and even of themselves. Except under pressure, people rarely think before opening their mouths. That's a bad thing for human affairs, but a good thing for novelists and short story writers. By what they blurt out, characters expose and reveal hidden things about themselves.

Q. HOW DO I AVOID CREATING STEREOTYPES?

A. By thinking not in terms of types or categories, but of specific and concrete actions, desires, and other qualities. The danger of stereotype is averted through specificity. If a character begins to come across as a stereotypical jock, he ceases to be one the moment we discover him reading Byron in his spare time, while stirring a Bolognese sauce.

Q. HOW DO I GIVE MY CHARACTERS DEPTH?

A. By evoking them through many or all of the following: physical description, dialogue (including what others say about her), internal dialogue (as conveyed through point of view), background information and flashbacks, and finally, most impressively, through action.

Q. HOW DO I MAKE SURE MY IDEAS ARE UNIQUE AND NOT "STOLEN" OR "BORROWED"?

A. The easiest way is to have your ideas generated by character, and not vice versa. If you have a character, and that character is motivated—that is, if her happiness depends on either destroying some irritant that has made her unhappy, or on attaining some goal designed to win her freedom or fortune—then the rest (theme, action, plot) will emerge uniquely from these ingredients, and the result will be yours and yours alone.

Q. WHAT ABOUT CLICHÉS: WHAT IS THE BEST WAY TO AVOID THEM?

A. Each of us has a built-in cliché detector that should be activated and exercised. The thing to remember is that clichés exist on all levels of writing, from ideas as a whole to phrases and, yes, even individual words when used under certain conditions. Sensitivity to clichés grows with training. Question what sounds familiar: It probably is. Ask yourself: Have I seen or heard that (idea/series of words) before?

Be vigilant, and clichés will avoid you, and vice versa.

Q. WHAT ABOUT MELODRAMA AND SENTIMENTALITY? HOW DO I AVOID THEM?

A. Melodrama is action in excess of motivation or circumstance; sentimentality is emotion in excess of the same. When writers resort to melodrama or sentimentality (tears, fistfights, operatic arias of emotion inspired by a hangnail) it's usually because they don't take the time to deal with the genuine, more subtle behaviors of their characters.

By slowing down and immersing ourselves more deeply and carefully in our characters' psyches, we avoid both traps.

Q. WHAT ARE THE DRAWBACKS AND BENEFITS OF USING AUTOBIOGRAPHICAL MATERIAL?

A. The benefits are obvious and consist almost entirely of convenience in the forms of total, unrestricted access to information of the most intimate nature. We know ourselves and our loves better than we can ever know anyone else's life or circumstances. So if we're to "write about what [we] know," what better material to work from?

But as with all things convenient the convenience comes at a price. We know too much about our own lives, with much of what we know unusable and amounting to clutter.

On the other hand, when we invent characters not based on ourselves—but based, say, on a glimpse of someone else, or a composite of glimpses—we tend to "know" only what really matters for our stories, and not much more. So our invented worlds come to us clutter free.

Matters of
Structure

Form: No Wine Without the Glass

Water, as Hermann Hesse wrote, "flows to seek whatever forms it finds." Ideas, however, must be given shape by us. As in architecture and engineering, form tends to follow function—except that artistic function is harder to observe or define.

Yet art comes with "laws" of its own. The first law may be that, whatever form our ideas may take, they must take *some* form. No wine without a glass. Even a form as energetic and seemingly chaotic as Jackson Pollock's drip paintings is a *form*, with boundaries and rules, logic, and limits

To put it in negative terms, every choice that we make presents us with limitations. The sum of these limitations adds up to form.

Having selected our material—the Substance—we face the question: How to present it? In what form? Through what scenes? From what point (or points) of view? Through an objective omniscient narrator, a subjective one, or one (or more) of our characters? Pacing: fast or slow? How much (if any) dialogue should we use? Direct or indirect? Emphasize atmosphere or action? Knowing we can't please all of the gods, which gods should we please?

Most of our structural choices may be dictated by the demands of our material, and thus organic in nature. But being too close to our material, we sometimes overlook the obvious. Sometimes it takes an outsider to say, "Since you're writing a novel about Siamese twins, wouldn't *alternating* viewpoints make more sense than a first-person narrative from only one point of view?"[22]

---

22 Shelley Jackson's novel *Half Life* tells the story of Siamese twins from a single point of view—that of Nora Olney who, after fifteen years of conjoinment, seeks to rid herself of Blanche, her comatose twin. Proof that to every principle or rule in this book, there are exceptions.

But when it comes to making structural suggestions, an editor or teacher must beware of crossing the thin line between instruction and interference. Any advice regarding structural choices should be offered tentatively, even reluctantly, as one possible solution among many—but it *should* be offered. It's up to the writer to accept or refuse the gift.

Plot: The Marriage of Substance & Structure

46} PLOT & A BOTTOMLESS COFFEE CUP

I've included plot here, as an element of structure, even though it belongs properly to the *tension* that results from combining substance and structure. That tension is what creates plot.

Given a fictional situation—an old man, having decided for various reasons to commit suicide, goes to have one last breakfast at the local diner—we must then make some structural decisions: When will we enter his situation, and from what viewpoint will we convey his experience?

Let's assume that we decide to enter the old man's life on the rainy morning when, having topped his Plymouth's gas tank and sealed all the cracks in his garage door, he steps out into the rain and heads down the hill into town for a last breakfast before returning to do the deed. We might then introduce a flashback or two. We might even decide to tell the story backwards, with the first scene showing the old man as he heads back up the hill toward his home, or as he sits in his Plymouth with the engine idling.

We decide to tell the story in the third person, from the old man's point of view, but we still have to decide how *deeply* we want to enter his psyche: how to strike a balance between our character's *subjective* thoughts and feelings and the narrator's *objective* descriptions of setting and action? There's no one-size-fits-all formula to apply; as when mixing gin and vermouth to make a martini, the choice is largely a matter of taste and disposition, and also enforced by the demands made by the story's unique material.

What does all this have to do with plot? Everything, for once we have answered these questions and set off with our characters on their physical and emotional journeys, "plot" pretty much takes care of itself. Plot is *what happens next* in a story, plus *that which makes you wonder what will happen next.*

I can tell you what happens to the old man, since his story is one of my own. He goes to the diner and orders what he assumes will be his last breakfast—and notices, near the bottom of the menu, the words, "OUR CUPS ARE BOTTOMLESS." Having vowed to re-climb the hill and kill himself after breakfast, it now strikes him that, in theory, anyway, given the bottomless nature of his coffee cup, this "last breakfast" might last forever. He decides to test his theory, ordering cup after cup of coffee until at last the owner of the diner cuts him off and sends him on his way. But the passion with which he has defended his right to a "bottomless" cup has awakened in our protagonist a renewed sense of vigor. When he climbs back up the hill, it is with the resolve to go on living. The plot hangs on the old man's discovery of the claim at the bottom of the menu—a discovery that I, the author, made with him while writing his story.

When written from outside, mechanically, schematically, plots and old staircases have two things in common: They're wooden and creaky. That's why I don't recommend formulas for plot, and why I don't even bother to talk about it all that much.

In talking about characters and situations and point of view, I am ultimately talking about plot, about the things that will determine and create our plots *so we don't have to.*

47 } I AM BUT MAD NORTH BY NORTHWEST: GOOD PLOTS, FOOLISH CHOICES

Most plots, especially those that are most active, depend upon characters doing foolish things. In movies with especially kinetic plots one sees this all the time. Without characters doing dumb things, most movie plots would spontaneously evaporate.

Just last night I stayed up late watching *North by Northwest,* one of my favorite movies. The plot turns on a case of mistaken identity: Advertising executive Roger O. Thornhill[23] (Cary Grant) is mistaken for a government counterespionage agent by the suave villain, Philip Vandamm (James Mason), who plots to have him murdered.

In one of the film's most famous scenes, Grant/Thornhill is attacked in a barren Midwestern prairie by a machine-gun outfitted crop-duster plane, a dramatic but highly impractical murder weapon that, indeed, proves ineffective. This particular foolish choice has been made by Vandamm/Mason; other plot points in the film depend on Thornhill's own foolishness, as when he decides to pursue the man for whom he has been mistaken. None of this detracts in any way from the pleasures of *North by Northwest;* but we realize that, absent the foolish choices made by its central characters, its plot would boil down to an easily cleared-up misunderstanding.

Hamlet (from which Hitchcock borrowed his title) happens to furnish an opposing example: a plot that is entirely dependent upon a character *not* doing foolish things. Hamlet's hesitations and vacillations (about which much fuss is made) are really what

---

23 "R.O.T." Asked, "What does the 'O' stand for?" Grant replies, "Nothing."

we might expect from a man faced with deciding whether or not to murder his uncle. Who wouldn't vacillate under the circumstances? Yet, given the nature of drama, we expect characters not to ruminate or reflect, but to *act*—which is why the character of Hamlet is considered such an anomaly. To have characters ruminate ("To be or not to be?") was considered antithetical to drama—antithetical to the very notion of plot, as it had been defined since Homer sent Ulysses home from Troy—when murder and suicide represented the perfectly logical, indeed mandatory, response to jealousy, threats, slights, or a broken heart.

Think of all the stories that would end before they begin if their characters gave careful consideration to the consequences of their actions.

48 } THE QUEST FOR HAPPINESS & OTHER IRRITANTS: TWO PLOTS—ONLY

Really, there are only two essential plots. In Plot A, a character who is unhappy with his lot in life takes action to change it (or, he's happy enough but seizes an opportunity to be happier). In Plot B, an irritant is introduced into a character's otherwise satisfactory existence. In Plot A, a character complicates his own situation; in Plot B, the situation complicates the character.

I can think of few plots that don't fit into one of these two formulas. Here are a few examples that do.

Kafka's "The Metamorphosis": Plot B. The "irritant" is the protagonist's overnight transformation into a giant beetle.

T.C. Boyle's "After the Plague": Plot B. The "irritant" is the plague that has spared the protagonist while killing nearly everyone else in California.

Kate Chopin's "The Story of an Hour": Plot B. The irritant is the news of the death of the heroine's husband. She finds herself rejoicing in her new freedom, only to learn that her husband has not died after all (a new Plot B).

Joyce's "Araby": Plot A. To win his beloved's heart and bring light into his dark existence, the protagonist sets out to buy her a gift, and fails.

Austen's *Pride and Prejudice:* Plot A. All five of Mrs. Bennett's daughters seek happiness and security, through marriage to an appropriate (that is, appropriately wealthy) suitor.

Hemingway's *The Old Man and the Sea:* Plot A. An aging fisherman attempts the biggest catch of his life, tempting failure and challenging his own courage.

Salinger's *The Catcher in the Rye:* Plot A. Frustrated by boarding school, Holden Caulfield spends a dissolute weekend in New York. (Practically everything about Holden's life irritates him.)

There are of course exceptions to the Two Plot Plan, but these tend to be stories and novels in which plots are scarcely discernible, like Stuart Dybek's short story "Pet Milk"—a tale of a pair of Chicago lovers who dine regularly at a Czech restaurant and kiss on the subway home. What holds such a thin "plot" together is the story's atmosphere, the Chicago milieu that the author so richly and lovingly evokes, along with a quality of nostalgia that seals the young lovers like fossils in amber.

Should you find your own stories a bit lacking in plot, look for the "irritant." If there is none, introduce one. Or find a less happy protagonist.

49} DRAFTING IN THE DARK: WHAT LIES AHEAD

My students ask me: "When plotting my work, how far ahead should I be looking?"

I'm uncomfortable with the question, which implies that "plotting" is a separate process, an independent act of volition—a verb that we force *into* our stories, rather than a noun that grows out of the process of writing them. But if the question is, "In writing a story, how much do I need to know about what's going to happen next?" my answer would be, "Probably not all that much."

As with life, the present moment in fiction counts far more than the past or the future. It is where all decisions are made—by the characters, of course, but also through them, by the author. We don't live *there, tomorrow,* or *yesterday;* we live *here, now, today.* If we're living our stories, the same rule applies to writing fiction. To second-guess our characters' futures is to leave their present lives behind, to remove us—and our readers—from their stories.

That doesn't mean you shouldn't have any *ideas* about the future of your plots. It's good to have a direction and even a destination. How we get there, and whether we get there or not, are other matters.

What I tell my students is this: When drafting a short story (which, by the way, is best done in one sitting), look to the middle, to an imaginary point midway between a vaguely perceived ending—that dim light on the distant shore—and the story's starting point. Imagine some event or occurrence near or at that middle point: the job interview, the Friday night dinner date, the doctor calling with the test results, the reversal where Mrs. Slocum decides to turn her son over to the police after all. Aim for that event or occurrence. Think of that point as a bell buoy with a red light flashing on it. Imagine that you have tied a rope to that bell buoy. Pull your story toward the bell buoy using that rope. If the rope breaks—fine, let it break: And let the currents carry you and your story where they will.

That's one way of doing things. Frank O'Connor, for one, did things differently. Planning his stories, O'Connor was far more systematic, even mathematical, reducing plots to an algebraic formula of usually four lines: "X marries Y abroad. After Y's death, X returns home to Y's parents, but does not tell them Y is dead."

Based on his algebraic formula, O'Connor would "block in the general outlines [of the story] and see how many sections it falls into, which scenes are necessary and which are not, and which characters it lights up most strongly." He called this blocked-in outline "a treatment," and imposed this method of plotting on his students—who hated it:

> They always want to begin right away with 'It was a spring evening, and under ice-cold skies the crowds were hurrying homeward along Third Avenue where the signs on the bars were beginning to be reflected in the exhausted eyes of office workers.' This is the sort of thing that makes me tear my hair out, because I know it is ten to one that the story should not begin on Third Avenue at all. …[But by then the student] has already surrendered his liberty for the sake of a pretty paragraph.

For O'Connor, the time for "fine writing" comes only when:

> … everything else is correct; when you know exactly how the story should be told and whom the characters are that you want to tell it about. …[E]ven then, when you have taken every precaution against wasting your time, when everything is organized and, according to the rules, there is nothing left for you to do but produce a perfect story, you often produce nothing of the kind.[24]

Somewhere between these two antithetical modes of working, mine and Mr. O'Connor's, you will (I hope) find your *own* way to plot a short story.

50} PLANTING STAKES IN THE ROAD: PLOTTING NOVELS

If you're drafting a novel, things work differently. Nature never intended for novels to be written in a day, let alone in one sitting.

---

24 From "One Man's Way," a radio lecture broadcast on *The Listener,* July 23, 1959.

Novels typically take six months to several years.[25] And the huge investment in time and labor precludes or anyway discourages the "seat of the pants" approach.

Unlike stories, which surprisingly often seem to generate themselves spontaneously, novels tend to require far more germination. The same three or four hours it takes a short story writer to rip through a first draft, a novelist might devote to staring out his window, or to a long aimless walk (along which he discovers that his heroine will drive to work rather than take the bus).

But novels, too, can be written in a fast, reckless way. Except in rare cases, the result is a "rough" or exploratory draft, a mere preview of the first or "working" draft that will emerge after we've discerned what it is we're really up to. That exploratory draft may then function as a sort of outline, or it may be jettisoned entirely.

All novelists have their own ways of writing stories. Some write an outline before proceeding, slowly and carefully, with a first working draft. "It's like driving a few stakes in the ground," is the way Lawrence Durrell described his process; "you haven't got to that point in the construction yet, so you run ahead fifty yards and you plant a stake to show roughly the direction your road is going, which helps to give you your orientation. But [my novels] are very far from planned in the exact sense."

Then there are novelists like Michael Ondaatje, who composes his novels like poems: carefully, line by line, section by section—in one draft, without looking forward or back. That's how he wrote *The English Patient,* which works, and how he wrote *Divisadero,*

Matters of Structure

---

25 One noteworthy exception: Hans Fallada's *The Drinker,* an autobiographical novel documenting the alcohol-induced psychic collapse of a respectable businessman, was written in two weeks in a German lunatic asylum in 1944. Far from seeming like a rush job, the result is a stylistically flawless prose narrative.

which doesn't.[26] The blame for the ear-popping descent from the first novel's brilliance to the second's failure can be laid squarely on the author's technique, which relies heavily on the hope that the sum of skillfully wrought parts will add up to a worthy whole. Sometimes it does.

In other words, Ondaatje's method can work—*if* you get lucky. Otherwise, do drafts and/or work from an outline.

Point of View:
Inhabiting Our Stories

No problem occurs more frequently in the fiction of inexperienced authors than a mishandled or misguided point of view. At bottom, point of view is a function not of the author's technical or mechanical prowess or choices, but of the author's *soul,* of his ability to inhabit his characters and their world—or not.

51} PLANNING SUBJECTIVITY: NO POINT OF VIEW, NO STORY

In fiction, means and ends are inseparable; method *is* substance.

At any given moment, a story or a novel must present us with a particular viewpoint, whether that of a character (or characters) in the story, or that of an outside observer—the so-called omniscient narrator.

---

26 The reviews, of course, glow, but they're reviewing the novelist and not the novel. Novelists like Cormac McCarthy and Michael Ondaatje, having written hugely successful works, enter the realm of the Sacred & Profound, and everything they write afterward—no matter how mediocre or trite— is pronounced wonderful by other novelists, who don't wish to offend the gods. This is why, just as baseball needs dedicated umpires, literature needs dedicated critics.

But, as with everything else artistic, a choice must be made. You can have all the ingredients—a plot, characters, dialogue, description, setting, conflict—but if they aren't bound by a specific, consistent, and rigorously controlled point of view, you end up with nothing. Which is why, when confronted with point-of-view errors in a workshop, I may write on the board in fat letters:

NO POINT OF VIEW, NO STORY

I'm not talking about minor gaffes and glitches ("As Sally gazed out the bedroom window the door clicked open behind her and there stood Albert"). I mean errors so fundamental that no amount of line editing can set them right, global blunders that call into question not only an author's grasp of a particular moment or scene, but of fiction's primary purpose—which is to render experience, and to do so as vividly, concretely, and authentically as possible.

The way to avoid such blunders is to *inhabit* our stories and characters—to write not from outside them, mechanically, but from inside, instinctively and intuitively. By positioning ourselves (and our narrators) firmly in the worlds of our stories, we render such blunders practically impossible.

52 } POINT OF VIEW:
THE SUBJECTIVITY FILTER

Fiction's stock in trade is subjectivity. And all experience is subjective. There's no such thing as a purely "objective" viewpoint in fiction (or, for that matter, in film: Simply by selecting close-ups and camera angles, the director injects biased—therefore subjective—content). Certain details are provided while others are left out, and to that extent the experience has been modified, customized, interpreted. It has passed through a *subjective filter*.

In fiction, things "happen" only when they affect our characters (see Meditation # 3). To be authentic, experiences must be processed through *someone's* subjectivity filter: that of a particular character whose mind and soul the author has chosen to inhabit, or of an omniscient narrator. Alternatively, events may be presented through an objective external viewpoint that *edits out* all internal emotional content (feelings and thoughts), allowing readers to supply the missing elements and thus create experience.

Hemingway's short stories illustrate an objective, external vantage point:

> He pulled back the blanket from the Indian's head. His hand came away wet. He mounted on the edge of the lower bunk with the lamp in one hand and looked in. The Indian lay with his head toward the wall. His throat had been cut from ear to ear. The blood had flowed down into a pool where his body sagged the bunk. His head rested on his left arm. The open razor lay, edge up, in the blankets.
>
> "Take Nick out of the shanty, George," the doctor said.

Here, as in most of Hemingway's Nick Adams stories, the viewpoint is expressed not by describing the protagonist's emotional responses to events, but purely *by selecting the events to which he responds,* with the responses themselves implied and left to the reader. Though void of subjectivity, a filter is very much at work here.

The point-of-view filter may enhance or it may extract, but there must be a filter. Information conveyed to the reader with this filter missing is equivalent to wine without a glass. That is—impossible.

53 } LILA'S GRANDFATHER: THE CASE FOR CONSISTENCY

A student has written:

> Hank could have passed for Lila's grandfather. His white mustache added to his years, yet he kept himself trim and thought himself as fit as the younger fathers. He was nuts about Lila, who

still loved him, though lately she had grown distant. She was no longer his little girl; in fact, she secretly wished that he would act his age. She especially hated it when he pretended to pull coins and other things out of her ears. Why was he so goofy? But all adolescent girls pass through a phase where they hold all fathers in mild contempt.

At first glance nothing seems wrong with the paragraph above. But on closer inspection problems arise. While the first sentence ("Hank could have passed for Lila's grandfather") is neutral, objective, the second sentence ("thought himself... fit") shifts us firmly into Hank's personal, subjective viewpoint. The third sentence (though it presumes to know Lila's feelings about him) could still be from Hank's viewpoint. But—unless we assume that Lila's secret isn't a secret—the fourth, fifth, and sixth sentences plunge us deeper into Lila's consciousness. The final sentence steps back to take a global, omniscient view of *all* adolescent girls' relationships with their fathers.

The cumulative result of all these subtle shifts is that the reader never knows quite where she stands. The point of view is never clear, the filter is distorted, and the reader's emotional response is therefore fuzzy and imprecise. We get the information necessary to construct a narrative; but constructing a narrative isn't the same as *inhabiting* one. If our readers are to inhabit our stories, we must first do so ourselves.

Point of view can never be incidental or accidental. As choices go, it is as fundamental as the choice between, say, present and past tense, or formal and informal diction, or dramatization vs. exposition.

54} POINT OF VIEW WITHOUT A PLAN: DEFAULT OMNISCIENCE

In a story about a waitress named Linda, we read this: "People didn't think Linda was as pretty as she used to be."

Arguably, this could be Linda's own view of things; if so, it's a harsh view, presented with the blunt objectivity of a Gallup poll. Early on in the same story we are told that "Linda was a waitress and an alcoholic; everyone knew that." Here, too, the point of view could *arguably* be Linda's, but for an alcoholic protagonist to have arrived at this blunt self-assessment would require something more in the way of character development. Since this pronouncement is made early in the story—in the first paragraph—a reader can't be blamed for taking it, not as Linda's subjective opinion, but as an omniscient narrator's objective verdict.

Ultimately, however, the story turns out to be Linda's, presented to us mostly from her viewpoint. As a reader, I'm thrown by those moments when the viewpoint turns omnisciently objective: "Lately, people had been all too concerned about [Linda]". Or is this still Linda's subjective viewpoint—wearing an omniscient, objective mask? At best it's confusing. At worst, it's inauthentic and unconvincing.

But the problem goes deeper than a few lapses. The problem is that the author hasn't taken the trouble to embed herself *thoroughly, consistently, and purposefully,* into her character's psyche—or into any other mind-set, including that of an omniscient narrator. Had she done so, none of these lapses could have occurred.

In another example, eight-year-old Aidan takes his first plane trip to France. The author sabotages his point-of-view strategy— and his story with it—in three ways. First, he strays into passive constructions: "It was the longest plane trip that Aidan had ever been on." This sentence locates the viewpoint just beyond the character's personal, subjective experience. (Compare: "Aidan yawned and shifted in his seat; he'd never been on such a long plane ride before.") Second, he drifts into omniscience: "[Aidan and his sister] knew they had better behave themselves." Finally, he slips into diction that pulls us thoroughly out of Aidan's eight-year-old psyche: "The only dietary adjustment was having to eat goat's milk for breakfast." (Compare: "Aidan spat out his breakfast. His mother had served it to him with goat's milk. It tasted like his armpit.") In each instance the author has failed to *be* Aidan, to plant himself—and the reader—decisively in Aidan's psyche: to see, feel, think, act, and react with him.

By resisting such immersion and commitment, by insisting on mixing our own views with those of our characters, we keep readers at a vague, inconsistent distance. The point of view I get here is neither Aidan's nor his sister's, nor that of a rigorously omniscient narrator, but what I call *default omniscience*: omniscience without plan, passion, or purpose. It fails to provide a consistent, reliable filter for the events described. Whatever it touches it muddies and mutes. It destroys the story as we read it.

No point of view, no story.

55 } BENEDICO, THE GREAT DANE: GENUINE OMNISCIENCE

Does this mean we shouldn't create omniscient narratives, that we should restrict ourselves to a single, limited point of view in our stories—or to two, or three? No, it means that we should enter omniscience knowingly and thoroughly.

Almost anything we do in our fiction, no matter how outrageous or experimental, can work if done consistently and with conviction. For proof, I offer this paragraph from Giuseppe di Lampedusa's *The Leopard*:

> Now, as the voices fell silent, everything dropped back into its usual order or disorder. Benedico, the Great Dane, grieved at exclusion, came wagging its tail through the door by which the servants had left. The women rose slowly to their feet, their oscillating skirts as they withdrew baring bit by bit the naked figures from mythology painted all over the milky depths of the tiles. Only an Andromeda remained covered by the soutane of Father Pirrone, still deep in

> extra prayer, and it was some time before she could sight the sil-
> very Perseus swooping down to her aid and her kiss.

Here, true omniscience allows di Lampedusa to enter the mind not only of a dog, but also of a mythological figure painted into the floor of the Sicilian villa in which his story is set—all in one paragraph. This, I admit, is omniscience taken to an extreme. Yet because it's done consistently and with conviction it goes down like a glass of good Sicilian wine.

The Naked and the Dead, Norman Mailer's doorstop World War II novel, is likewise omniscient:

> Nobody could sleep. When morning came, assault craft would
> be lowered and a first wave of troops would ride through the
> surf and charge ashore on the beach at Anopopei. All over the
> ship, all through the convoy, there was a knowledge that in a few
> hours some of them were going to be dead.

No one character in Mailer's novel can possibly know how *every-one* sleeps or thinks. When wanting to break from omniscience, Mailer uses a device borrowed from Dos Passos that he calls "The Time Machine"[27]—interchapter flashbacks that take us deep into the stream of consciousness of individual members of his doomed troop of soldiers. He thus gives us the best of both perspectives, omniscient *and* intimate.

Less obvious examples of genuine omniscience may be found in many (or most) novels written before 1950, including Carson McCullers's first—and in my view best—book, *The Heart Is a Lonely Hunter.* Unlike Mailer, who was already a decrepit twenty-five-year-old geezer when he wrote *his* masterpiece, McCullers was only twenty-three. Two dozen pages into her book we read:

> [The New York café] was still not crowded—it was the hour when
> men who have been up all night meet those who are freshly wak-

---

27 Dos Passos called his "The Camera Eye." He uses it in his U.S.A. trilogy.

ened and ready to start a new day. The sleepy waitress was serving both beer and coffee. There was no noise or conversation, for each person seemed to be alone. The mutual distrust between the men who were just wakened and those who were ending a long night gave everyone a feeling of estrangement.

Here, too, there is a clear filter—and no question that the filter is omniscient, since it allows us to perceive the feelings of everyone in the town. Unlike di Lampedusa and Mailer, who plunge headlong into unabashed omniscience, McCullers makes her way slowly, gradually, starting off in what might be mistaken for third-person objective, or even for the voice of a peripheral narrator.[28] In the third sentence she even hedges her omniscience with "seemed," implying that her "omniscient" narrator can't be entirely sure. Indeed, large chunks of the novel are written from a single character's viewpoint. It's only when taken as a whole, and in paragraphs like the one quoted above, that the overall omniscience becomes obvious.

In literary fiction, full-throttle omniscience isn't used as much these days. To inhabit whole platoons of soldiers and Great Danes takes a big soul, and perhaps souls have gotten smaller. Or maybe the concept of an "epic" consciousness no longer fits the times. Perhaps we recognize now, more than in the past, the autonomy of individual natures: that every human heart is distinct. And maybe we are all, to some extent, alone in our own worlds.

Moreover, authorial omniscience (since we know it's not possible) can *feel* trumped up, a parlor trick, in an age where information and "facts" are considered so much more valuable than the fruits of imagination. It fails our "authenticity" test—the same test that reality shows, like *Survivor* and *The Bachelor,* apparently pass.

---

28 One could argue that there's little difference between an omniscient narrator and an invisible peripheral one—that is, a peripheral narrator who plays no role in the story being told. The difference, if any, is that we wisely refuse to acknowledge the latter's existence.

56} TOPGALLANT YARDS: RIGGING A SHIP CALLED FICTION

Too often writers simply neglect point of view completely, failing to make this most crucial of choices. They perhaps think point of view is unimportant, or can be fixed or added later. This is thinking from *outside* the story and its people, rather than from inside them and their world.

Most teachers fail in trying to teach point of view (as I have mostly failed, too) for just this reason. We speak of "third-person subjective" and "limited omniscience" as if we are describing topgallant yards and second futtocks in rigging a tall-masted schooner—the *SS Fiction*.

But point of view doesn't work that way. Trying to revise or "fix" the point of view of a story is like trying to rig a ship that's at the bottom of the sea. Point of view is a *mind-set*: not just a way of seeing, but a complete set of interpretive criteria—a sensibility through which readers experience a fictional world, by seeing, feeling, tasting, smelling.

This mind-set stems from *character*: either a member of the fictional cast, or an omniscient yet invisible host or narrator, or the character of the author himself. Even the most objective, "camera-like" point of view entails a rigorous selection process.

To write without a firm grasp of point of view is much harder than to write with it. It's harder because we find ourselves writing from outside of our material, mechanically, rather than from inside, organically. We rely entirely on intellect, and our intellects are no match for the sensibilities of our characters.

57} GETTING JACK HOME: WALKING IN A CHARACTER'S SHOES

That may explain why a passage like this one fails to engage us as much as it might have:

Jack lived a half mile from the mill. His house was on the other side of the river just past Tanner's machine shop. To get there he would take a right at the American Legion, then a left on Passaic Drive, then another right on Elm Street until he got to the bridge. His house was the third on the right past the bridge, squeezed in between the Hotel and the Café. Jack, his wife, and their three kids lived on the second floor. In good weather the kids would be out playing; in bad they would stay indoors watching television. If she wasn't working at the diner, his wife would be making supper, in which case Pat, their oldest, would reheat whatever she'd cooked the night before. Jack would change out of his work clothes and boots, wash up, and set the table.

But instead of going straight home, Jack decided to stop in for a shot or two at the River House Café.

The passage fails because it's been written from outside of the character, and outside of the scene itself. It could succeed were it written without providing Jack's own sensations, from the vantage point of a detached, camera-like objective observer following Jack home. Or the scene could be written from a godlike, omniscient perspective, allowing equal access to both his objective circumstance and his internal, subjective experience. *Or* the scene might have been written from Jack's point of view, filtered entirely through his sensibilities. Instead of the Mapquest-like itinerary of street names and directions, we'd have the experience of a character moving through space, feeling the hot sun or cold air, smelling his dinner cooking, or leaning on the café bar.

None of those approaches is taken here. Here, somehow, through the miracle of *default omniscience*, Jack manages to be both at home with his wife and children *and* hoisting a few at the River House Café, simultaneously. Which tells us—since people can't be two places at once—that Jack is *nowhere:* that he inhabits no particular time or place. Jack is not a flesh-and-blood character, but only a construct in an author's mind.

Unless we inhabit our characters and the worlds in which they live, and watch them *as if* we ourselves were characters operating within that world, our characters will wander through our stories like ghosts; or, worse, they'll exist merely as bits of information scattered across our pages. Compare:

> The main street was quiet and hot, almost deserted. He had not realized until now that it was Sunday and the thought of this depressed him. The awnings over the closed stores were raised and the buildings had a bare look in the bright sun. He passed the New York Café. The door was open, but the place looked empty and dark. He had not found any socks to wear that morning, and the hot pavement burned through the thin soles of his shoes. …

In the earlier passage, the point of view was tentative to nonexistent. In this scene from *The Heart Is a Lonely Hunter,* the point of view is deep, firm. Carson McCullers inhabited her character and wrote the passage *from inside him.*

58 } A FICTIONAL HOUSE DIVIDED: SPLIT POINT OF VIEW

That we should inhabit our characters doesn't mean we should inhabit them all, or all at once.

In a short story especially, it's usually wise to focus the reader's viewpoint on a single character. As a reader, I have a limited supply of empathy to invest, so I prefer to concentrate on a single character. Two points of view are not always better than one.

In a story about two brothers competitive in all things (with Jason always falling short of his older brother, Andrew), adopting a split point-of-view approach works both *for* and *against* its subject. On the one hand it heightens the characters' differences: Andrew shrugging off his conquests, scarcely aware of his little brother's raging envy, and Jason yearning to be better than

Andrew at something, *anything*. On the other hand, the reader never quite knows which character to root for. When all is said and done, I find myself in the interesting but uncomfortable position of empathizing with Jason while admiring Andrew, meaning my feelings are mixed. Ultimately, I care less about *both* characters than I might have cared about either one.

Had the story been written from one point of view—it wouldn't matter which—I'd have cared more. Alternatively, the author could have written a two-scene version of the story, with Scene 1 strictly from Jason's viewpoint and Scene 2 strictly from Andrew's (or vice versa)—understanding that the character who gets the last word will leave the deeper impression.

Whatever strategy you choose, remember that your reader has a limited supply of empathy. Make sure it's invested wisely.

59} INHABITING CHARACTERS: A SIMPLE EXERCISE

I give my students a simple exercise. I ask them to write a scene in which a man waits for a bus, and to write it from the man's point of view. You'd be surprised what can go wrong.

Student # 1 reads aloud what he has written:

> Frank had been waiting for the bus for nearly forty minutes when his ex-wife, Wilma, who happened to be crossing the street, saw him standing there with his hands in his pockets.

"Stop there!" I interrupt. My student looks up. His face asks:
What's wrong?
"You've violated Frank's P.O.V."
"I *have?*"
"Unless his ex sees him through *his* eyes, then yes."
"Oh, right."
Student # 2 reads:

> On a gray winter morning, Harold J. Fingerhut III, a short, plump, and otherwise insignificant-looking fellow wearing a porkpie hat, stood at the corner of Oak and Elm waiting for the Number 9—.

"Stop!"

"What?"

"You say Mr. Fingerhut is an 'insignificant-looking fellow'?"

"That's right."

"According to whom?"

My student looks perplexed, then responds, "Why, Fingerhut."

"This is how Fingerhut sees himself?"

"That's right."

"Are you sure? Are you sure that's not how *you* see him?"

"What if it is? What's wrong with that?"

"Your opinion of Mr. Fingerhut is irrelevant."

"How can it be irrelevant if I'm his creator?"

"It's only relevant if you intend to write the scene from *your* point of view, but the assignment was to write the scene from *the man's* point of view. Or did you forget?"

"I guess I forgot," my student responds sourly.

Student # 3 reads:

> Damn these busses, do they always have to run late? For the fifth time in ten minutes Howard Baxter looked at his watch. If that damned bus didn't come soon there'd be no chance of catching the end of the Super Bowl. He had left work early hoping to get home ahead of the rush, but now already traffic had thickened along Fifth Avenue and it looked as though he was in for it . . .

I let this student keep reading. She has become Mr. Baxter waiting for—and finally boarding—his bus. The story writes itself. No need for me to say, "You've done it." It's obvious to all of us.

One might have to listen to five or six students before declaring, like Colonel Pickering in *My Fair Lady,* "By George—you've got it!" But sooner or later the point gets made. And the point is this: NO POINT OF VIEW, NO STORY.

I'll say it again:

NO POINT OF VIEW, NO STORY.

Point of view is the rock on which solid fiction is built. It can't be added or subtracted afterward, any more than the canvas can be added to a painting.

Let either your character's or your omniscient narrator's viewpoint serve as the organizing principle for your narratives, the source of all the ideas and feelings expressed and information conveyed. *Nothing should reach the reader that hasn't passed through the point-of-view filter.*

Once more, for old times' sake:

NO POINT OF VIEW, NO STORY.

Once Upon a Time: Beginnings

"Many years later, when he faced the firing squad, Colonel Aureliano Buendía would remember that distant afternoon when his father took him to discover ice."[29]

Many structural problems are solved when we enter into the worlds of our stories. But other fundamental problems remain. How do we structure our stories temporally, chronologically? And most nagging of all: *Where to begin?*

Beginnings have always driven writers crazy. Since so much depends on readers being grabbed by the opening words of our novels or stories, we tend to fret over them. We tend to assume that great beginnings are born amid lightning bursts of inspiration—forgetting that most of those great beginnings probably weren't written as

---

29 Gabriel García Márquez's life-spanning opening to *One Hundred Years of Solitude.*

beginnings to begin with. Many or most were arrived at by jumping to a strong passage somewhere deep within the manuscript, a passage written with no intention of grabbing anyone.

Still, whether we consciously write our beginnings or we select them from parts already written, decisions—choices—must be made.

60} BIBLICAL OPENERS: BEGINNING WITH BACKSTORY

Every word of a story is, in a sense, a beginning. And each beginning is diving off a cliff into the ocean. To have done so and survived is a relief; to contemplate doing so is agony.

In composing this section of the book you are reading, I confront the same problem. I stand at the edge of the cliff asking myself: In discussing beginnings, where to begin? Well—why not with the most famous beginning of all?

> In the beginning God created the heavens and the earth.
>
> And the earth was without form, and void; and darkness was upon the face of the deep. And the Spirit of God moved upon the face of the waters.
>
> And God said, Let there be light: and there was light.[30]

Unlike most of us, God has no problem getting His story off the ground. To be divine helps, as it helps to have a story to tell that truly does begin at the *very* beginning—and so there's no question of going back any further, say, to the day *before* God created the heavens and the earth. Nor is the Bible's omniscient narrator by any means tempted to drift into flashback or backstory, since, well, there is none.

---

30 In *Restaurant at the End of the Universe,* Book II of Douglas Adams's five-book Hitchhiker's Trilogy, he gives us this version of that beginning: "In the beginning, the universe was created. This made a lot of people very angry, and has been widely regarded as a bad idea."

The same can't be said for our stories. Whatever beginning we choose, there's always another behind it, and another behind that. Our stories aren't those of divine creators, but of mortal men and women whose characters are formed not only by their present circumstances, but also by past experiences. Bergson[31] declared, "Consciousness is memory." In creating living characters we can't overlook what makes them human— namely, their histories, what they remember, and even a few things that they may *not* remember but which have formed them all the same.

Therefore, implied or overt, *every* story has a backstory. And since the consciousness of our characters—like our own—reflects the memories and experiences of all those who've proceeded them, that backstory goes back and back and back all the way to the beginning of time, all the way to *In the beginning, God created the heavens and the earth*—the theoretical opening line of all our stories.

Fortunately, theory and practice differ—or else all stories would have a biblical prologue, like James Michener's saga *Hawaii*:

> Millions upon millions of years ago, when the continents were already formed and the principal features of the earth had been decided, there existed, then as now, one aspect of the world that dwarfed all others. It was a mighty ocean, resting uneasily to the east of the largest continent, a restless ever-changing, gigantic body of water that would later be described as pacific.

Michener didn't feel compelled to create the earth first before flooding it. Still, in reaching way, *way* back for his opener, he suggests the epic proportions of the work to follow. In a similar way Charles Dickens opens *A Tale of Two Cities* epically, with the rhetorical equivalent of what, in a movie, would be a very long, wide-angle crane shot:

---

31 Henri-Louis Bergson, French philosopher, 1859–1941.

It was the best of times, it was the worst of times, it was the age of wisdom, it was the age of foolishness, it was the epoch of belief, it was the epoch of incredulity, it was the season of Light, it was the season of Darkness, it was the spring of hope, it was the winter of despair, we had everything before us, we had nothing before us, we were all going direct to Heaven, we were all going direct the other way—in short, the period was so far like the present period, that some of its noisiest authorities insisted on its being received, for good or for evil, in the superlative degree of comparison only.

Rather than plunge us into the hearts of their stories, each of these openings serves as a sort of *framing device*—an imposing, ornate gate through which we pass to get to the story (see Meditations # 68–70). Call it the red carpet treatment. But gate and carpeting are there not just to flatter, but to orient us. Along with all the pomp and paradox, Dickens lays out the history of the period in which his story is set, a time when plain-faced queens and large-jawed kings (and vice versa) occupied the thrones of England and France.

61 } FINN AGAIN, BEGIN AGAIN: WHEN STORIES SWALLOW THEIR OWN TALES

Some stories end where they start, and vice versa.

Madison Smartt Bell's *Ten Indians* starts: "Don't know I can say how it all started, but I tell you how it almost finished up." Similarly, when Orham Pamuk's *My Name Is Red* begins, his protagonist is already dead, the corpse speaking to us from the bottom of the well where his murderer has deposited it. *The Lovely Bones,* Alice Sebold's 2002 novel, likewise comes to us from the beyond, with the narrator in heaven following her brutal rape and murder.

Trading beginnings for endings is an old trick—but not a bad one. Though we may be unsure where to begin our stories, we tend to know how they'll end. Martin Amis knew:

This is a true story but I can't believe it's really happening.

> It's a murder story, too. I can't believe my luck.
>
> And a love story (I think), of all strange things, so late in the century, so late in the goddamned day.
>
> This is the story of a murder. It hasn't happened yet. But it will. (It had better.) I know the murderer, I know the murderee. I know the time, I know the place. I know the motive *(her* motive) and I know the means. I know who will be the foil, the fool, the poor foal, also utterly destroyed. And I couldn't stop them, I don't think, even if I wanted to. The girl will die. It's what she always wanted. You can't stop people, once they *start creating.*[32]

Amis can't believe his luck. He knows exactly when and how to begin his story: not with the beginning, but with the end, or close to it.

On the other hand the distinction may be entirely false, since in cases like this who can say that the beginning *isn't* the end, and vice versa? This is very much the case with *Finnegans Wake,* Joyce's last, most ambitious and least read (and least readable) novel, where beginning and ending are united. Joyce's novel begins (and ends):

> riverrun, past Eve and Adams, from swerve of shore to bend of bay, brings us by a commodius vicus of recirculation back to Howth, Castle and Environs.

The same novel ends (and begins):

> Whish! A gull. Gulls. Far calls. Coming, far! End here. Us then. Finn, again! Take. Bussoftlhee, mememormee! Till thousandsthee. Lps. The keys to. Given! A way a lone a last a loved a long the

As never achieved before or since, Joyce solves the problem of beginnings and endings by having *neither*—and both at once. Like the universe it attempts to hold, *Finnegans Wake* has no center or boundaries. Also like the universe, some would argue, Joyce's book has no purpose.

---

32 From *London Fields.*

62} A SURFEIT OF BEGINNINGS

Our stories and agendas may be humbler than God's, or the Bible's, or Dickens's, or even those of Mr. Joyce. But we still face the difficulty of beginning. And we face it knowing that, with each of our opening lines, line by line and word by word, we make a covenant with our readers: We lay down the laws of the world that they will live in as long as they keep reading.

So—again—*where to begin?*

The question needs to be split in two: (1) where do our stories begin, and (2) where do we start telling them?

As storytellers, we're not obliged to follow any straightforward (linear) timeline of events. Experience exists in a state of flux, a rushing, swirling stream: We can dip or dive in wherever and whenever we choose.

In a story about a woman who has a love affair while vacationing in Venice, we might begin with her first glimpse of her paramour sipping a *caffe* at an open bar along the Zatterre. With his sweater draped capelike over his broad shoulders, he puts our heroine in mind of a count: Indeed, she learns that he *is* a count, Count Vittorio Visconte. Or we might start with her boarding the Alitalia flight, or earlier still, when she meets with the travel agent. Or we could begin in the middle of their affair, with the lovers embracing to the sloshing of the canal, or the morning after their first night of lovemaking (alas, Vittorio is impotent). Perhaps we begin with the drive to his palazzo, a dozen miles outside of Venice—which she finds almost in ruins, with fig trees growing throughout and rain coming through holes in the terra-cotta roof. Or does the story start with our heroine packing on the night before her departure, or is she crying her eyes out aboard a Boeing 747 as she flies back home? Do we telegraph the ending up front, or pave the way to it slowly, slyly, from an auspicious start through a series of reversals?

Any or all—or none—of these hypothetical beginnings might work. To know where the story is going helps; in fact it's crucial, since the beginning has to at least *agree* with the ending. Otherwise we may find ourselves in the position of the architect who builds his dream house only to realize, after all of the floors are in place, that he's neglected to plan the staircase.

63} SLAPPED AND HURRIED ALONG: LITERARY BIRTHS

Though most writers prefer to dive straight into the centers of their stories, beginning at the beginning has advantages. It lets readers experience events "in real time," as they unfold, without having to make temporal adjustments as they go. Real life happens this way, so why not fictional life? In fact many stories (usually longer ones, novels) begin at the beginning of their protagonist's lives, with their births. Remember *Robinson Crusoe*?

> I was born in the Year 1632, in the City of York, of a good Family ...

Since Defoe used the technique in 1719, other writers have given birth to their protagonists before our eyes, on the first page. Dickens titles chapter 1 of *David Copperfield* "I am born," and opens with his narrator wondering whether he'll turn out to be the hero of the novel we hold—a doubt we don't share, having seen the words *David Copperfield* stamped across the book's title page. As opening gambits go, it's not especially sincere, so we can't entirely blame Holden Caulfield when, a hundred and one years later, he calls it crap:

> If you really want to hear about it, the first thing you'll probably want to know is where I was born, and what my lousy childhood was like, and how my parents were occupied and all before they had me, and all that David Copperfield kind of crap, but I don't feel like going into it, if you want to know the truth.

Holden's views notwithstanding, among more than a few contemporary authors Dickens' strategy still holds:

> I was born in the city of Bombay . . . once upon a time.
> —SALMAN RUSHDIE, *Midnight's Children*

> The child was born on a night of moon and thunder and a wind that sang high, sweet and clear, naming this a night of miracles.
> —KATHRYN LYNN DAVIS, *Sing to Me of Dreams*

> I was born inside the belly of a white elephant during a thirty-day dry Nor'easter.
> —CHRISTOPHER COOK GILMORE, *Atlantic City Proof*

> I was born twice: first, as a baby girl, on a remarkably smogless Detroit day in January of 1960; and then again, as a teenage boy, in an emergency room near Petoskey, Michigan, in August of 1974.
> —JEFFREY EUGENIDES, *Middlesex*

The narrator of *The Magus,* John Fowles's first novel, describes his origins only to point out that they're the *wrong* origins, unsuited to what fate has in store for him. No sooner does he present us with his past than he tosses it into the weeds like roadkill:

> I was born in 1927, the only child of middle-class parents, both English, and themselves born in the grotesquely elongated shadow, which they never rose sufficiently above history to leave, of that monstrous dwarf Queen Victoria. I was sent to a public school, I wasted two years doing public service, I went to Oxford; and there I began to discover that I was not the person I wanted to be.
>
> I had long before discovered that I lacked the parents and ancestors I needed ...

By contrast, the eponymous hero of Lawrence Sterne's *Tristram Shandy* is all too aware of the import of *his* birth—an awareness not shared by his parents:

> I wish either my father or my mother, or indeed both of them, as they were in duty both equally bound to it, had minded what

they were about when they begot me; had they duly considered how much depended upon what they were then doing;—that not only the production of a rational Being was concerned in it, but that possibly the happy formation and temperature of his body, perhaps his genius and the very cast of his mind;—and, for aught they knew to the contrary, even the fortunes of his whole house might take their turn from the humours and dispositions which were then uppermost:—Had they duly weighed and considered all this, and proceeded accordingly,—I am verily persuaded I should have made a quite different figure in the world, from that, in which the reader is likely to see me.

One obvious *disadvantage* of starting our stories with the birth of our heroes is that the experience isn't likely to form part of our hero's consciousness, since it can't possibly be remembered. Well, *most of us* don't remember being born. As with all things fictional, here too we find exceptions:

> I was slapped and hurried along in the private applause of birth—I think I remember this. Well, I imagine it anyway—the blind boy's rose-and-milk-and-gray-walled (and salty) aquarium, the aquarium overthrown, the uproar in the woman-barn ...

Thus Harold Brodkey's *The Runaway Soul* (which runs away to 833 pages and took Brodkey twenty-seven years to write) squares up to us with the audacity of a man who dares—*dares*—to tell us what colors he saw in the womb. We are thereby more than sufficiently prepared for the coming performance. And "performance" is the word: Brodkey's protagonist has yet to emerge and already the world applauds, or so he imagines.

64} IN MEDIAS RES: NOT A DINOSAUR

The trouble with beginning our stories at the beginning is that the story, if it has begun at all, has *barely* begun. It will take some time to warm up before we bring it up to speed on the highway.

This is why most stories start *in medias res* (Latin for "in the middle of things"). The ancient Roman poet Horace advised aspiring epic poets to go straight to the heart of their stories instead of starting at the beginning. That "heart" may be somewhere near the end of the string of events that form a story, but the idea is to begin the telling with the action already underway.

Katherine Shonk's 2001 story, "My Mother's Garden," about a woman trying to convince her mother to abandon her home in a suburb of Chernobyl, begins *in medias res*:

> Spring had come to my hometown. When I got off the bus at the entrance to the contamination zone, Oles was standing at the guard station in a lightweight uniform instead of his padded military jacket, his gun swung loosely over his back. The thaw seemed to have improved his unusually sullen mood; he nodded his appreciation of the flowered fabric I'd brought for his wife and let me pass through the gate without even looking at my documents.

Typically, though they may start in the middle of the protagonist's journey through life, stories that start *in medias res* don't actually start in the middle of the story itself. Instead they start with or close to an *inciting incident:* an event that propels the protagonist out of her status quo and into new circumstances that put that status quo in new perspective. Shonk starts this way, with the arrival of the daughter to her mother's doomed home— and not, as she might have, with her learning about the Chernobyl disaster.

65 } SETTING OUR STORIES ON FIRE: THE INCITING INCIDENT

Most contemporary narratives are written with the inciting incident occurring (or alluded to) within the first page or pages. Here is the opening to Scott Spencer's novel *Endless Love*, about a boy whose obsessive adolescent love affair leads to tragedy:

> When I was seventeen and in full obedience to my heart's most urgent commands, I stepped far from the pathway of normal life and in a moment's time ruined everything I loved—I loved so deeply, and when the love was interrupted, when the incorporeal body of love shrank back in terror and my own body was locked away, it was hard for others to believe that a life so new could suffer so irrevocably. But now, years have passed and that night of August 12, 1967, still divides my life.

That was the night when, in a bid to gain his beloved's attention, David Axelrod set her house on fire, nearly killing her and her family. Starting with that crisis, we discover the obsessive love affair that led to this act, an affair that the novel's next hundred pages re-create. That's a *long* flashback, long enough to indicate that the fire scene is really a *framing device* (see Meditation # 70). However since the novel extends to 418 pages, with most of the plot resulting from that action, the fire still qualifies as an *inciting incident*.

Often the inciting incident is conveyed by the first sentence:

1. They threw me off the hay truck at noon.

2. None of them knew the color of the sky.

3. One August afternoon, when Ajay was ten years old, his elder brother, Aman, dove into a pool and struck his head on the cement bottom.

The first quote, from James M. Cain's *The Postman Always Rings Twice*, explains how Frank, a drifter, winds up at the diner where he falls for Cora, wife of Nick "The Greek" Papadakis, the diner's owner, whom Frank and Cora eventually plot to murder. Had Frank not been thrown off that hay truck, the most famous crime novel ever would lack an inciting incident.

In Quote # 2, the characters in Stephen Crane's short story "The Open Boat" don't know the color of the sky because they're too busy rowing, or hanging their heads in exhaustion, aboard the lifeboat that has delivered them from a shipwreck—the inciting incident.

Quote # 3 is from Akhil Sharma's short story "Surrounded by Sleep," about a young Indian boy who believes himself marked by his brother's accident; to comfort himself, he conjures a cardigan-wearing God, half Clark Kent, half Mr. Rogers. The demarcation between Ajay's previous (status quo) existence as a happy child and his present exceptional circumstances is clearly marked. To begin with the pool accident seems not only wise, but compulsory.

In other stories, the inciting incident is less dramatic. In John Cheever's "The Swimmer," Neddy Merrill's decision to swim across the county by way of a string of swimming pools has no motivating event beyond that it's a nice day, "one of those mid-summer Sundays when everyone sits around saying, 'I drank too much last night.'" Indeed, as much alcohol as water lubricates Ned's journey home. However whimsically or drunkenly arrived at, Ned's decision qualifies as an inciting incident, and so Cheever starts there.

66} TESTING FITZGERALD: GETTING TO THE INCITING INCIDENT

Sometimes the setups of our stories take too long, as in a story about a former small-town football star who finds the answer to his midlife crisis—and a possible means to rekindle an old flame—in joining a third-rate heavy metal band.

The problem is it takes thirteen pages of loud music to get to where Jimbo first sees Stacey after a gap of sixteen years. The author might consider getting to that inciting incident much sooner, perhaps even in the first sentence: "At first he didn't recognize her, her hair was so short and the strobe lights made her look like some silent movie ghost . . ." Establish the main facts: girlfriend in high school, time gone by, Jimbo's move to Boston in a failed bid for a law degree, etc. Then flashback to their last moment together—no more than a page—before plunging into the deeply fleshed-out scene of the reunion.

That's the main dish here—a *reunion scene*.[33]

Once you know what main dish you're serving—the central action or event that your words are leading the reader toward—then each of those words should set up that action or event, should be a life support system for that dramatic scene.

67 } BEGIN IT NOW: GOING GOETHE'S WAY

"I write the first sentence and trust in God for the next."

—LAWRENCE STERNE

Often the line between a character's status quo and the events that thrust him into a brave new existence is too broad or blurry.

In a story about an alcoholic man's downward spiral, is the inciting incident the alcoholic's first drink, or his hundred-and-first—the one that he swears will be his last? When does a drunk *begin* to be a drunk? When he thinks he's become one, or when his friends tell him so? Or when he wakes up one morning in jail, or in the psychiatric ward of a hospital? Or when he gets fired from his job? Or when his wife and children leave him? Or when he finds himself begging for coins and cigarettes on Skid Row?

We're stuck with the same old question: *Where to begin?*

---

33 It helps to give your scene a name. Sometimes, as an exercise, I have my students go through their works-in-progress and label the "types" of scenes that they're writing: love scene, dinner scene, classroom scene, argument scene, waiting scene, sex scene, and so on.

Perhaps the best advice comes from Goethe:

> Concerning all acts of initiative, there is one elementary truth the ignorance of which kills countless ideas and splendid plans: the moment one definitely commits oneself, then Providence moves too. All sorts of things occur to help one that would never otherwise have occurred ...
>
> Whatever you can do or dream you can do, begin it. Boldness has genius, power and magic in it. Begin it now.

Sure, Johann Wolfgang, but *where?*

Faced with the choice between beginning nowhere and beginning anywhere, why not begin *anywhere?* After all, when it comes to our stories, we are gods creating entire worlds. And once you've created your world, if you should find that the beginning no longer works, you'll have a much easier time finding a beginning that does.

In beginning to write we also begin to create boundaries; we create limits. These limits tell us where to go next, and where *not* to go.

False Starts, Flashbacks, & Framing Devices

68} COMING SOON TO A THEATER NEAR YOU: COMPETING WITH MOVIES

Having been raised on movies and television, we're used to having our stories diced, shuffled, and sliced; flashbacks and flashforwards turn time itself into a card trick or a carnival ride. Fiction writers feel compelled to play similar games with time. Hence the proliferation of stories and novels jammed with flashbacks and framing devices.

Since the first silent films went public, stories and novels have been influenced by movies. "By the time you read this," Jodi Picoult's *Nineteen Minutes* begins, "I hope to be dead." These are Peter Houghton's words, the words that precede his high school shooting rampage. As prologue, Picoult presents these words in Peter's handwriting—a fragment of his diary? A note to a girlfriend? We turn the page and, headed by a portentous, burned-in time stamp ("March 6, 2007"), we read, in a regular typeface:

> In nineteen minutes, you can mow the front lawn, color your hair, watch a third of a hockey game. In nineteen minutes, you can bake scones or get a tooth filled by a dentist; you can fold laundry for a family of five ...

Clearly the point of view here has shifted, but the motive is consistent: to raise curiosity and impel readers to keep reading. It works.

In *Nineteen Minutes,* Picoult is surely competing with movies (and television), treating timely, sensational subjects with as much drama and dialogue as she can pack between covers. She succeeds not only because she's a clever writer, but also because her thorough research gives us an authentic experience.

Norman Mailer's use of interchapter flashbacks in *The Naked and the Dead* takes us into each of a platoon of soldiers' pasts—and more specifically into their sex lives. This cinematic device would have been inconceivable before movies.

The use of flashback—also called *analepsis*—goes back much farther than movies, to the first millennium B.C.E. and the *Mahabharata,* a sacred epic poem (the longest ever written) whose multiple narratives unfold through an elaborate series of flashbacks and framing devices.

Trained by movies and television, readers have grown accustomed to flashbacks, orienting themselves with the dexterity of falling cats to even the most disorderly narratives. Some writers feel compelled to come up with new ways to disorient their readers. For most of us, though, trying to compete on any level with movies and television is a mistake. Movies and television have technology on their side. They have stars and multimillion-dollar budgets. They have passive audiences slumped in plush seats. They dazzle their viewers with special effects. We can't, and shouldn't have to.

Readers—at least the kind I write for—read because they love stories and the language itself. They don't want pseudocinema; they don't need special effects. What they demand from works of literature they don't expect from movies, and vice versa.

Raising the question: *What can writers give people that movies can't?* For an answer, see Meditation # 99.

69} BAIT & SWITCH SYNDROME: DISAPPEARING SCENES

The seductive flashback tends to be overused and abused. When, a page or two into a story, I'm yanked out of the present action and into a flashback, I often feel cheated. I had invested in a set of characters and circumstances, only to see my investment nullified: I have to start investing all over again.

A novel opens with someone getting up, getting dressed, brushing his teeth. As he stands before the bathroom mirror, his mouth foamy with toothpaste, he recalls his date of the previous night. White space: The scene shifts. We're in the Côte d'Azure lounge, where we spend the next eight pages with the protagonist on his date. What of the toothbrushing scene? Gone, never to be seen again. Though the loss may be insignificant, the reader can't be blamed for wondering why the author wrote that banal opening at all, only to jettison it.

A good flashback increases and deepens my investment in the story, the one I've already begun. If it sweeps me out of the present action, it docs so only temporarily, just long enough to add to my appreciation and understanding of the characters in their present situation.

Many novice writers use flashbacks more or less as a pilot uses his ejector seat, to bail out of a story that's not working. Occasionally the ejector button parachutes us into a better story—but why open with a poor story to begin with? Why not start with the good one?

70} FRAMING DEVICES VS. FLASHBACKS

Many flashbacks aren't really flashbacks at all, but stories embedded within other stories, or framing devices. Sometimes the author doesn't realize he's framing his story: He confounds the frame with the picture.

A student turns in a story about a Croatian soldier who has stepped on a booby trap. Instead of a story, however, we're treated to a sermon about war and politics, framed by the device of having the soldier poised to blow himself to smithereens. But a framing device does not a story make; it only helps put an already existing story into a distinct context or perspective (sensationally, in this case).

The real story—the picture in the "frame"—might be the soldier's own story before he puts his boot down on a mine. The implied narrative of all framing devices is something like, "all this has led our protagonist here, to this time and place and to this situation." What events have led our hapless soldier to *his* present moment? Did he volunteer for combat? We're told that he and a friend enlisted. What factors inspired him to enlist? Patriotism? Love? Coercion?

If the author were to line up the events that led his protagonist to this doomed moment, he'd have more than a sensational frame for a generalized treatment of war. The protagonist's death can be given authentic power and purpose.

Like framing devices, flashbacks, too, should be motivated.

In a story about a young girl lamenting her father's fall from grace (he has suffered a huge financial setback and taken to drink), she remembers him as he looks in an old photograph that she once saw of him—triggering a flashback.

But the memory feels unmotivated and merely digressive. Something should *make* Jessica remember that photograph.

Perhaps, while searching in the attic for a carton of Christmas tree ornaments, she stumbles on the photo in a shoebox of old photographs. Maybe she takes the photo and keeps it with her at all times, as a sort of talisman against the specter of her father as he appears to her in real life, slumped next to a bottle at the kitchen table. The photograph can play an active role in the story, motivating the flashback(s) it inspires.

TO SUMMARIZE: Flashbacks should be necessary, motivated, and distinguished from framing devices, which should themselves serve some end more noble than novelty or cleverness.

Suspense, False & Real: Dispensing Information

71} FLIRTING WITH DANGER: FALSE SUSPENSE

Writers abuse flashbacks for one of two reasons: 1) they don't know *where* their stories really begin, or 2) they aren't sure *what* story they're telling. This brings us to *false suspense*.

A fiction writer's job is to *tell* stories, not to *hide* them. This should be obvious, but isn't. Often—as a workshop leader and as editor of a literary journal—I read stories where, within the first pages,

I find myself asking: Who is this person? Is this a man or a woman? What is his/her name? How old is he/she? And—the ultimate question born of such questions: *What am I reading, and why?*

In effect the author is saying: Keep reading and I'll *tell* you my heroine's name and what country she's in and who has just flung open the door to her boudoir and announced, "Vidor is dead!" (And who in blazes is Vidor? That information, too, will presumably be furnished in good time.)

The problem with such a strategy is that it assumes enormous forbearance on the part of readers. We do not read in order to learn information already known to the characters, but to share in their experiences and to learn, with them, the answers to more interesting questions, like: What will happen next? How will X respond? And what effect(s) will X's response have on Y?

These, you'll note, are *plot* questions.

While a writer may aspire to raise philosophical questions in his readers, plot questions are what keep them reading. And whatever else we do, we have to keep our readers reading—always bearing in mind that *readers are rude*. Unless they're taking a required freshman course, nothing compels them to keep turning pages. The vaguest twinge of hunger, or bladder urge, or itch, may prompt them to table your masterpiece and never pick it up again.

Readers hold all the cards. They can be rude; you can't. And one way to be rude is to tease people. Writers who capriciously withhold information are teasing. They do so for the same reason they abuse flashbacks: because they don't trust their story, or they have no story to tell.

72 } AND THEN SHE WOKE UP: CAPRICIOUS WITHHOLDING OF VITAL STATISTICS

The classic example of a strategy based on withholding information is the "and then she woke up" story, where the reader discovers, at the last possible moment, that what he's been reading was only a dream. All this time Pamela has been sound asleep and safe in her bed, with no giraffes chasing her after all!

That's good news for Pamela, but a terrible way to tell a story, and a worse way to treat your reader, who invested in Pamela's giraffe-plagued universe only to have it yanked out from under him. The perpetrator of this strategy might defend himself by saying, "Well, Pamela didn't *know* she was dreaming, so I'm not withholding any information to which my character is privy." *She* may not know she's dreaming, but the author knows damn well, and if he's being honest with himself and with his material he will provide clues to indicate that we are reading, not reality, but a dream. (He might also go fish for another plot.)

I call this strategy *false suspense*. If your reader is sufficiently patient or gullible, it may carry him along for a few pages, or even for most of your story. But sooner or later the jig is up; you have to show your hand. At that point, the few readers who've stuck with you will be disappointed and resentful. The longer this strategy "works," the more resentful your readers will feel.

73} SEEING RED: TRICK—OR TREAT?

A story whose strategy depends entirely on deceiving the reader is likely to fail, since readers don't want to be deceived. This is why withholding information is usually a bad idea.

An author sets out to fool readers into thinking they're reading a murder mystery, with the bodies of two children splayed out on a kitchen floor. No alternative reason is given for why the kitchen is in disarray, why the knife drawer is left open, why the bodies are lying in "red puddles."

In fact, the blood isn't blood but strawberry syrup. It's Halloween, and the children have decided to pull a gruesome prank on their parents. *Trick or treat?*

Alas, for the reader, no treat, just a trick. The story doesn't work—or if it does, the effect is merely annoying. To make the "trick" work, the author had to cheat on her point of view. She couldn't tell the story from the children's viewpoint, since that would give the game away by making it clear that they're quite alive. And she can't tell the story from the parents' point of view without spilling the beans that it's Halloween and they'd been out trick-or-treating an hour earlier. She can't even employ a peripheral narrator: A bystander would instantly notice the family dog calmly lapping up the "blood"—which, incidentally, smells like strawberries. Any reasonable witness would guess within seconds what's going on—but the author wants her effect to last a page and a half. To pull it off, she resorts to a sort of objective default omniscient point of view: i.e., no point of view at all.

False suspense often goes hand in hand with inconsistent or nonexistent viewpoint. Moral: Don't trick readers, or they may see red.

74 } BLACKMAILING PAMELA: COYNESS VS. SUSPENSE

If there's a line between false suspense and coyness, it's a fine one. With false suspense, an author deliberately constricts the flow of information to keep readers disoriented, betting that—rather than jump off—they'll stay with it until they've gained all the facts. A coy author withholds information more subtly, aiming not to disorient readers but to keep them on their toes.

Then there are authors who *provide* information as a way of teasing. I'm always telling my students, "Don't withhold information." However, when one student turned in a story that began, "Pamela was late for her meeting with the extortionist," I had to question that advice.

In this case, a key piece of information was trumpeted in order to grab me "by the throat." I would have preferred to be ushered into the story more subtly, with Pamela arriving late for her rendezvous with a man she knows only as "Mr. Smith." We see Pamela running, checking her wristwatch, threading her way through Grand Central Station. Why is she running? She gets to the terminal, wipes the sweat from her forehead, searches for a man wearing a "wash coat." Could that be him over there? What *is* a wash coat, anyway? By the time we encounter "Mr. Smith," we'll know this meeting isn't casual or pleasant, and that Mr. Smith, whoever he is, is not to be trusted.

I hear you say: Isn't this "withholding information"?

Yes, and no. To be sure, the reader is not being told everything. Who is "Mr. Smith"? What does he want? Why is Pamela so frantic to meet him?

But these are all *plot* questions, questions that keep us reading without frustrating our ability to appreciate what's going on in the present moment. That Pamela is being blackmailed is not immediately relevant. She's not thinking, *I'm being blackmailed.* She's thinking, *Did he say information booth or ticket window?*

By writing such a scene from *inside* our protagonist, we find ourselves besieged by the present moment, rather than thinking in headlines.

75 } DARK MATTER: TOO MUCH LEFT OUT OF A STORY ABOUT CHILD ABUSE

By now it should be clear: One of a writer's biggest challenges is knowing how much information to give to the reader, and when. In every story some information is given to the reader directly, through bald statement, and some through implication. By involving readers' imaginations and intellects more directly and deeply, implication is usually more effective.[34]

---

34 "Science must exhaust all possibilities; art presents only so much as to allow the imagination to divine the essence."—Schopenhauer.

On the other hand, it's possible to leave too much to readers' imaginations. In a story about two children who have been abused by their father, the prose is swift and sure: The sentences flow, and almost every sentence carries action. The writing is tense, dramatic. But I have two questions:

1. Who is the narrator (the unnamed girl) telling her story to?

2. Why is she telling it?

The narrator knows something is wrong; she intuits that what has happened to her with her father in the past was bad and wrong, something that shouldn't have happened. She sensed it then, and she senses it more clearly now that she realizes the same thing may be happening to her younger sister.

That much is clear from what's written. What isn't clear is just *how much* the narrator understands. If she understands as little as she appears to, why is she telling the story at all, and why now?

If the circumstances are dire enough, if the first-person narrator understands that what has happened to her may be happening to her sister—if, in other words, the story has some real urgency behind it—then the narrator's sense of urgency should compel her to tell her story as clearly as she is able—not vaguely and hazily, as in the given story.

Maybe the narrator is writing a letter telling an outsider what has happened, trying urgently to convey what she has witnessed, to express her fears about something she only partly understands, something she intuits is bad but without knowing any of the technical terms or the exact reasons why. Yet she must make everything as clear as possible. That should be her *motivation,* and her author's, too. Coyness has no place in a story where the stakes are so high.

What's the difference between being coy and conveying information through implication? The difference is one of intention. If an author tells us either too much or too little in order to manipulate us, then she's being either melodramatic or coy. But if she's being true to the characters and their situation, then she's not being coy, she's being subtle; she's not being melodramatic, she's being direct.

Give your readers what they need to know to understand and appreciate what they're reading. Nothing more, and nothing less.

76} TOO MUCH DIRECTLY STATED IN A STORY ABOUT CHILD ABUSE

But of course, when it comes to writing fiction, no general laws or principles apply consistently to all cases—so I'm about to contradict myself (or seem to). That is the nature of art: Establish a rule and see it broken.

Another student turns in a story with a similar theme, about Katie, an eight-year-old whose father has been abusing her sexually. The story is written from the point of view of Katie's slightly older sister, Lizzie. The chosen point of view makes the story as much about communication as about sexual abuse—about how anger, confusion, and betrayal are both expressed and suppressed in the same person.

By filtering the story through Lizzie in the third person, however, the author keeps the reader at a distance from the dramatic experiences that are at the heart of the story. It's like watching a play through a gauze curtain. If the story is about what Lizzie understands and interprets based on the actions and suggestive utterances of her little sister, it might be more effective to write it in the *first person*, making Lizzie the "I" of the story (as a peripheral narrator/eyewitness).

Also, if the story is about the way a little girl communicates her distress in the face of trauma, the style should probably be as subtle and indirect as Katie's limited means of communication. By having Lizzie question her sister directly about her father's conduct, thereby making the subject of child abuse *explicit* rather than *implicit*, the story loses much of its potential power. [35] It might be more effective to indicate the sexual abuse through implication—perhaps with the rocking horse in Katie's bedroom serving as a symbol for her desire to escape.

As writers we always have to walk a thin line between giving too much and too little information. The trick is to suggest or imply (rather than state) as much as possible, but without being coy, causing confusion, or generating false suspense.

Suggested readings: Joyce's "An Encounter"; D.H. Lawrence's "The Rocking Horse Winner"; William Carlos Williams's "The Use of Force" (about a pediatrician examining a little girl with diphtheria).

77 } GENEROSITY: PROVIDE, PROVIDE

They say it's better to give than to receive. It's also better, when writing fiction, to be generous than to withhold. Here is the proof:

> My father wanted to show me something, but he wouldn't say what. He only said I should go get my gun, my thirty-six-aught-six, and follow him. This happened just outside Bend, Oregon, where we lived in a ranch house surrounded by ten acres of woods. I was twelve at the time: old enough to shoot a gun, young enough to fear the dark.

This opening to Benjamin Percy's story, "Refresh, Refresh," about a group of young men at loose ends in the Oregon countryside, following the deployment of their reservist fathers to combat in Iraq, is nothing if not generous.

Look at the amount of information given. The protagonist is a twelve-year-old boy who is afraid of the dark and whose father

---

35 See the discussion of Hemingway's "Hills Like White Elephants" in Meditation # 23.

presumably hunts. The setting: Bend, Oregon. The passage is pure information, pure generosity. I think of that Robert Frost poem, "Provide, Provide." That's what the author does here: He provides his readers with information. He communicates; he shares, he gives. He is bountiful; he holds nothing back. So different from the author lounging in an upholstered chair, chatting us to death while swirling the brandy in his snifter.

Originally published in *The Paris Review*, "Refresh, Refresh" was subsequently selected for *Best American Short Stories 2006, The Pushcart Prize XXXI, Best of the Small Presses,* and the *Plimpton Prize.* It pays to be generous.

That's what I try to teach my students, and what I try to practice in my own writing: to give everything away and hold nothing back, while leaving as much room for implication as possible.

78} MAKING IT WORTH THE CLIMB: THE VIEW FROM MT. FICTION

When you ask readers to read a short story (let alone a novel), you're asking them to take a journey with you up a steep climb of exposition, or rising action, to the summit, where a climax of some kind will occur. Following this climax, readers will stand alone on this precipice with an unhindered view of the world they've just experienced, and even, perhaps, of life in general.

As author you're charged with equipping the reader with all the tools and information necessary not only to arrive at the summit, but to appreciate the view from there. That means withholding nothing crucial or basic, while at the same time providing nothing unnecessary or sooner than necessary: The journey is arduous, and every unnecessary bit of information makes it more so.

False suspense weighs your reader down with useless yet burdensome questions. It not only makes the climb much harder, it also spoils the view from the top.

The solution is straightforward: Have a story to tell and tell it. *Never withhold crucial information.* Eudora Welty said so, and she knew a thing or two about telling stories.

Setup & Payoff, Climax & Resolution

79} EPIPHANIES & EXPLOSIONS

One test of a story's success is whether it exhausts its own possibilities, and how it exhausts them.

Think of a fireworks display. In his arsenal the pyrotechnician has Roman candles and bottle rockets as well as multi-tube devices packed with pounds of colorful explosives. Just when we think we've witnessed the loudest, biggest blast of all, he treats us to one even bigger.

Our stories and novels should work the same way, with nothing "set up" that doesn't "pay off" later. Small payoffs lead to greater ones, and finally to the greatest payoff of all.

Not every story works this way, of course; not every story comes packed with explosives. All of Joyce's stories in *Dubliners*, like many stories by Chekhov and Cheever, rely on subtle emotional upheavals or awakenings—what Joyce called *epiphanies*: moments of sudden deep awareness that alter a character's view of the world and his place in it.

Typically, some sort of climax ends or resolves the crisis brought on by the inciting incident. In my story "Swimming," a seventy-two-year-old man's marriage is threatened when he meets—or thinks he has met—a younger woman named Juliet while swimming in the lake where he and his wife, Dorothy, are summering. The inciting incident is his first encounter with the mysterious younger woman. Will Frank be tempted into an affair with Juliet (who also swims; his wife doesn't)? To save his marriage from stasis, Frank decides, he must teach Dorothy to swim. The crisis is resolved when, in his attempt to do so, he nearly drowns her. This scene gives the story its *climax.*

Not all stories will blast us with explosives, and not all stories resolve themselves neatly. Gentle stories can have gentle resolutions and may move us without concussing us. But explosive or gentle, our stories must have a climax.

80} SETUP & PAYOFF: THE BOMB UNDER THE TABLE

In a short story, *everything* is either setup or payoff. So when a writer opens a story with a long description of the curtains blowing in his heroine's bedroom, the reader has every right to expect those curtains to pay off somewhere later in the story. If not, we have a setup with no payoff. And when, in a scene where she finally confronts her puritanical mother, sixteen-year-old Jenny tells Mom how she kissed her new boyfriend, we get the opposite: payoff with no setup. The confrontation would have worked much better had we been led in some way to anticipate it.

Without setup, there can be little or no suspense. Hitchcock gives the example of a movie scene set at a board of directors' meeting. We watch the members of the board going about their business, making motions and doing whatever it is that board members do, and suddenly—BOOM! There's an enormous explosion; everyone is dead. Unknown to both the board and the audience, a bomb had been ticking away under the table. A shocking scene, and one that's all climax with no suspense; all payoff with no setup. To inject suspense into the scene, in the midst of the board meeting the director would need to cut away to a close-up of the bomb ticking under the table. Without such an establishment shot, there's nothing for us to anticipate, no cause for suspense.

In the story mentioned above, the one with the curtains, what moment is being set up in the first scene? Where do those blowing curtains point? Maybe they point to the scene where Jenny finally confronts her largely absent mother, who is dying of lung cancer at home, and whom she must now take care of. The curtains blowing in the first paragraph? Do they breathe for her mother's ailing lungs? Or maybe that breeze is the fresh air of catharsis.

Chekhov offers the example of the gun over the mantle in the first act of a play which, to justify itself, must be discharged in the third act. In Flannery O'Connor's "A Good Man Is Hard to Find," the story's first paragraph alerts us, almost in passing, to the news that a convict known as the Misfit has escaped from the federal penitentiary and is headed for Florida, where a grandmother, the story's protagonist, and her family happen to be vacationing. What are the odds of Grandma and the Misfit encountering each other? In real life, pretty low. In a work of fiction, 100 percent.

Less blatant examples will serve. Early in Joyce's most famous story, "The Dead," we read, "Gabriel's warm trembling fingers tapped the cold pane of the window" —which sentence sets up the tapping of snow on another window in the story's ultimate paragraph ("A few light taps upon the pane made him turn to the window.").

Ideally in a work of fiction, and especially in shorter works, every line is a life support system for the final scene, image, or line. "Call me Ishmael," with its Biblical overtones, sets up "And I only am escaped to tell thee" (Job 1.).

Try and see to it that the climaxes that bloom at the ends of your stories have been seeded in your opening pages, and vice versa. Or better still: Look for the seeds that are already planted there, but that haven't germinated.

81} REVERSALS 'R' US: A TOY STORE ANTICLIMAX

A successful resolution *thwarts* our expectations; it doesn't (fully) satisfy them.

I'm reading the story of a single mother who learns that her fifteen-year-old daughter has been secretly seeing an older boy (a man, practically) and lying about it. She discovers the stranger's identity and sets off, with her seven-year-old son Max in tow, in a blind rage to the toy store where her daughter's lover works, to give the cradle-robber a piece of her mind.

Such a setup raises obvious expectations: a violent confrontation between enraged mother and the lothario. Maybe she'll slap him in the face, or strike him with her purse, or simply threaten to have his reproductive parts fricasseed and served to him for brunch if he so much as sets eyes on her daughter again. Since these are our obvious expectations, it stands to reason that they will *not* be satisfied. Something—but what?—must offer some resistance to these "logical" outcomes.

Inside the Toys 'R' Us, Max wants every toy he sees. To placate him, Mom grabs a shopping cart and lets him fill it. It takes the mother forever to track down the cradle-robber. By the time she locates her quarry, the shopping cart totters with toys. Behind the counter she finds not a lothario or hulking ape, but Albert: a shy, awkward, acne-ridden, bespectacled eighteen-year-old.

Payoff? Not quite. Even a shy eighteen-year-old can be the ruin of a young girl. Albert's "sweetness" doesn't in itself resolve anything. There needs to be a more satisfying resolution. What can Mom do? Bribe? Threaten? Plead? Make Albert swear he won't lay a finger on her daughter till she's reached the age of majority?

Albert is either an impediment to action, or a gun waiting to go off, or both.

Or maybe Mom responds so favorably to something in him that she ends up wanting him for herself.

Whatever the payoff, more must happen than Mom deciding that Albert is okay after all. The setup is too good for the story to end with a whimper. Having won Mom over, perhaps Abert asks *her* for a date? That should get the ball rolling again.

But whatever you do, remember Chekhov's gun, and don't let it backfire—or worse, go off with a whimper.

Last Thoughts on Structure

82 } PAVED WITH INEVITABILITY: THE ROAD TO THE END

Every great story is a life-support system for its ending. Every scene and chapter and section is there to set up The End, to provide whatever is needed in order for the final words to send a shiver up readers' spines. You might say that every word of a story is setting up the ending, and therefore that, even as we begin our stories, we are already in the process of ending them.

I have tried this test with some of my favorite novels and stories: I imagine that each line of the story is the *last* line, and I ask myself, as the last line, would it resonate, would it send a little shiver up (or down) my spine?

With great works, the answer is very often, "yes."

We speak of great endings as "feeling" inevitable—with "yes, of course" following immediately on the heels of "Oh, my God!" But in a great piece of writing every paragraph, every sentence, even every word carries this quality of inevitability, which may help explain why in great literary works *every* line might function as a last line.

Those who live life most fully are said to live every day as if it were their last. The same philosophy applies to writing. When down to your last draft, try to write each sentence as if it were your last, to treat each word as if it were the final word, a last breath of life.

Matters of Structure

Plot springs from the marriage of substance and structure. Plot is dictated less by our own choices than by those of our characters, who seek either to gain happiness or to rid themselves of an irritant preventing it.

The more we try to dictate or force the plot, the less satisfactory the result. Rather than force it, we should *discover* it along with our characters, through inhabiting a viewpoint located *firmly within the world of the story itself,* not outside it.

Similarly, beginnings are best arrived at by simply following the impulses suggested by our materials, and not by resolving to "grab" readers by the throat (or any other body parts).

Unless they serve an urgent or organic purpose, flashbacks and framing devices should be shunned.

The writer's first impulse should be to provide information, not to conceal it to generate false suspense and tease readers.

A good climax is one that exhausts all the possibilities suggested by the setup of a story, while subverting—or at least not satisfying—readers' expectations.

A great ending is surprising *and* inevitable. It is supported by everything that comes before it. It is like the night-blooming Cereus that blooms once, then closes its petals for good, but not before exuding its exquisite, lingering scent.

Q. WHAT'S THE BEST WAY TO COME UP WITH A PLOT?

A. Through characters with motivations. Remember that there are really only two plots: Plot A, where a character is routinely unhappy and suddenly seizes an opportunity for happiness, and Plot B, where a character is routinely happy but some circumstance or irritant destroys or undermines his happiness, and he must act to reinstate his status quo. The solution to plot is to make sure you are dealing with one of these situations.

Q. WHAT ABOUT POINT OF VIEW? HOW DO I KNOW IF I'M HANDLING IT CORRECTLY?

A. If your story or novel isn't working well, if the scenes don't quite come off, if the characters feel shallow, if the structure isn't satisfying, or if you're finding the writing process itself an uphill struggle, question your point of view.

Do you *have* a point of view for each of your chapters or scenes? Have you embraced that point of view purposefully, thoroughly, and consistently (understanding that you may be switching points of view)? If you are writing from the limited perspective of one character, have you immersed yourself (and the reader) sufficiently in that character's psyche? If you are writing objectively, presenting your material with no subjective content, is that unusual choice serving your purpose? If you are writing omnisciently, have you—from paragraph to paragraph—immersed us purposefully, thoroughly, and consistently in whatever P.O.V. applies to the moment in question?

Remember: Omniscience is not a license to be sloppy or half-baked; on the contrary, it requires more, not less, effort than a limited viewpoint.

Q. HOW DO I COME UP WITH THE STRONGEST BEGINNING?

A. Not by worrying about wonderful opening sentences or paragraphs, but by asking, "Where does the story really start?" and starting as close to there as you can. Where does the main character's life veer away from his or her status-quo existence? What inciting incident or event causes that veering away? At what point is the character first prompted to take some action—defensively or offensively—in order to achieve the goals of either Plot A or Plot B? Begin there. The wonderful opening will then generate itself.

Q. WHAT IS THE BEST STRATEGY FOR USING FLASHBACKS OR FRAMING DEVICES?

A. The best strategy is to avoid them if at all possible. Assume that the same Aristotelian ideal that applies to drama—unity of time, action, and setting—applies to stories and novels as well—and why shouldn't it? If you could possibly dramatize a character's condition in one setting, with a single scene, through a single action, why would you choose to use six scenes, a prologue, two flashbacks, and to mount the entire story in some clever framing device? You wouldn't, and shouldn't want to.

Think of Hemingway's "A Clean, Well-Lighted Place" and how simply and beautifully it not only conveys the lot of a depressed old man, but the whole human condition, through a single dialogue of a few short pages.

Q. AND SUSPENSE? HOW DO I BUILD SUSPENSE?

A. By raising questions in your reader through *providing* information, not by withholding it. False suspense results from such withholding; it makes readers wonder not what's going to happen next, but what's happening, and why, and to whom? Real suspense raises real *plot questions.* A story that begins, "One morning Gregor Samsa awoke from troubled dreams to find himself transformed into a giant beetle," provides us with a good deal of information that in turn raises genuine plot questions ("How did this happen? What will he do? How will his family react?").

Poor writers assume that by being stingy with information they can entice readers to beg for more. Good writers know that the opposite is true: that the more generous they are with information, the more readers will want to know.

Q. WHAT ABOUT SETUPS AND PAYOFFS? HOW DO I KNOW THEY ARE BEING ACHIEVED?

A. Often we don't; they just happen by themselves. But just as often we need to go back into our drafts and make sure that effects achieved at the ends of our stories have had their seeds planted in the beginning, and vice versa, that many if not all of the seeds planted early in our stories germinate and bloom at or toward the end.

Q. HOW DO I KNOW IF I'VE WRITTEN AN EFFECTIVE CLIMAX?

A. Two characteristics mark a good climax or ending: First, it should surprise us; second, it should feel inevitable. Typically the reader experiences these two qualities almost simultaneously, with, "Oh, my God!" followed immediately by, "But of course!" An ending or climax that is surprising but not inevitable—in fact not even all that plausible—isn't going to satisfy much. Likewise, an ending that is inevitable but on the other hand totally predictable won't do much for readers.

And remember, too, that a climax needn't be violent to be effective. It can even be anticlimactic, provided it still satisfies the requirements of surprise and inevitability.

Matters of
*Symbol, Myth
& Metaphor*

On the Meaning(s) of Things

"Now the word symbol scares a good many people off, just as the word art does. They seem to feel that a symbol is some mysterious thing put in arbitrarily by the writer to frighten the common reader—sort of a literary Masonic grip that is only for the initiated."

—FLANNERY O'CONNOR, *"The Nature and Aim of Fiction"*[36]

A symbol is more than a sign. A sign represents something express-ible: for example, a skull and crossbones = "poison"; a running deer = "Caution: Deer Crossing." A symbol represents something *inexpressible*, or having a wide range of potential meanings or interpretations: A thorny rose might represent flawed perfection, or beauty undermined by deceit, or taboo and temptation, etc.

The world is full of symbols. Practically everything can be a metaphor. A window, a puddle, a pair of shoes; a dog, an itch, a road, a mirror, a stone, the far side of the moon—everything stands (or can) for something else. The mirror is a reflection; the stone a burden; the itch an urge; the road a journey (with its implied bends, hazards, and detours). Depending on whose shoes those are, you may or may not want to be in them. And the view through the window may be sunny or foggy—or of a brick wall.

If the world is lousy with symbols, literature is doubly infested, overrun first with symbols intended by authors and then by sym-bolic meanings discovered by well-meaning critics, scholars, and pedagogues. In grade school most of us endured the silliness of sift-ing through *The Scarlet Letter* in search of alternative interpreta-tions of the red *A* that poor Hester is forced to wear on her bosom

---

36 From *Mystery and Manners, Occasional Prose.*

(American, Able, Angel, Adam, Eve's Apple, The Great Alpha!, Mater Adolerata), or mulling over the holy significance of the Whiteness of the Whale. If patriotism is the last refuge of scoundrels, sifting for literary symbols may be the last refuge of dull-witted or lazy English teachers. At best it's about as challenging as fishing with dynamite; at worst it turns even sensitive and gifted students against literature with a capital L (for Lame).

But symbols *do* exist in literature. And there are symbols in literature that the author may never have intended. An author needn't plant symbols deliberately for them to take root and flourish in the minds of readers. That said, contemporary authors treat symbols quite differently than their classical forebears did. In the *Metamorphoses,* Ovid celebrates gods and goddesses who in turn represent empirical phenomena (Mithra, god of solar fire, protector of abundance; Ceres, goddess of wheat and other food plants). Today's writers tend to celebrate the meanings of ordinary things.

If Ovid had gods and goddesses, we have windows and wallpaper. In Kate Chopin's "The Story of an Hour," published in 1894, Mrs. Mallard's bedroom window is the portal through which a new sense of freedom takes violent possession of her soul soon after she learns of her husband's death in a railway accident. When the report of Mr. Mallard's death turns out to be false—and he appears, intact, at their front door—the sudden loss of her newfound freedom leads to her abrupt death. That window, with its patch of blue sky, is the central metaphor or symbol in Chopin's story.

In an equally famous work by Charlotte Perkins Gilman published just five years later, the windows facing out to a sunny garden are barred, much as the story's protagonist is barred from leaving the nursery where her physician husband has ordered her to rest and recuperate from what he calls "a temporary nervous depression."

The story is called "The Yellow Wallpaper";[37] and it is the wallpaper in the nursery, not the barred window, that furnishes the protagonist with a "view" to her own predicament, that of a woman isolated and trapped within the jaundiced patterns of a patriarchal society.

83} SYMBOLIC COLORS & TEA LEAVES: GOOFING AROUND WITH SYMBOLS

Since everything is relative, nothing is without associations.

Take the color yellow itself. It has both positive and negative connotations. In the positive column: sunlight and bright flowers (happiness, joy); egg yolks (new life); butter (sustenance, luxury). Negative: fear, cowardice, nasty bodily discharges (urine, pus, vomit). There are warning yellows (traffic lights, street signs), screaming yellows, yellows sulfurous, smoldering, and smutty. In Gilman's story the clash of the imprisoning wallpaper and the natural daylight—different shades of yellow—reflects the irony of the protagonist's supposed "cure," thrusting her ever deeper into her "illness" (yellow = pallid, jaundiced, sickly).

The game of attaching symbolical meanings to such things as colors in literature is seductively easy to play. I have a writer friend who invariably interprets whichever paintings of mine hang in my home, launching into a detailed analysis to illuminate my Christian or pagan imagery, discovering unconscious parallels with the Annunciation or with Inanna's descent into the underworld. Fine with me, though I thought I'd painted an innocent bowl of cherries. (Professional readers of palms and tarot cards do no less, and make livings from it.)

---

37 An interesting aside: Silas Weir Mitchell, the physician on whom Gilman based the character of the husband (and who did, indeed, prescribe to her his "rest cure") was a pioneer of neurological medicine who, among other things, treated Civil War soldiers suffering from gunshot wounds. Mitchell was also himself a quite successful author of novels and poetry—much better known in their time than Gilman. They were good friends.

Given that everything is already a metaphor, there's seldom cause for authors to introduce metaphoric content into their work. If the work has been produced honestly, authentically, with integrity, it's already there, imbedded in the raw materials.[38] All we authors have to do, and only occasionally, is take note of the associations (metaphors) when they occur and reinforce them, through repetition or by some other means: by positioning them more prominently, or pointing to them in a title or chapter heading, or finding other ways (placenames, characters' names) to thread them through the work.

In early drafts especially, trust your impulses and instincts. Later, as you work to shape and clarify those first impulses, keep an eye open for the very best metaphors: the ones you never planned or intended.

84} HOGSON'S GROPINGS: A SLIPPERY METAPHORIC TADPOLE

Though symbols arise organically, it takes the conscious work of an artist to weave them into a story so they can be fully appreciated.

In a story of a rural girl's coming of age, several organic symbols arise, like mushrooms, as if unconsciously, from the soil of the material. An opening scene with Sally and her friends catching tadpoles in a pond not only gets the story off to a good start, but embodies its main theme: As tadpoles must turn into frogs, so little girls must turn into young women.

However, as constructed, the tadpole-catching scene comes off merely as a colorful aside, its symbolic potential unrealized.

Having recognized a good symbol or motif, the trick is to introduce it more than once and in key places. The green light at the end of Daisy's dock in *The Great Gatsby* is a good example. In early drafts of

---

38 Did Jean Giono, writing *The Man Who Planted Trees,* plan the symbolism of those trees—or need to? Our symbols should all grow as naturally from the soil of our stories.

the novel, the green light appears only once, as an atmospheric aside. Having recognized it as an effective symbol, or anyway as a captivating image, Fitzgerald decided to "refrain" it—not just anywhere, but as the novel's closing image. Recall Chekhov's rule: "If there's a gun on the mantelpiece in Act I, it should discharge in Act III." Symbols abide by the same rules as loaded guns.

In our coming-of-age story, the antagonist, Mr. Hogson (Sally's teacher, who gropes her in the bleachers during a basketball game) should teach not history but *biology*, forcing his students to dissect *frogs* (motif reiterated)—an activity that Sally engages in with equal parts fear, repulsion, curiosity, and yes, arousal, as she endures Hogson's gropings. And Sally's fear and loathing of him is at least in part a fear and loathing of her own emerging sexual impulses and feelings, over which she has little control, feelings that force her into an adulthood she isn't prepared for.

My student titled her draft "The History Teacher." Suggested alternative title: "Tadpoles."

In another story, the author's third-person narrator makes repeated allusions to characters in Greek mythology, and especially to Charon, pilot of the ferry that carries the souls of the departed across the River Styx. In class we asked, "Where does your protagonist come by these allusions?" The writer didn't know. Then we asked, "What does the narrator do for a living?" The student had no idea.

But in the subsequent draft he knew. He was a mortician.

85} BRIDGES & CHICKEN BONES: ARMATURES OF MEANING

A fiction writer's job isn't just to convey experience vividly and viscerally, through scene and concrete description. It's to illuminate, to shine the bright light of metaphor and meaning, to make the hidden interrelatedness of things clear enough for those meanings to resonate with readers.

Case in point: A missed opportunity in a story about a drawbridge attendant and his daughter, who wants him to retire before something terrible happens to him and his bridge. The author might reinforce the girders of her story's metaphoric "bridge." She could make everything in it relate to bridges, to connections, to transitions. Things should add up. When the narrator reaches out to hug her father, her arms form a metaphoric "bridge" between them, a bridge that each character approaches with a mixture of trepidation and relief.

As writers we should build as many of our own metaphorical bridges as possible to strengthen the connections latent in our stories. We need to pay attention not just to our characters' actions, including small ones, but to our descriptions—of characters, settings, weather—and to recognize their implications and associations, to seize on these associations and reinforce them.

I worked on a story for years about a failed young actor, Justin, who, having hitchhiked to New Orleans, ends up sharing the bed of an older homosexual who is also alcoholic. I wrestled, among other things, with my choice for a title. In the beginning I called it "Café Doomed"—the nickname of the restaurant where the protagonist takes a job, and where he meets Don, his future roommate. I liked the title, but wasn't sure it pointed to the heart of the story, as good titles should. Before I could find the story's ultimate title, I'd have to uncover its main theme.

It took an image from the story to point the way.

In the scene where Don first shows Justin (the hitchhiker) his very humble apartment, he leads Justin down a narrow alley lined with "tinfoil pans piled high with table scraps and chicken bones." Don explains that this mess is the doing of his landlord's daughter, Mildred, who feeds the neighborhood strays.

"Chicken bones?" said Justin.

"More cats and dogs die of Mildred's generosity than of all other natural causes combined. I guess she thinks it's better for them to choke to death on a chicken bone than to starve on nothing."

This bit of dialogue about Don's landlord's daughter and those chicken bones pointed the way to the story's central metaphor and its ultimate title. The story, I realized, is about how the need for love is stronger than the instinct for self-preservation. This theme is underscored by Don's inability to end his masochistic relationship with Sherman, his former roommate, who abuses him throughout the story. When Justin, who finds in Don a source of protection and affection unavailable to him from his own parents back home, attacks Sherman, Don turns violently on him.

Final title: "The Bones of Love."

86} TEARING DOWN THE HOUSE: GOING TO EXTREMES

For a metaphor or symbol to resonate, it should send out tendrils of implication in several directions, pointing both toward and away from its immediate or obvious meanings. It should function on more than one level.

And it should explore those implications to their limits.

In a story titled "Resurrection," a construction worker vents a lifetime of frustration on a home renovation job he's been hired to do for a disagreeable couple. That's a solid, intriguing premise, if that's the premise. On the one hand Nick seems intent on destroying the home he's been hired to restore; on the other he seems to want to do the job properly, to code, even if it means sacrificing the authenticity of those lovely two-hundred-year-old beams and wide-planked floors.

Sometimes to restore one must first destroy, and in the end nothing may be left of the original. That's what's implied here thematically. But what can we find in Nick's life that makes this a *metaphor*, and not just a law of carpentry?

Throughout the story are scattered clues of Nick's dissatisfaction with his life: his nagging, no-longer-sexually-available wife; his affair with a much younger woman; his bratty, spoiled son; his distaste for his clients. Yet none of these dissatisfactions is sufficiently developed in the story—not enough, anyway, to convince me that Nick would sledgehammer himself out of a lucrative job. What is Nick (metaphorically) banging away *at*? His wife? His kid? His marriage? His clients? Himself? All of the above? Or is he symbolically "banging" Margie, his young mistress—in which case the words "monotonous, dull thrusts" take on an altogether different meaning?

Adding to the story's thematic murkiness is the fact that Nick succeeds neither in renovating nor destroying the symbol-laden house. A burst sewage pipe intervenes, robbing Nick of the opportunity to seal his own fate—and robbing readers of the satisfaction of a story that follows through on its own implications.

Some stories demand extremes. Nick could either destroy the house completely, tearing it down to the rafters, or do a superb renovation job that costs him ten times what he's being paid, using aged wood and old-fashioned plaster and lath. As it is, the story teeters without making a decisive move in either of these tantalizing directions. The burst pipe, as a *deus ex machina*, wrests the story away from its protagonist. Better to have Nick dismantle it, or tear down his *own* house for parts with which to restore that of these strangers, leaving himself and his estranged wife to carry on their null marriage in the dismantled, frigid shell of what might have been their happy home.

When it comes to our drafted stories, we'd best all be Freudian or Jungian analysts, and interpret them as though they were other people's dreams, taking nothing for granted, assuming that

our choices weren't arbitrary, but there for a reason, that everything means something.

87 } SKELETONS IN THE CABINET: SYMBOLIC FURNISHINGS

Sometimes we need to look more deeply into what we already recognize as symbols, to exploit their capacity for meanings.

An elderly woman struggles to fend off a contractor who has
been hired by her children to remodel her kitchen. In the remod-
eling he'll have to destroy a cabinet built by her late husband—a
piece of furniture that symbolizes both her bittersweet marriage
and her own place within the family.

In his play *The Price*, Arthur Miller puts furniture to great
symbolic use: The "price" for which an armoire is sold represents
the value of a forsaken life. Here my student does likewise. And
the writing is good; the details are precise and convincing. I get a
clear picture of the old woman's home, and especially of her staircase with its "photographs arranged like the stations of the cross."
(Given the painful arthritis that accompanies the protagonist
down those stairs, and her subsequent martyrdom to a cause, the
implications of this simile can't be ignored.)

What's missing is what's *inside* that cabinet symbolically, or
what should be inside it. The cabinet is supposed to represent the
old woman's marriage, and her love for her deceased husband and
his dedication to her. And there is the suggestion of a rift between
children and parents—or at least between children and father—
since in their eagerness to provide their mother with a convenient, modern kitchen, her offspring show little attachment to
their father's handiwork (and, by implication, to their dead father).
But then, the old woman herself showed indifference to the cabinet: After all, she did agree to have her kitchen remodeled. Why

does she react so strongly now that it's too late, with the contractor about to go at the cabinet with his crowbar?

My guess is there's more to this story than the problem of what to do about an old cabinet. There's the story of a marriage between a husband who never failed to do things in a half-assed way (witness that poorly built, warped cabinet) and a wife who loved and, at times, and with good reason, hated him—him and that damned cabinet he built for her because he was too cheap to buy her the Hoosier cabinet she wanted. Yet she won't desecrate his memory.

Open your symbolic cabinets. You'll find skeletons in there.

88} THE OPPORTUNISTIC FIG TREE: SYMBOLS IN SEARCH OF A STORY

Since we can't always rely on readers to discern, let alone properly interpret, our symbols, our stories should benefit from, but not depend on, such interpretations.

In a story about a daughter coming to terms with her mother's invalidism, the narrating daughter's complex attitude toward death and decay is symbolized by a fig tree growing incongruously in the hospital courtyard—a symbol that, as things stand, takes the place of a plot, rather than augmenting it.

As symbols of sex and death go, that fig tree couldn't be riper. Old and New Testaments alike burst with symbolic figs, starting with the fig leaves that Adam and Eve turn into bikinis, and proceeding through the Parable of the Barren Fig Tree (Matt. 21: 18-22) to the Redemption of the Fig Tree (Luke 13: 6-9)—with the fruit symbolizing God's bounty and blessing or, when withered, Yahweh's judgment and the coming Apocalypse. Figs play a symbolic role not just in Christianity, but in Islam, Buddhism, Hinduism, and Jainism. Siddhartha found his *bodhi* (enlightenment) under a sacred fig. On a more earthly plane, figs are neither flowers nor fruits, but both. They date back to the Mesozoic era, seventy million years ago, and bloom year round. Fig trees are also opportunistic. Nearly every ruined farmhouse in Europe has one growing up through its rotting rafters as a harbinger of barrenness and decrepitude, a tree whose roots supplant other, more polite forms of life.

But take the fig tree and its allusions away from our story and little if any story remains. Just as *The Great Gatsby* would survive without the green lantern at the end of Daisy's dock, a story ought to survive (even flourish) without its symbols. What's missing from my student's story is *conflict*. Mom's reluctance to accept her old age isn't conflict enough. In fact—and in spite of her vertigo— she's good-humored, so it's hard to understand why her daughter is so upset with her. The closest thing to an emotional journey in the story is that taken by the daughter as she contemplates the heavily symbolic fig tree—an emotional journey that, because it's so thinly motivated, feels sentimentally forced.

The author should consider organizing this story around a solid central conflict. Then the symbolic fig tree won't grow out of nowhere. It will take root in firmer soil, and bear its golden ripe fruit less awkwardly and obviously.

Though a symbol or symbols may enhance a story, they are not substitutes for one.

Titles & What They Tell Us

89} WHAT'S IN A TITLE: MYTHICAL SNAKES IN THE GRASS

As with a first sentence, a title raises expectations. When those expectations aren't met, readers may be left unsatisfied. On the other hand, when writers must struggle to title their stories, it's often an indication that they haven't yet found the central metaphor or meaning of what they've written.

A student titles his story "Sucker Punched." A sucker punch is an unexpected blow, an assault that catches its victim off guard, a definitive but fiendish clout that leaves no room for argument or fair play. A cheap shot.

Sometimes (the story tells us) fate deals the sucker punch. His breath smelling of booze, Ava's drunken father teaches his daughter to throw a sucker punch as a means of defending herself against the bully who for weeks has been tormenting her at school. But Ava's dad is oblivious to the even crueler blow dealt by fate to his offspring in saddling her with an irresponsible, alcoholic, inadvertently harmful father: himself.

Here, theme and story are perfectly wed. And—like those little thermometers that come with frozen turkeys to tell you when they're cooked—the title "pops."

In other cases, our titles tell us that our stories aren't fully baked. In "Eurydice's Shadow," a woman who once aspired to be a concert pianist has sacrificed that dream at the altar of motherhood. Louise is married to a benevolent but distant man, saddled with children she can barely tolerate, and locked away in a provincial rural setting far from the cities where she might have pursued her musical dreams (and possibly a little romance on the side).

At least Emma Bovary could have an affair! But Louise's plight is familiar not only through classic works like *Madame Bovary* and *Anna Karenina,* but contemporary ones like Richard Yates's *Revolutionary Road*, Michael Cunningham's *The Hours* (and the film based on it)—or novels by popular contemporary authors like Barbara Taylor Bradford, who specializes in stories of women trapped in dreary marriages and "willing to pay any price" (to quote one dust jacket blurb) "for their dreams."

The exhausted theme here gets a facelift through its title, which refers to the myth of Eurydice and Orpheus, a couple who were inseparable in their love until one day Eurydice was bitten by a serpent and cast down to Hades. To rescue her, Orpheus appeals to the overseer of the underworld with his lyre, playing a tune so sweet and moving he is allowed to descend and reclaim her, but only on one condition: Orpheus must not look back; he must trust that Eurydice is following him out of Hades. At the last moment, of course, Orpheus breaks his vow and looks back, and Eurydice is snatched back into the underworld.

Here, wrapped like a mummy in a myth thousands of years old, is the story-within-the-story—not yet unraveled by its author. Instead we get the static tableau of a character trapped in a dead marriage, when what's called for is a character trapped in a dead marriage who *does something* about it, or tries to, and pays a price.

In the spirit of hypothetical reflection, I offer you my own take on the story—one of many possible treatments of the material suggested by its title.

Wishing to earn extra income and keep a hand in her playing, Louise gives private piano lessons to locals, including Oren, a farmer who lives down the road and who lacks any musical talent. Nonetheless, Louise is taken with him, with his rugged looks and his guileless innocence. She falls in love and in doing so begets her own downfall: While making love to Oren in a soybean field she's bitten by a rattlesnake. At ten miles-per-hour in his International Harvester tractor, Oren "rushes" Louise to the emergency room. On the way they're intercepted by an SUV driven by Louise's husband, and their affair is exposed.

This scenario exploits the Eurydice myth. Louise survives, and her husband agrees to stay married to her on several conditions: that she will give up piano playing and teaching, devote herself fully to her children, and never cast eyes on Oren again.

But just like Orpheus, Louise can't keep her word. In the last scene we see her playing Clark's *Requiem for Lost Children* loudly, in an empty house, as her husband pulls out of the driveway with the children in his packed SUV.

"Eurydice"? "Rattlesnake"? "The Snake Bite"? "The Serpent"? Each of these titles points to the myth exploited by the story, and to the heart of the story itself.

Look to your titles as keys to what your stories are—or are not—about.

90} ENDYMION ON BOURBON STREET: A TITLE FLOATS THROUGH A STORY

Occasionally a title stares us in the face, yet we fail to see it or to connect its metaphoric meaning to the material at hand.

During Mardi Gras in New Orleans, a woman decides to end her love affair with a married man. Heartache, guilt, lust, confusion—all set against a seedy New Orleans backdrop. How can the author go wrong?

Indeed, much goes right, including having the image of Endymion hover over this tale of a woman's need for companionship and sex. Endymion was a mortal, the lover of the moon goddess Selene, who kissed him to sleep nightly and who begged Zeus to grant him eternal life so she might embrace him forever. But Zeus went a step further, putting Endymion into an eternal sleep on Mt. Latmus. In the story, Endymion is the subject of a garish float parading through the French Quarter during Mardi Gras.

It's an apt symbol, but one the author hardly exploits; instead it is served up as a splash of local color and discarded.

In the story's main action, Laura, a married woman on vacation with some friends, makes her way through the already thronged streets of the Quarter to a hotel where her illicit lover waits. Perhaps the heroine thinks of her paramour as her Endymion;

perhaps his features remind her of the pagan god of lust? Maybe the story ends with the image of Endymion floating past her along Bourbon Street?

In any case, such a strong symbol demands to be put to good use. That particular float should be described in such a way that it sticks in the reader's mind, vividly.

The story might open with Laura making apologies to her friends, perhaps saying that she has a business appointment. Then we see her out on the street looking guiltily over her shoulder, making sure she's not being watched as she passes by policemen and parade floats being outfitted. Approaching her lover's hotel, she relives their first meeting, and her later discovery that he's married. She mentally replays their whole sordid affair, complete with vivid lovemaking. She gets to the hotel and has the concierge ring up for him, or maybe she rushes into the elevator—an old-fashioned caged elevator—and starts up to his suite. In the elevator (reeking of the aged elevator operator's cheap drugstore cologne), Laura has her epiphany. By the time she reaches her floor she has come to her senses. She scribbles a quick note and slides it under Jason's door, then hurries to rejoin the parade with her friends.

As her friends toss doubloons and beads she watches Endymion glide toward—and then past and away from—her.

My student titled her story "Affair in New Orleans." This sums up the situation, but does little justice to the story or the myth it embodies. Other suggestions?

91} TRIMALCHIO IN WEST EGG: MORE ON TITLES

Great titles are made, not born—and made often with great deliberation and struggle. To some they come easily, to most not. Few books get published with their original titles, and that may be a good thing. Jane Austen's original title for *Pride and Prejudice* was

First Impressions. Tennessee Williams's original titles for the play that became *A Streetcar Named Desire* were *The Moth* and *The Poker Night.*[39] Joseph Heller wanted to call his first novel *Catch-18*, but his publisher asked him to change it when another World War II novel, Leon Uris's *Mila 18*, came out the same year.[40] Had Ezra Pound not talked T.S. Eliot out of it, *The Waste Land,* the greatest of all modernist poems, would have been called *He Do the Police in Different Voices.* Before (and after) arriving at *The Great Gatsby,* Fitzgerald weighed a dozen other possible titles for his masterpiece, including *Trimalchio in West Egg, The High-Bouncing Lover* and *Under the Red, White, and Blue.*

Women in Love was originally *The Wedding Ring; The Red Badge of Courage: Private Fleming, His Various Battles. From Here to Eternity* was originally titled *If Wishes Were Horses. Gone With the Wind* began as *Tote the Weary Lode; A Farewell to Arms* was *They Who Get Shot.* And so on.

Not all title changes are for the better, nor are they always the inspirations of authors. Often publishers pull rank, and for good reason. Does anyone question why *The Village Virus*, Sinclair Lewis' original title for *Main Street*, didn't survive his publisher's marketing department? And among fans of James M. Cain's *The Postman Always Rings Twice,* how many would prefer his original title, *Bar-B-Q?!*

But publishers don't always err on the side of literary or commercial success, and occasionally their choices even raise doubts about their sanity. The publishers of the English translation of Primo Levi's *Se questo è un uomo* (literally, *If This Is a Man*)—his poetically stark memoir of life in a concentration camp—chose, none too bravely or wisely, to retitle it *Survival in Auschwitz,* confining the book's vision while diminishing its broader human implications.

---

39 Also *Blanche's Chair in the Moon*—a title Williams himself called "very bad."

40 For similar reasons *Catch-11 (Oceans 11)* was rejected, as was *Catch-17 (Stalag 17),* until Heller finally hit on the "funny" number 22.

Although they don't always get the final word, authors do have a strong say in the titling of their works. And so, though I may not judge a book by its cover, I don't hesitate to read meaning into its title.

Titles are great carriers of information. They tell us not just what we're reading, but what we're writing, about its thematic, metaphoric, or symbolic content (or lack thereof). If there are going to be problems with a novel or story, those problems often announce themselves in the title, like the smell of ozone before a storm.

A story called "The Boiler Room" forms a solid image, piquing my interest and connoting (for me) a dark world of fiery but suppressed desire, an Inferno; another, called "Daydreaming," connotes nothing and lowers expectations—as does any work titled "Untitled."

Good titles don't have to be complicated, poetic, or clever in any way. Often the greater the work, the simpler the title: *The Odyssey, Hamlet.* Of course, any truly great work lifts its title to greatness, explaining why so few great works have awful titles.

Titling our stories forces us to arrive at a deeper understanding of what they are about—what central metaphor operates in them. They give us our focal point, or make it clear that we have none.

I encourage you to arrive at a working title as early as possible, and to modify it often as your vision of the work-in-progress grows clearer.

Streams (& Oceans)
of Consciousness

92} NAVIGATING STREAM OF CONSCIOUSNESS

Through free association, our random thoughts churn up symbols.

Many years ago, while living in Connecticut, I spent a few months apart from the woman I was then engaged to, traveling in the Pacific Northwest. The whole time I was out there, two Beatles songs kept going through my head: "Ticket to Ride" and "Yesterday." When I came back East, I noticed a strange toothbrush in my fiancée's medicine cabinet. Needless to say, our engagement was off.

Had I played closer attention to those songs served up by my unconscious, I might not have bothered coming home; I might even have seen that the reason I went away in the first place was that I didn't really want to get married.

In its swirling eddies and sweeping currents, the stream of consciousness carries observations and associations, implications and omens.

But the stream of consciousness is more than a body of water that sweeps us along like little sailboats through our days. The stream *defines* us; it is who we are. Our minds may seem incoherent, discharging electrical impulses and sparks in wild disarray, and yet the thoughts and feelings generated by those sparks, in all their randomness, merge somehow to produce a coherent "I."

Our characters, too, make use of stream-of-consciousness thinking, through what's called "interior monologue."

The opening chapter of a student's novel, set during a seaside idyll, makes heavy use of the stream-of-consciousness techniques pioneered by James Joyce and Virginia Woolf. The former's *Ulysses* holds the most famous interior monologue in English, a passage that, capping an unpunctuated sentence of 2,500 words, ends with what Joyce called "Molly Bloom's acquiescence at the end of all resistance":

> ... I was a Flower of the mountain yes when I put the rose in my hair like the Andalusian girls used or shall I wear a red yes and how he kissed me under the Moorish wall and I thought well as well him as another and then I asked him with my eyes to ask

again yes and then he asked me would I yes to say yes my mountain flower and first I put my arms around him yes and drew him down to me so he could feel my breasts all perfume yes and his heart was going like mad and yes I said yes I will Yes.

Stream of consciousness attempts to capture characters' inner thoughts while moving them through time and space (or, in the case of Molly's soliloquy, as she lolls in bed). The flowing "stream" must in fact be carefully organized and orchestrated, so that what appears to be chaotic on the surface is actually focused and to the point. Precisely because it lacks any obvious form or structure, stream of consciousness demands a high degree of craft and rigor. Think again of Jackson Pollock's paintings: All those "arbitrary" drips, swirls, blotches, and spatters are very much in the artist's control.

In another novel we meet a character named Kim. Fresh from a broken, sexually charged affair, she has just learned that a childhood friend has brain cancer, and processes her emotions as she moves through a seascape. The author has turned composer, creating a symphony of words consisting of a few interwoven themes expressed in a handful of movements. These themes might be: the ocean, the wind, Kim's sadness over her failure to win acceptance to Julliard (she's a violinist), and the possible loss of her friend.

All these themes might run together while maintaining a quality of randomness, spontaneity, and surprise, forming a free-flowing "stream" of consciousness. As Kim herself reflects (while rehearsing a violin concerto in her head), "Framework: intro, supporting, supporting, supporting, conclusion."

None of this is or ought to be arbitrary. If successful, the music should build, movement by movement, to a satisfying conclusion or crescendo, with all of the thematic rivers joining before flowing together into the sea. Otherwise the disassociated strains will trickle off to nowhere.

As with any tour-de-force approach, stream of consciousness typically requires much revision and many drafts. And control of punctuation and syntax is crucial.

In my student's chapter, Kim's reveries lead her into the ocean itself, where she nearly drowns after breaking through a fittingly symbolic warning signboard ("ACCESS PROHIBITED"). Her stream of consciousness is literally broken by her fall. The subsequent scene of her rescue shifts us out of reverie and into action, implying that the heroine has nearly drowned in her thoughts.

In your own compositions, pick out the themes and see how they inform and underscore and interact with each other like instruments in an orchestra.

93} DRINKING THE OCEAN: WHEN SYMBOL & SUBSTANCE PART WAYS

There are authors who ignore, or refuse to acknowledge, the less-than-positive implications of their own symbols.

I'm reading a convincing story about a nine-year-old's infatuation with the sea, a fixation based entirely on postcards and photographs and on what she has imagined or dreamed, since she's never actually been there. All this is rendered by the author with great heart and skill, with delightful turns of phrase and descriptive passages. Sara is shown stretching her neck in the backseat of the car en route to the seashore, the landscape rolling by with its "mountains filled with shanty houses of exposed brick, and tin roofs built haphazardly up and down the steep hills." In the same paragraph I read, "She didn't want any ugliness to come between her and her ocean." Lovely.

And, though I admire the title, "Drinking the Ocean," it makes me question certain aspects of the story that seem to me less than fully realized. This is, after all, the story of a young girl's love affair—not with a man but with an entity, with the ocean. But the implications and hazards of such an infatuation are not sufficiently or satisfactorily explored. Emotionally, physically, or both, something needs to happen in a story. And in this one, essentially, nothing happens. Sara starts out in love with the ocean; then she meets the object of her dreams, which lives wholly up to her fantasies.

Not only is that unsatisfying, it's unrealistic. Dreams rarely live up to reality. And so there must, I think, be a moment of reckoning in the story, the moment when reality obliterates fantasy, when symbol and substance part ways. The green-blue sea in a dream or in a postcard is not the same sea that we swim in. That beautiful azure color is only a mirage: As soon as we cup the water in our hands the magic color disappears. Maybe Sara swallows water, or is caught in a riptide? Suppose she gets stung by a jellyfish, or steps on a stingray? The unrealized story arc here is:

(a) girl has naive fixation with the sea

(b) girl goes to the sea

(c) girl finds reality has little to do with fantasy

(d) girl is disappointed

(e) girl comes away with a new, realistic, and mature love based on experience rather than fantasy (the water that she brings home in a bottle is salty and bitter, but she loves it in spite of its harsh taste).

The loss of innocence metaphor is inescapable. The bitterness of the sea is the bitterness that must accompany any relinquishing of innocence or ideals.

A story generates its own unity out of the meanings latent in its raw materials. Those latencies must be made slyly overt; that is the writer's job. Not to inject stories with artificial or forced meaning, but to suss out the meaning(s) already there, so the reader can, with a little effort, appreciate them.

94} THE SUBLIME EXISTS: DON'T FORCE IT

Of symbols, poet John Ciardi has written:

> A symbol is like a rock dropped into a pool: It sends out ripples in all directions, and the ripples are in motion. Who can say where the last ripple disappears? One may have a sense that he at least knows approximately the center point of all those ripples, the point at which the stone struck the water. Yet even then he has trouble marking it precisely. How does one make a mark on water?[41]

Should we force symbols, metaphors, myths, or meanings into our stories? No. Never. Should we go looking for them like big game or mushroom hunters? No. Better to let our symbols find us, and welcome them when they do.

Matters of Symbol, Myth & Metaphor

---

41 From *How Does a Poem Mean?*

Matters of Symbol, Myth, & Metaphor

The best things that happen in our writing happen not because we *will* them, but because we let them happen. This is true of all the arts, of painting and music and film and photography, and of the sciences, too. Of all the attitudes, techniques, and approaches available to us as creators, grim determination is certainly the worst. Though likely to produce results, it's also a source of nervous ailments—exhaustion, depression, insomnia, anxiety, headaches, stomach cramps, and delusions of grandeur alternating with bouts of low self-esteem.

But the worst of the ailments induced by grim determination is *self-consciousness*, a state of hyperawareness or overvigilance with respect to one's own performance. As when a dancer watches his feet, self-consciously produced art is at best forced, overdetermined, and inauthentic.

Nothing is more contradictory than the grim pursuit of the sublime. It's like trying to make someone love you. It never works. The sublime exists. It presents itself most willingly to those who seek it least aggressively and with the most generous ambitions (see Meditation # 151). This is why artists need humility and faith, and it is perhaps why Vincent van Gogh—whose original ambition was to be a priest—succeeded so well as an artist.

To "believe" in art is to recognize nature's hidden patterns and symbols. It is to believe in the structure, order, and meaning latent in events that, at face value, seem meaningless and chaotic. The artist/priest coaxes life's hidden patterns and implications from their dark hiding places into the clear light of day: as a writer, through the medium of words. When language works this magic, it is largely due to what we call style.

Q. HOW DO I KNOW WHETHER I'VE WORKED ENOUGH SYMBOLS INTO MY NOVEL OR STORY?

A. You don't, and you really shouldn't. Symbols are the reader's problem, not yours. Your job as writer is to recognize them when they occur *naturally,* and to make the most of them when they do.

And keep in mind that everything is a latent symbol. I have a friend who makes it her business to see the symbolism in everything: clouds, gestures, accidents … Sometimes she drives me crazy with her endless analytical interpretations.

And yet as readers of our own drafts this sort of Freudian excess can pay off. For instance, when we realize that the backyard sinkhole a character has been trying unsuccessfully to fill for years is a symbol of his faithless marriage.

Q. WHAT ABOUT NOVELS AND STORIES THAT EMPLOY SYMBOLS? CAN YOU RECOMMEND ANY?

A. Since (as my friend will tell you) symbols are everywhere, they're also everywhere in works of art, especially in great works. Finding them is as easy as looking for them. And so there's no point, really, in presenting you with a list of works that make special use of symbols, because, like beauty, symbols are in the eye of the beholder.

Just bear in mind—as you read great books—that everything is a potential symbol. The potential is in *you,* the reader, as much as it is in the book.

Once a story is in the hands of a reader, it's the reader's to interpret as he wishes. If a reader decides that Sherlock Holmes's violin playing symbolizes his repressed homosexual passion for Dr. Watson, then, for that reader, so it is.

Matters of
Style

Style: Nutriment, not Condiment

We'd meet in his Greenwich Village apartment, a creaky duplex across the street from the Jefferson Market. During prohibition it had been a speakeasy; the Judas window was still there. An oval recess in the ceiling commemorated the existence of a small stage. We'd sit side by side at his long dining room table walled in by books. Except where a set of tall drafty windows (whose sills his wife, Nancy, had adorned with cobalt bottles) faced Sixth Avenue every inch of the place, from its warped floorboards to its stamped tin ceiling, groaned with books.

Armed with his Mont Blanc fountain pen, my mentor slashed through my sentences, slathering them with ink, making me read first my version and then his, to see that his was superior. For eighteen months we did this, until I bridled at my mentor's "improvements." By then it didn't matter; I'd learned what he had to teach me: Never allow a dead, sawdusty, or droopy sentence, a sentence not worth reading twice.

In those eighteen months, thanks to Donald Newlove,[42] I became the next best thing to a poet: I became *a stylist*.

95} HAUGHTY HOBOS & HAIRY CASSOULETS

Style is nutriment, not condiment: not the ketchup, mustard, or gravy of good writing, but, as much as subject, the meat and potatoes. Structure, substance, style ... except for purposes of

---

42 Author of *First Paragraphs,* one of a series of "Handbooks for the Soul" aimed at writers (the work that first prompted me to seek him out)—as well as *Those Drinking Days: Myself and Other Writers,* a searing confessional of the sloshed life.

discussion, none of these elements can truly be separated from the others. When you can see the cracks, you need to worry.

For example, reading a story about a hobo, told in first person (or even close third), I stop short on encountering words like "complacency," "obliterating," and "mandatory." Unless the hobo is a Rhodes scholar with an inflated vocabulary, the choice of language needs to be examined—especially if the same narrator also uses words like "ain't," "golly," and "shucks."

Half of a good style is consistency; the other half is modesty.

Cleverness for its own sake kills.

Take the following sentence from a story submitted recently to *Alimentum,* a journal of creative writing relating to food: "There are hardly any, though possibly a few, hairs in my cassoulet. I don't notice. I take them to be feathers from the duck." At first the sentence seems to make sense. But on closer examination there are at least three contradictions here. Are there hairs in the cassoulet, or not? Are they noticed, or not? Or does the narrator see duck hairs? At the altar of cuteness the author sacrificed meaning and precision. I confess I didn't finish reading.

Even Nabokov, who could do almost anything with words, knew that to justify the verbal and intellectual pyrotechnics of *Lolita* he had to make Humbert Humbert, his narrator/protagonist, a hypercultivated, highly articulate man, and so he did. This gave him carte blanche to do as he pleased with the English language,[43] provided he did it well—and he does, very.

As for Melville's Ishmael, you might think there is no excuse for a tramp seaman's lancing us with Biblical prose. But Melville's masterpiece is *consistently* incredible and excessive. Melville doesn't just break all the rules, he breaks them constantly, flagrantly, in great bursts of rhetorical brio.

---

43 The same can't be said for *Ada, or Ardor,* Nabokov's six-hundred-page exercise in mandarin self-gratification.

Saul Bellow is equally daring with diction in this passage from *Herzog*, where the title character watches his lover apply her makeup:

> First she spread a layer of cream on her cheeks, rubbing it into the straight nose, her childish chin and soft throat. It was gray, pearly bluish stuff. That was the base. She fanned it with a towel. Over this she laid the makeup. She worked it in with cotton swabs, under the hairline, about the eyes, up the cheeks and on the throat. Despite the soft rings of feminine flesh, there was already something discernibly dictatorial about that extended throat. She would not let Herzog caress her face downward—it was bad for the muscles. Seated, watching, on the edge of the luxurious tub, he put on his pants, tucked in his shirt. She took no notice of him; she was trying in some way to be rid of him as her daytime life began.

Though Bellow does it so casually and confidently that we may not even notice at first, the above paragraph holds no fewer than a half dozen shifts in diction. The first sentence is neutral, its tone neither formal nor informal. But "bluish stuff" drops us firmly in colloquial territory. Then we get three more neutral or plainspoken sentences, each short, creating a staccato effect, as of a recipe or grammar school primer: See Spot run. In the next sentence, via multiple subordinate clauses, Bellow ratchets his voice higher, but only slightly. But with sentence seven he vaults fully into formal diction, starting with the word "despite" and arriving at the summit of pomposity with "discernibly dictatorial." From that haughty zenith Bellow has nowhere to go but down, and down he drops, to "*bad for* the muscles," another colloquialism. From there, the passage reverts to its plainspoken style—as if, having tolerated Herzog's highbrow presence for as long as possible, his now fully made-up mistress has worked him and his bombastic vocabulary out of her system.

Proof that, with fiction, you can do almost anything, provided you do it with purpose, conviction, and confidence.

Plainspoken vs. Poetry
& Minimalism

96} WATER FROM WINE:
IN PRAISE OF THE PLAINSPOKEN

That last passage shows us style being played for all it's worth by a master who's not afraid to take risks.

You may not want or need to take such risks. To achieve style, or even poetry, you do not need fancy words or phrasing, or even complex ideas or imagery.

Simple thoughts expressed in plain language will do, as in this opening of a short story by *Big Fish* author Daniel Wallace:

> As sad as it was, I guess it was about time my mother died. She had become so old. Who knew a person could live so long? Her body looked like it had been soaked in water for a week, then dried out on an asphalt parking lot on the hottest day in August. She had no teeth, and her tongue could hardly move at all. A far cry from the tongue that could tie cherry stems in a knot with her mouth closed (the only trick she knew).

Few would argue that this passage isn't poetic. And yet any search for "poetry" within the individual lines will turn up nothing. It's the arrangement of simple thoughts, the clarity of images, and the honest earthiness of the narrator's voice, along with his attention to details and generosity with information ("the only trick she knew") that charms the reader while striking a poetic chord.

A plainspoken style has much to recommend it. At the very least it *doesn't* get in the way. Witness this passage from Charles Simmons's novel *Salt Water:*

> Father and I used to fish off the shore for king, weak, blues, and bass. The bass gave the best fight and were the best eating. We pulled in a lot of sand sharks too, small, useless things we threw back. Sometimes we went for real sharks, with a big hook, too heavy to cast. We'd fix on a mackerel steak, and I'd swim out with the hook and drop it to the bottom. I did this even when I was small, except then I'd float out on my inner tube, drop the hook, and Father would pull me in with a rope.

"The best technique," Henry Miller once remarked, "is no technique at all." Which is probably true. But Miller might have added that to attain "no technique" takes years of study and practice. Plainspoken writing *looks* easy. But to write plainly, transparently, takes modesty, discipline, and saintly restraint. The result goes down like a glass of clean cold water, and is as hard to argue with.

The popularity of the plainspoken style owes much to Hemingway, who owed much to Sherwood Anderson, and to the wire service reporting that taught him to be thrifty[44] with words.

97 } LESS IS MORE—OR LESS: MINIMALISM

When severity of language and description is taken to extremes and applied to unexceptional characters in banal situations, we call the result *minimalist fiction.* Of the so-called "minimalist school," Raymond Carver, Amy Hempel, Bobbie Ann Mason, and Ann Beattie are considered leading exponents. Unlike Hemingway's prose[45]—which cuts to the bone while implying worlds of unstated sensations and ideas—minimalist prose emphasizes superficial qualities:

Matters of Style

---

44 I wrote "parsimonious" first, then struck it.

45 "I always try to write on the principle of the iceberg. There is seven-eighths of it under water for every part that shows."—Ernest Hemingway.

> The kitchen was filled with specialized utensils. When Dale Anne couldn't sleep she watched TV, and that's where the stuff was advertised. She had a thing to core tomatoes—it was called a Tomato Shark—and a metal spaghetti wheel for measuring out spaghetti. She had plastic melon-ballers and a push-in device that turned ordinary cake into ladyfingers.
>
> I found pasta primavera in the refrigerator. My fingers wanted to knit the cold linguini, laying precisely cabled strands across the oily peppers and beans.

This passage—from an Amy Hempel short story, in her collection *Reasons to Live*—exemplifies "kitchen sink realism." I'm no big fan of minimalism, but in her writing Hempel achieves a perfect balance of brevity and density, richness and rigor, and her short, spare tales play like sad, catchy tunes.

My problem with most so-called minimalist fiction is that its economy isn't achieved through a process of elimination. What's left out was never there to begin with, and is therefore *not* implied: Less is simply *less*. If I use the "m" word to describe a story, I mean that the author implies more than what is stated.

Minimalism, too, has its risks. And you may want to take them. But such risks should not be taken blindly.

Moby-Dick and *Herzog* notwithstanding, the emphasis in this section will be on clarity, logic, accuracy, and consistency: in other words, on rules. The fearless among you will break as many of them as they wish. One definition of a fearless person is someone who needn't be told to be fearless.

For the less brazen I present the following injunction—written in monumental letters across the blackboard:

THERE ARE NO RULES

Following which I add, in smaller letters:

However …

Worth Reading Twice:
Pedestrian vs. Poetic

"Words, he said, have a certain value in the literary tradition and a certain value in the market-place—a debased value."

—James Joyce, *Stephen Hero*[46]

"Unconscious action leads to style, conscious action to mannerism."

—Max J. Friedlander

98} HOW THE GAME IS PLAYED: WHY SHAKESPEARE DRIBBLES

Style *is* substance. In good, durable writing, no dichotomy between the two exists. To last, writing must withstand numerous readings with little or no diminishment of pleasure. If the style is good enough, each fresh encounter between text and reader will bring greater pleasure than the last.

Without a great style there can be no great art. The subject of art is, in part, its style: *how* what is said (or painted or danced or photographed or filmed) has been said. There are invisible styles and styles that call attention to themselves; styles that go down like water and others that taste like whisky, wine, molasses, or motor oil.

The poet claims he doesn't "capture" feelings. Rather he builds with words monuments to commemorate them. Fiction works similarly. Do we create experience? Do we "capture" it? No: We, too, build monuments of words, though our monuments

46 Joyce's first stab at what would become *A Portrait of the Artist as a Young Man.*

commemorate *characters* and *scenes*. And if they are to last, our monuments must be made of something durable—a strong style.

Except for its style, the content of most works of fiction can be successfully conveyed by other means, by movies and television, media that have indeed stolen much of fiction's fire. Who needs fiction, anyway? With such slick and dazzling media at our disposal, why bother with plain, old-fashioned words? Why work with a medium so challenging—for both writers and readers?

I'm reminded of an undergraduate's complaint about Shakespeare: "Why does he make everything so hard? Why can't he just say things *straight?*"

I asked the student if he ever played basketball. He did.

"Do you dribble?" I asked.

He squinted at me. Of course he dribbled. Everyone dribbles.

"Why? Why don't you just walk down the court with the ball?"

"That's not how the game is played."

"Oh? Why not?"

"Because—it'd be too easy. It wouldn't be any fun."

The rules to basketball are fairly straightforward; the rules of style aren't. While there's no arguing with someone else's style, we can choose not to put up with it—just as you may choose not to put up with some of the advice that follows.

99} WORDS INTO MUSIC: WHAT WRITERS CAN GIVE PEOPLE THAT MOVIES CAN'T

If books merely convey plots and characters, why, in the age of cinema, read a book? What can books give us that movies can't?

In two words: beautiful writing.

Screenplays can be brilliant, but language isn't their medium. The language of a story or novel *is* the point.

Here's something movies can't do:

> Ships at a distance have every man's wish on board. For some they come in with the tide. For others they sail forever on the horizon, never out of sight, never landing until the Watcher turns his eyes away in resignation, his dreams mocked to death by Time. That is the life of men.
>
> Now, women forget all those things they don't want to remember, and remember everything they don't want to forget. The dream is the truth. Then they act and do things accordingly.
>
> So the beginning of this was a woman and she had come back from burying the dead. Not the dead of sick and ailing with friends at the pillow and the feet. She had come back from the sodden and the bloated; the sudden dead, their eyes flung wide open in judgment.

With these opening words of her best-known novel, *Their Eyes Were Watching God*, Zora Neale Hurston strikes deep into the heart of what fiction does best: language. Prose poetry. This language doesn't just reconstitute itself in the mind as images, plot, and characters; like music it imbues us with feelings.

But Hurston soon gets down to telling her story. This opening prose poem is merely appetizer.

Like many a great opener, this one tells us, from the start, that whatever else the forthcoming tale is about, it will be also be about the power and beauty of words.

100} INDELIBLE SENTENCES: SIGNATURE STYLES

However we define style, who doesn't want to be known for hers? What aspiring author doesn't dream of producing prose so distinct readers can identify her from one or two indelible sentences?

Even among the most celebrated, very few writers achieve that standard. How many of the following quotes can you link to their authors?

1. "Americans are very friendly and very suspicious, that is what Americans are and that is what always upsets the foreigner, who deals with them, they are so friendly how can they be so suspicious they are so suspicious how can they be so friendly but they just are."

2. "The heaventree of stars hung with humid nightblue fruit."

3. "The sun shone, having no alternative, on the nothing new."

4. "With two thousand years of Christianity behind him ... a man can't see a regiment of soldiers march past without going off the deep end."

5. "In the fall the war was always there, but we did not go to it anymore."

6. "We had to empty our pockets; they were after knives and matches and such objects of harm."

7. "Sunday is always a bad day. A sort of gray purgatory that resembles a bus station with broken vending machines."

8. "I don't like jail, they got the wrong kind of bars in there."

9. "A lady's imagination is very rapid; it jumps from admiration to love, from love to matrimony in a moment."

10. "The great revelation perhaps never did come. Instead there were little daily miracles, illuminations, matches struck unexpectedly in the dark."[47]

Unlike the so-called graffiti "artist" who sprays his indecipher-able scrawl on the tenement wall, the first wish of those who wrote the sentences above wasn't to call attention to their style, but to

---

47 1. Gertrude Stein; 2. James Joyce; 3. Samuel Beckett; 4. Louis-Ferdinand Céline; 5. Ernest Hemingway; 6. Saul Bellow; 7. Lorrie Moore; 8. Charles Bukowski; 9. Jane Austen; 10. Virginia Woolf.

communicate clearly. *Unconscious action leads to style, conscious action to mannerism.*

The great character archetypes of literature—Emma Bovary and Leopold Bloom and Raskolnikov—resulted not from their authors' desire to create archetypes, but from their desire to create authentic individuals. Similarly, great style tends to be a result, not a cause.

Style happens while we attend to other, more important matters.

101} ENGAGING THE SYMPATHETIC IMAGINATION

When I say "communicate clearly," I'm not being very clear.

Communicate what? Do I simply mean information: who, what, where, when? Newspapers give us this. But a work of literary art must create a fictional world; it engages not just the brain's cognitive functions, but a higher organ: the *sympathetic imagination.*[48]

And this is where style begins to assert itself.

Until the reader surrenders to his imagination, he will not enter the world of a story. If he does not, the blame falls not on the reader but squarely on the writer. Every stylistic glitch or blip, every unnecessary or jarring word, every misplaced punctuation mark, unintentional rhyme, or alliteration, every droning or backwards sentence—anything that draws the reader out of the story to strand him on a shallow sandbar of mere words—undermines the fictional experience.

This is why writers, good ones, study poetry. Not to compete with poets in their prose, but to learn from poets how to use language—not just efficiently, but perfectly.

---

48 The ability of a person to penetrate the barrier between himself and his object, and to secure a momentary but complete identification with it. "If a sparrow comes before my window," wrote Keats, "I take part in its existence and pick about the gravel."

102 } A RESORT IN THE LAURENTIANS: POETIC VS. PEDESTRIAN PROSE

When I speak of poetic prose, I don't mean *purple* prose. Purple prose is bad poetry —overly rich; it's corned beef hash *with gravy.*

Poetic prose is prose tempered by poetry, as in this passage from "Maedele" by Gabriella Goliger:

> Staring at a stubborn spot of ice that resists the battering of the windshield wipers, Rachel sinks down into her seat and drifts. She constructs a fantasy, beginning with a premise and adding details, a dab of color here, another there, until the vision wraps her in its fuzzy warmth. The premise is that Mr. Blustein's gone to Paris. A gallery there is exhibiting her work. Meanwhile Blustein waits for Rachel on the front steps of his apartment building. He paces with impatience, then catches sight of her youthful figure up the street. His eyes glow when he sees her, graceful, nonchalant, her hair streaming in the wind (it has lengthened and straightened itself by some miracle). He grabs her arm and guides her upstairs. No. He whistles for a cab, and they go to the Queen E. Hotel for a second breakfast. No. They drive to a resort in the Laurentians. That's it, a resort in remote, snow-filled woods. He reaches for her hand across a dining room table and his eyes, brilliant with all that he knows and feels and has a hold on, those eyes burn toward her, reduce her to cinders.

I call this writing poetic not because it functions as poetry—it doesn't. The author isn't writing a poem; she's telling a story. It's poetic because it exploits poetic devices.

What are these devices? *Precision* (not just a "resort" but one *"in the Laurentians"*). *Concision* (that "stubborn spot of ice" says all we need to know about the weather conditions). *Compression* (from the resort in the snowy Laurentian woods the author cuts to the lovers holding hands across the dining room table, implying everything in between). These devices combine with musical attributes, with an ear for rhythm and cadence: "he *pa*ces with im*pa*tience"—the internal rhyme clearly intended.

Here, a lesser version of the same passage:

> As Rachel drove her car in the blizzard she fantasized about Mr. Blustein. In one of her fantasies Mr. Blustein had gone to Paris to attend an opening at a gallery that was exhibiting Rachel's paintings. In another fantasy she met him at his apartment building, where he stood waiting for her on the sidewalk in front of his door, seeing her approach, looking extremely gorgeous and sexy to him, with her long brown flowing hair blowing in the stiff breeze. In the same fantasy he took her by the arm and took her upstairs to make love to her, or maybe they went to have breakfast in a fancy hotel. As Rachel drove through the snowstorm more fantasies went through her mind, like one of Mr. Blustein taking her to a far away, remote resort, where, over a candlelit dinner, he would gaze lovingly into her eyes.

Pedestrian prose.

Writers' workshops, even those belonging to the fanciest and most righteous MFA programs, say little about poetic prose, though it represents an ideal for fiction writers to aspire toward. Prose needn't be "poetic" to have style. But fiction not worth reading twice—not just for the plot, but for the joy of encountering its well-chosen words in the same artful order—isn't worth reading at all.

Poet Richard Hugo warns us: "Once language exists only to convey information it is dying."

103} A QUAYSIDE IN THE RAIN: THE JOURNEY FROM JOURNALESE

Pedestrian prose is sometimes called "journalese."

Though they have things in common, journalese isn't the same as journalism. Journalese is writing that gets all the information down in the right order, but in language that's flaccid, flat, not worth repeat readings.

An author needs to create in her narrators not a dry reporter who gives us the facts, but a seductive storyteller whose voice is unique and memorable—or at least delivers some poetry or wit.

Here's a passage raised, in three stages, from journalese to *stylish* prose.

> **STAGE 1:**
>
> It was raining. I was standing on the pier reading a notice about drowning victims. There were no other people or cats on the wharf. There were a few railway trucks parked under a row of cranes. All of the warehouses were closed. There were only a few dim lights burning on the *Lotus,* which didn't look very inviting.

> **STAGE 2:**
>
> I stood in the rain on the quayside reading a large sheet of printed instructions for resuscitating the apparently drowned, which was the only information of any sort available to passersby. The wharf was deserted. The cranes huddled together in a row, a few railway trucks crouched between their legs; the warehouses were shut, locked, and abandoned even by the cats; the *Lotus,* lit with a few dim lights, looked as uninviting as a shut pub.

> **STAGE 3:**
>
> I stood in the quayside mizzle reading a broadside for resuscitating the freshly drowned, the only information available to a passerby like me. At that hour the wharf was unambiguously deserted, occupied only by six dinosaur-like rusty cranes, with railway trucks crouching at their feet. Even the local alley cats had deserted the warehouses in favor of more welcoming places. The *SS Lotus,* her massive black hull pierced by a spattering of feeble porthole lights, looked about as inviting as a shuttered pub.

The second of the three passages is from Richard Gordon's 1953 novel *Doctor at Sea.* Into it he has injected some of his narrator's wit, which takes the form of droll observations ("the only information of any sort available to passersby"), personifications (cranes "huddled," trucks "crouched") and character-inspired simile ("uninviting as a shut pub" suggests the narrator's non-aversion to a cozy nip now and then). The result isn't poetic, but it's not journalese.[49]

In the third revision I've perhaps gone too far with my tweaking, removing dead wood ("apparently," "together"), nixing all but one conjugation of that dead verb *to be,* and—since the book is about shipboard life—changing "abandoned" to "deserted" and "large sheet of printed instructions" to "broadside" (both new words have nautical connotations). "Shuttered" feels more solid to me than "shut." As for "mizzle," it means "a very fine rain" but sounds like "mizzen" as in "mizzen mast," and so, for me anyway, it casts a maritime aura. Other of my "improvements" are by way of injecting personality. You may take issue with "unambiguously," as I usually do with adverbs; it is there not just to color the adjective, but to tint the narrator's psyche. You'd cut it? Fine, cut it.

As a stylist, you, too, won't resist tinkering with other people's prose. The better the prose, the more it invites tinkering.

Overwriting, Obscurity, & Mannerisms

104} BART'S SHIRT: SPURTING PROSE

Going too far out of our way to avoid journalese can lead to overwriting, or trading accuracy for effect. As in this sentence:

"Spurts of liquid lava hurled from Susan's eyes onto Bart's shirt, creating a random pattern of dark spots on the sky blue fabric."

---

49 When we inhabit our characters deeply, their souls lend color and texture (poetry) to our prose. The best way to avoid journalese is to write from inside our characters.

The sentence is ego-driven, working too hard to impress the reader, who doesn't want to be impressed but to visualize the thing being described. "Spurts of liquid lava"? I assume these are tears, which don't spurt but merely drip onto Bart's celestial shirt. *Creating a random pattern?* Sure, but the reader doesn't need to be told so; it's obvious. What all this means is something like, "Susan's tears fell on Bart's shirt." That gets the point across without spewing any lava.

Pitching your voice higher doesn't mean finding complicated ways to say simple things; it means paying attention to syntax and rhythms, to precision; creating vivid images out of words chosen for their solidity, accuracy, and efficiency. Eliminate any word, phrase, or sentence that doesn't help the reader see—or worse, that *interferes* with his seeing accurately.

Though not poetic, "Susan's tears fell on Bart's shirt" isn't a bad sentence: It does its job; it wastes no words; it's swift and lean, with a pleasing iambic cadence. The moment demands nothing more. That Bart's shirt is sky blue tells me nothing I really need to know (if it were of raw silk, or denim, that might add something).

It's not the words in a sentence that make it work well, but the *thought* behind the words. A sentence works because it's true, it's solid, it's authentic. Whereas the idea behind volcanic tears creating an archipelago of dark spots is trumped up, insincere, sentimental. Forced.

Write solid sentences that waste not a word, and already you've moved beyond journalese.

105 } A PURPLE HANDSHAKE: OVERWRITING

People who overwrite are often among the most gifted novices. Still, because it takes talent to overwrite doesn't mean you should do it.

Say you've written this paragraph:

> Erin took a half step towards Sam; he countered with his hand. Unnoticeably she balked, and then quickly extended her hand as well. They shook and Sam's strong hands one last time pressed against her disillusioned flesh, and he squeezed her hand softly, regretfully, universes of meaning behind one simple handshake.

Leaving aside the glaring excesses ("universes of meaning"), we quickly feel that emotions are being forced on us. The author isn't just letting her characters shake hands; she's pumping up emotion and "meaning." Nearly every verb drags along its adverb like a dog with a tin can tied to its tail; and adverbs tell us *how* the scene is being played. They crowd out the reader's imagination.

Suppose, instead, that we already know Erin and Sam well. We know their circumstances, where they work, how they live, their habits, what they look like, the sounds of their voices, their thoughts, their hopes, their dreams. Now when the author puts her characters into a scene together, she and her adverbs can buzz off and leave her characters alone to talk. Before parting the lovers shake hands.

At that point, if the author has done her job properly, in place of the above purple passage she might write:

> *They shook hands.*

A chill may visit the reader's spine, because he knows, without being told, what that handshake *means*—that these characters may not see one another again.

106} SIMPLE ACTIONS DEMAND SIMPLE WORDS: IZZY'S SNORES

Simple sentences, too, are part of a good style. They add texture and variety. They also steer us away from convolution.

A student writes: "As Izzy's snores continued to ricochet all around the room, Becky's eyes were the only ones that remained wide open." *Translation*: "Izzy's snores kept Becky awake."

While complex thoughts may demand complex language, simple thoughts are seldom well served by fancy language. The trouble with journalese is not that it uses simple sentences; it's that it never reaches beyond them even when the occasion calls for it, as it *doesn't* here. The sentence, "Izzy's snoring kept Becky awake," is unimpeachable. It wastes no syllables and puts the emphasis where it belongs.

Concise, straightforward sentences are the mortar between bricks—those complex sentences that swoop and turn, that convey vivid imagery or subtle observations through metaphor, rhythm, or other poetic devices. They are a part of stylish writing, but without simple sentences stylish prose can't function or even exist.

107 } MORE SENTENCES LOST IN TRANSLATION

Of John Updike's habitual forays into overwriting, Norman Mailer once gibed: "Like many a good young writer before him [who] doesn't know exactly what do when action lapses ... he cultivates his private vice, he writes. "[50]

Although they may not be as accomplished in this "private vice" as Updike, that hasn't stopped many of my students from engaging in it.

"Writing" in italics (or quotation marks) is *bad* writing. It's writing that makes mountains out of anthills, that's affected or pompous or both. And the harder these writers try to impress us, the less impressive they are.

---

50 From *Advertisements for Myself*, in which Mr. Mailer has something unkind to say about all his literary brothers except James Jones.

When I come across examples of *writing*, my first impulse is to translate.

"She wore a type of expression that invariably promises a subsequent question from most people, a quizzical expression that echoes the question 'why?' before the word is ever spoken." *Translation*: "She cocked her head."

"Suddenly their conversation was interrupted by the sound of the doorbell." *Translation*: "The doorbell rang."

108} HAIR GEYSERS: TOO MUCH OF A GOOD THING

Sometimes an author's strengths and weaknesses are combined in the same sentence. Here are some mixed examples:

> Knotty red hair geysered in a crude ponytail from the apex of her head, giving the impression of a mad cheerleader, and the apartment smelled of cocoa.

Here "geyser" makes a welcome fresh appearance as a verb. I also appreciate the judicious nose for apartment odors. But the two sensations feel sort of jammed together against their will. And how to reconcile a *geyser* with a *cheerleader*? And since a ponytail isn't likely to erupt from elsewhere, "apex of her head" seems strained.

Later in the same story: "being a hostess that night had merely happened to her the way she might get splashed by a passing car." The comparison is funny and apt, but a bit awkwardly phrased (try, "like getting splashed by a passing car").

Later still: "She lifted her hands from the steering wheel; her unmanned sedan tracked straight and true down the carpool lane, like a bowling ball down the gutter." Thanks to that gratuitous simile, the sentence itself bowls a split.

Tone: Violence & Heavy Breathing

109} VINCENT PRICE SYNDROME: PANTING PROSE

Remember Vincent Price—the horror movie actor known for his funereal demeanor and chilling voice? The Master of Menace, the King of Creepy, the Sovereign of Sinister. But like many a stereotyped performer, Price eventually fell victim to his own shtick and turned into a Hollywood joke.

This psychological thriller—about a daughter whose relationship with her widowed dad is threatened by his possessive, vindictive girlfriend—is marred by what I'll call Vincent Price syndrome:

> She stares into the glassy lifeless eyes. His jaw drops open; his mouth is so dry his lips stick to his teeth. Suddenly things begin to move very, very slowly.
>
> A harrowing black speck appears in the corner of his left eye, barely visible at first but growing miraculously larger and larger until it slides down his cheek leaving an ominous trail along the side of his nose around the edge of his mouth down to his chin where it freezes for a heartbeat before breaking off. The young girl follows with quavering anticipation the single blood tear's straight and sudden descent to the white tiled floor of the foyer.
>
> And suddenly things begin moving very, very fast.
>
> "Mom!" Kara screams, but more like this:
>
> *"Moooooooooooooooooomm!"*
>
> Expelling all the petrified breath from her lungs her cry carries into every room of the house. Meanwhile outside a light powdery snow is falling on frozen grass and the windows of the house begin to light up one by one.

This is full-blown Vincent Price syndrome: over-the-top emotions and breathless prose, aided and abetted by an overuse of modifiers ("miraculous," "harrowing," "petrified," "ominous"). The characters' actions are themselves over the top—at one point the protagonist pees in her pants out of fear (see Meditation # 30).

This is sentimentality, unearned emotion. It can try readers' patience, leaving them not numb with fear, but just plain numb. With its panting modifiers and ominous asides ("… little did Loretta know …"), such writing never trusts a reader's powers of perception and intuition. Like a bad instructor, it does all the work for them.

In their predilection for panting, over-the-top prose, novices are hardly alone. More than a few established authors, and even some mega-bestselling ones, set the tone. Staggerered, lunged, heaved, collapsed; thundering, gasping, cavernous, chillingly close, mountainous, ghost-pale; stammered, defenseless, perfectly immobile, ghostly, surge of adrenaline—this breathless glossary studs just the first page of Dan Brown's *The Da Vinci Code.*

To date, that book has sold over 45 million copies in hardcover alone. But you and I don't aspire to make millions, only to produce great works of art. Right? *Right?*

110} TAKE A HOSE TO YOUR PROSE: COOL LANGUAGE/OVERHEATED IMAGES

"Reporting on the extreme things as if they were average things will start you off on the art of fiction."

—F. Scott Fitzgerald

In relating violent actions and emotions, verbal restraint is important. Violent emotions are best painted in "cool" colors, clinical blues and sober industrial grays—the antithesis of overheated language, aflame with modifiers, that shouts in garish reds and flamboyant yellows. (Modifiers seem to be the first things writers grab for in the heat of emotion.)

Wordsworth wrote, "Poetry is the spontaneous overflow of powerful feelings; it takes its origin from emotion recollected in tranquility." When powerful emotions are conveyed by hysterical language it has (for me) a double-negative effect: The heightened, intense, frantic language *cancels out* heightened, intense, or frantic emotions.

Style ought to complement content rather than collide with it. When dealing with violent material, cool your prose down; take a hose to it.

Tone: Humor, Satire, & Literary Humor

111} PEN IN CHEEK: SATIRE

A *New Yorker* cover got much more attention than the magazine bargained for. It shows then-candidate Barack Obama as the new President of the United States: He stands in the Oval Office, decked out in full Muslim regalia, knocking knuckles with his wife Michelle, who sports army fatigues and an AK-47. In the background, a portrait of Osama bin Laden hangs over the fireplace in which an American flag burns.

Democratic and Republican campaign spokesmen alike described the cover as "offensive," "tasteless," and "disgusting." But *New Yorker* senior editor David Remnick had a different word for it. He called it "satire."

"What I think it does," said Remnick, "is hold up a mirror to the prejudice and dark imaginings about Barack Obama's—both Obamas'— pasts, and their politics."

Maybe that's what Remnick *thought* he and his cover artist Barry Blitt were doing. Others didn't see it that way. For them, the cover played straight into the hands of those whose ideas and opinions it was meant to satirize. And it was in poor taste.

When writers knowingly and purposefully set out to ridicule, pillory, burlesque, or otherwise hold up characters to censure or derision they are, at best, *hopefully,* writing satire, a literary genre wherein through usually acerbic wit an author attempts to attack or at least call attention to some societal ill or injustice.

The form dates back to ancient times, to *The Satire of the Trades,* a text composed at the start of second millennium B.C.E. that attempts to assure weary scribes that their lot in life is far superior to that of "ordinary" men. Of the early satirists the Greek dramatists Aristophanes, whose play *The Clouds* slandered Socrates and may have led to his execution, is by far the best known. More recently satire has been used by novelists Sinclair Lewis and Joseph Heller to scorn, respectively, the vacuity of the American middle class and the insanity of war.

In Meditation # 4, I discuss the danger of prejudging our characters and thus limiting their dimensionality, while preventing both our selves and our readers from arriving at deeper levels of understanding and empathy. With satire a prejudgment of some kind is mandatory if only to ascertain that a character or subject *deserves* satiric treatment.

But there are different levels of satire, and of judgment. There is the kind of judgment that labels, defines, or categorizes—that puts characters in a box and refuses to let them escape. And then there is a kind of judgment that is ongoing and subject to revision, that allows for empathy, understanding, or even forgiveness, that doesn't pigeonhole or condemn outright, from the start (though the resulting story or novel may amount to a condemnation). Such is the type of "open-ended judgment" rendered by satirists like Flannery O'Connor, who—though she certainly has her views, and though her characters reflect certain values in society that she disapproves or deplores, are still living, breathing, dimensional characters (the grandmother in "A Good Man Is Hard to Find"). Great satirists judge, but they don't condemn.

We run two other major risks with satire, and the two go hand in hand: bad taste, and being misunderstood.

With a cartoon, we at least know that humor is *intended,* even if (like Queen Victoria) "we are not amused." With written satire, the potential for misunderstanding increases by an order of magnitude. Jonathan Swift got a famously hostile reception for his essay, *A Modest Proposal,* which proposed cannibalism as the means to prevent the children of the poor from becoming a burden to society. Not only was Swift accused of bad taste, he came within a hair of losing his royal patronage.

Contemporary satire can backfire as badly, as the editor of one campus newspaper learned when he published an article titled, "Rape Only Hurts When You Fight Back":

> Most people today would claim that rape is a terrible crime almost akin to murder, but I strongly disagree. Far from a vile act, rape is a magical experience that benefits society as a whole. I realize many of you will disagree with this thesis, but lend me your ears and I'm sure I'll sway you towards a darkened alley.

The writer—no doubt envisioning readers rolling with laughter—goes on to tout the "advantages" of rape, proclaiming that, if not for rape, "how would [ugly women] ever know the joys of intercourse with a man who isn't drunk?" Whether or not they got the joke, no one, least of all the president of the university, was amused.

Satire is dangerous. It is meant to be so. From Ovid's *Art of Love* to the novels of Chuck Palahniuk, library shelves sag under the weight of satirical masterpieces, with few if any subjects immune from the satirist's pen. This short list of topics, and the authors who satirized them, spans centuries: Nigel of Canterbury *(Speculum Stultorum):* monks and universities; Walter Map *(De Nugis Curialibus[51]):* court life in medieval England; Erasmus *(In Praise of Folly):* corrupt clergymen; Voltaire *(Candide):* optimism; George Orwell *(Animal Farm):* Stalinist Russia; Flannery O'Connor *(Wise Blood):* religious hypocrisy; Vladimir Nabokov *(Lolita):* statutory rape; Joseph Heller *(Catch-22):* war; Terry Southern *(Candy):* sex; Don Delillo *(White Noise):* consumerism.

The key to successful satire is to establish the satirical tone early and maintain it consistently, as Heller does with the famous first lines of *Catch-22:*

> It was love at first sight. The first time Yossarian saw the chaplain he fell madly in love with him.

Tonally, these first two lines give us permission to laugh at anything and everything that follows, including men getting disemboweled by shrapnel or being bombed on orders from their fellow officers. Heller's opening continues:

> Yossarian was in the hospital with a pain in his liver that fell just short of being jaundice. The doctors were puzzled by the fact that it wasn't quite jaundice. If it became jaundice they could treat it. If it didn't become jaundice and went away they could discharge him. But this just being short of jaundice all the time confused them.

If you've ever had jaundice, you know it's no laughing matter.[52] It can be a harbinger of hepatitis or cirrhosis or other liver diseases,

---

51 Trans: *The Courtier's Trifles*

52 Ironically, this is the title of one of Heller's other books, about his struggle with Guillain-Barré syndrome—a paralyzing affliction that struck Heller down in 1981 but from which he recovered.

including cancer. Yet Heller makes it clear, through his deadpan delivery and switchback sentences, that his intent is humor, that we're not to take Yossarian's illness too seriously. In fact, Yossarian is faking it.

But even where the pain and suffering in Heller's novel are meant to be real (as when Snowden, the radio-gunner of Yossarian's B-24, spills his literal guts), we see the author grinning in the wings (at least, I do). Yet Heller's grinning doesn't stop me from taking his theme, the insanity of war, seriously. When he tells us that wars are bonkers, he means it. *Catch-22* is satirical, but its message is, if not in earnest, sincere.

Within the first few lines of a story or novel the author makes a pact with the reader, letting him know what to expect and establishing the level of sincerity and earnestness. Stray from those levels and you break the bargain.

112} JOHN UPDIKE OR HOLDEN CAULFIELD: A DICHOTOMY OF DICTION

Diction comes down to the words we use. We can evoke a world merely through restricting the vocabulary used by our narrators (and by other characters).

As with most things in fiction writing, consistency is king. The narrator who, on page one, says, "And we're off like a dirty sheet!" cannot say, on page 18, "Vehicles had difficulty with the ascent." Our narrators can't be John Updike and Holden Caulfield at the same time.

Nor is a New Millennium Supermom likely to dress like Mrs. Dalloway. One student's story, with a postmodern flavor, is studded with grace notes (and occasionally whole chords) that echo *To the Lighthouse* and other writings by Virginia Woolf. But what does Woolf's world have to do with this protagonist—an obsessively competitive contemporary urban mom?

The result is a disconnect between subject and tone. It's as if, having found herself in possession of Mrs. Dalloway's voice, the writer applied it to a character it doesn't belong to—like a little girl trying on her mother's dress.

Story and characters cannot be parted; neither can plot and theme, nor metaphor and plot, nor style and substance—nor can any one or two or three elements or components of a work of fiction be parted from the others.

In works of art, unity is eveything. When you make a stylistic choice, especially one likely to draw attention to itself, it should relate to *something in the material.*

Better still, the demands of the material should limit our choices, and make, or help make, them for us.

113 } BRAMWELL GROVELS: LITERARY HUMOR

Writing can get overconvoluted through an author's attempt at *literary humor.* This is humor that relies on *how* a thing is said—usually, in a pompous, pretentious, euphemistic, or otherwise verbose way—rather than on *what* is being described.

"Being of a decidedly delicate nature, Mrs. Phelps was obliged to dispatch herself with utmost promptitude to the nearest place of easement."

Translation: "Mrs. Phelps ran to the bathroom to throw up."

A longer example:

> It would seem that the cosmic tumblers have aligned, and Kyle, our two-year-old, is at this precise moment congealing into a perfect storm of incoherence, mobility, and fastidiousness. This temporal mania is hardly mitigated by his reluctance to avail himself of even the briefest and most token of naps; and soon thereafter (that is, after the nongranted reprieve), with the

arrival of his playgroup cronies, said mania is thrust into maximum overdrive.

If these examples have a distinctly Victorian flavor, that's because literary humor is essentially Victorian, born out of an exaggerated (and, by current standards, perverse) sense of decorum. When I read, "She would sit properly and decline to enter into the conversation," I imagine that the sofa or chair on which the lady sits is overpadded and stiff, set in a stuffy parlor jammed with lace doilies and bric-a-brac—even though the story takes place in 1997. The stilted language packs more pomp than meaning.

Victorian circumlocution has its place: namely, in Victorian prose. Here is part of a letter written by Charlotte Brontë's younger brother Bramwell, an aspiring poet:

> Sir,
>
> It is with much reluctance that I venture to request, for the perusal of the following lines, a portion of the time of one upon whom I can have no claim, and should not dare to intrude; but ... I could not resist my longing to ask a man from whose judgment there would be little hope of appeal. [After half a dozen lines of florid flattery and a paragraph of apology, Bramwell proceeds:] ... I seek to know, and venture, though with shame, to ask from one whose word I must respect: whether, by periodical or other writing, I could please myself with writing, and make it subservient to living.

When Bramwell wrote his groveling letter, such self-abasement was not only tolerated, it was de rigueur. A blunter instrument would likely have gained no reply. In Queen Victoria's England, among the educated classes, propriety was everything. Because those values no longer apply, humor based on them feels inauthentic and forced.

To be funny, you need to be as true and specific to the characters and their circumstances as possible.

Let language carry humor, rather than create it.

114 } FUNNY ON PAPER: PUNCTUATION = TIMING

With humor, on the written page as in life, timing is everything. The following examples come from another student's story.

> "He told me he was married, but only on paper. I asked, 'What kind of paper?'" [Two sentences and already the author has gotten a laugh out of me.]

> "I was always asking the wrong questions." [Endearingly harsh self-judgment.]

> "I was new at this." [The world loves its ingénues.]

> "He said he was separated; I pictured oil and water in a puddle." [The analogy works perfectly, the image conveyed in a lightning flash.]

> "I pictured an egg gently tapped along the edge of the mixing bowl with blue flowers, my mother pouring the yolk between each split-half shell, the slippery whites oozing over the edge." [Specific, authentic.]

> "I didn't ask, 'Separated from what?' I was learning." [Here, the speedy response of the first sentence has built momentum toward the slow wink of "*I was learning.*"]

No matter what you hear to the contrary, and *The Chicago Manual of Style* notwithstanding, punctuation is an art, not a science. Exactly what a comma is for no one can say for sure without qualification.

Punctuation is a breath, a pause, a stutter, a foot on the brake, a downshifting of the transmission. Like any art it must be mastered. We should learn the supposed rules that we may break them as the Italians drive their Alfa Romeos: *with confidence.*

Magic & Anthropomorphism

115} BIRD BRAINS: WRITING ANTHROPOMORPHICALLY

In writing stories with nonhuman animals as their protagonists, we follow a practice going back to ancient times. The Pompeians took mischievous delight in putting animals' heads on human bodies, anticipating Bugs Bunny and Porky Pig by two thousand years.

More recent antecedents include Jack London's *The Call of the Wild*, relating the adventure of a wolf, and reached a pinnacle thirty years ago in the novels of Richard Adams—especially *Watership Down*, his first and most famous, about a warren of supremely brave and noble rabbits. Adams's bestseller spawned an epidemic of anthropomorphic fiction that ultimately initiated its own decline. Enough with the talking apes and bunnies. Anthropomorphic fiction today has been relegated to children's books.

So my first question for the author of an anthropomorphic story about a parrot is this: Who are you writing for? What is your "target audience" (in the marketing cliché)? We want our work to be published and read. So the author should consider the ultimate form her story will take. A children's book? For what age group? With or without illustrations?

As with all kinds of writing, Rule # 1 of anthropomorphic writing is consistency. This is true in writing for children:

> The Mole had been working very hard all the morning, spring-cleaning his little home. First with brooms, then with dusters; then on ladders and steps and chairs, with a brush and a pail of whitewash; till he had dust in his throat and eyes, and splashes of whitewash all over his black fur, and an aching back and weary

> arms. …[H]e suddenly flung down his brush on the floor, said
> 'Bother!' and 'O blow!' and also 'Hang spring-cleaning!' and
> bolted out of the house without even waiting to put on his coat.[53]

—or for adults:

> My father was a St. Bernard, my mother was a collie, but I am
> a Presbyterian. This is what my mother told me, I do not know
> these nice distinctions myself. To me they are only fine large
> words meaning nothing. My mother had a fondness for such; she
> liked to say them, and see other dogs look surprised and envious,
> as wondering how she got so much education.[54]

—or writing a satirical parable with a deeply serious social and
political agenda:

> The pigs had an even harder struggle to counteract the lies put
> about by Moses, the tame raven, who was Mr. Jones's especial pet,
> was a spy and a tale-bearer, but he was also a clever talker.[55]

The author of anthropomorphic fiction needs to arrive at a firm
set of principles governing how her anthropomorphized creatures
think, in what terms, and with what vocabulary. To what extent
do they see things as humans do? Having established such guide-
lines, the author must stick to them fearlessly. The moment the
code is broken—the moment the reader stumbles on inconsisten-
cies—credibility is lost, the conceit crumbles, and the reader is no
longer willing to suspend disbelief.

In the student story about parrots, the same parrot that
calls human hair "feathers" refers to the "Amazon" rain forest.
Wouldn't a parrot have his own name for the forest? Would he call
it, for example, the "Green World"? The chief interest of anthropomorphic fiction is imagining what it's like to be a member of

Matters of Style

---

53 Kenneth Grahame, *The Wind in the Willows.*

54 Mark Twain, "A Dog's Tale."

55 George Orwell, *Animal Farm.*

some other species (in this case, a parrot). If the writer hasn't done that, what's the point?

116} REQUIEM FOR A CLICHÉ: MAGIC REALISM TO THE RESCUE?

From time to time, authors combine the tone (and clichés) of two disparate genres, as if two wrongs might make a right.

I'm presented with a tale set in the world of boxing. Within the first round, the story is K.O.'d by clichés. There's the boxer's grumpy trainer (a character seen before, played by Keenan Wynn/ Burgess Meredith) and his dutiful, horror-stricken, nice-girl wife (Angie/Adrian/Julie), who watches from a ringside seat as "gouges of Mickey's bright red blood flew through the air." When not clichéd and hyperbolic, the writing feels synoptic, like the sketch of a film treatment—fitting, since much of the story is lifted straight from movies (*Rocky, Requiem for a Heavyweight, Somebody Up There Likes Me*).

But then, halfway through the narrative, the story takes an abrupt turn into *magic realism*—as does Bernard Malamud's *The Natural,* a baseball story that owes its rescue from cliché to an imported dose of this exotic genre.

Magic realism is a broad term that denotes a seamless blending of illogical and/or surreal events with "realistic" characters and settings. The genre is associated with Latin authors, especially Jorge Luis Borges, Gabriel García Márquez, and Alejo Carpentier, and exemplified by the scene in García Márquez's "A Very Old Man With Enormous Wings," in which, at the story's end, the title character (who may or may not be an angel) literally flies away. Barbara Kingsolver, Italo Calvino, and Salman Rushdie have been (respectively) North American, European, and Asian exponents of the genre.

In this case, when the author has Angie literally *feel* the blows as they are dealt to her husband's face, the author has dipped into magic realism's bag of tricks. Later, when Angie visits her priest, a dash of religion is added, like Tabasco, to the already heady mixture. This might have worked well, were religious symbols woven into the story from the start—with Angie (for instance) giving her husband a St. Christopher medallion to wear for good luck in the ring.

Near the end of the story, as a way to surmount her dread of the sport, Angie takes up boxing herself; she proves to be a "natural," and in her white gym outfit she achieves angelic status among her fans (the lights of the arena creating a "golden halo" around her head). At this point, all realistic bets are off: We feel that the story has made a forced landing somewhere in Venezuela, where such things happen. The magic feels tacked on to the "realism"; it doesn't arise organically from the materials because its seeds weren't planted from the start (see Meditation # 80).

The magic in magic realism should feel inevitable and not convenient. Otherwise it's just an excuse to take flight from your own stories.

Some Tense Choices: To Be or Not to Be

117 } THIS GUY WALKS UP TO ME: PAST VS. PRESENT TENSE

If you listen closely to people telling anecdotes at social gatherings or to stand-up comedians telling stories (that turn into jokes), you'll notice that often they'll start telling their tale in the past tense ("Last week I was rolling my cart down frozen food aisle at the supermarket") and then—so seamlessly that if you weren't listening closely, you probably wouldn't notice—they switch to present tense ("when all of a sudden this lady walks up to me"). Their stories are told this way for two reasons: (1) it comes naturally, and (2) the stories seem to work better.

Writing stories on paper is a far less spontaneous process than telling them out loud, and choices—even about such matters as tense—are often made with great deliberation. Still, the stand-up comic and the raconteur have something to teach us: Whether they realize it or not, they're getting the best of both worlds.

By starting their stories out with the past tense, they plant a seed of expectation. The words "Last week" or "The other day" tell us we're in for a story, one that occurred at some point in the past, whose outcome is already well known—but only to the teller. His knowledge shapes and colors his story, and allows him a degree of perspective. In the first line of *The Good Soldier,* Ford Madox Ford announces that what follows is "the saddest story ever heard."

The present tense, on the other hand, is all immediacy, no perspective; it allows for no reflections and no foreshadowing ("little did Susan expect"). As with plays and movies, with the present tense the past is gone and the future doesn't exist; everything is happening *now.* The point when the raconteur and the stand-up comedian switch to present tense is usually when the story shifts into active or dramatic mode. Suddenly we're no longer simply *listening* to a tale being told; we watch it flicker and unfold on the mind's movie screen.

Like the raconteur and the comedian, fiction writers have been known to slide from tense to tense to great effect, as John Rechy does incessantly in *City of Night,* his first novel, and as Kerouac does occasionally in *On the Road:*

> I bought my ticket and was waiting for the L.A. bus when all of a sudden I saw the cutest little Mexican girl in slacks come cutting across my sight. She was in one of the buses that had just pulled in with a sigh of airbrakes and was discharging passengers for a rest

> stop. … A pain stabbed my heart, as it did every time I saw a girl I
> loved who was going the opposite direction in this too big world.
> "Los Angeles coach now loading in door two," *says the announcer
> and I get on.* I saw her sitting alone. …[Italics added.]

Kerouac slides so deftly from past to present and back again that we barely notice. This sort of trick requires not just a good, but a great, ear.

Thomas Harris embeds present-tense descriptions of Hannibal Lecter into his past-tense novel, *The Silence of the Lambs.* Charlotte Brontë's Jane Eyre (the narrator of the novel) slides from past tense to present tense when describing episodes charged with emotional significance, as if experiencing them anew with us. In *The Constant Gardener,* John le Carré uses tenses counterintuitively, conveying present action using past tense and flashbacks using the present tense.

More typically, novels are set in one tense or the other. And though past tense has always been the gold standard of storytelling, Joyce Cary, John Updike, and Chuck Palahniuk (among others) have written entire novels—and long ones—in the present tense. Pynchon's *Gravity's Rainbow* (eight-hundred pages) begins:

> A screaming comes across the sky. It has happened before, but
> there is nothing to compare it to now.
>
> It is too late. The evacuation still proceeds, but it's all theater.
> There are no lights inside the cars. No light anywhere. Above him
> lift girders old as an iron queen, and glass somewhere far above
> that would let the light of day through. But it's night. He's afraid of
> the way the glass will fall—soon—it will be a spectacle: the fall of
> a crystal palace. But coming down in total blackout, without one
> glint of light, only great invisible crashing.

The sense of immediacy in this opening passage and the suspense conveyed by it are enough to set even a jaded reader's teeth on edge. Reading it feels like sitting in a dentist's chair, watching him lay out his shiny implements, with that first *now* as menacing as any syringe or drill: *This may hurt a bit.*

But while successful long works have been written in the present tense, there's still the danger of wearing readers out—a danger not faced by the stand-up comic or the raconteur, or by movies. Unlike written stories, which demand constant interaction from their readers, movies do all the work for us, allowing us to be totally passive. Reading a novel written in the present tense can feel like *reading* a movie—or like reading the screenplay of a movie, where we have to direct, design sets and costumes, and play all the parts: a lot of work. And unless the "movie" is action-packed, the blow-by-blow assault of subtle thoughts and microscopic gestures may feel, as one blogger describes her experience of Helen Dunmore's *The Siege,* like "being hit repeatedly over the head with a teaspoon."

But the biggest problem with present tense is that it greatly restricts the use of flashbacks, flash-forwards, backstory, and any other matter not pertaining to the present action. While the choice of tense is highly personal and subjective, if a novel isn't working in present tense, I gently suggest that the author consider switching to past tense, where the element of suspense is readily implied.

Similarly, first-person narration is difficult to sustain for the length of a novel. The combination of first-person/present-tense narration in a novel is therefore especially challenging, like doing the Tour de France on a unicycle.

118 } YOU TALKIN' TO ME? SECOND THOUGHTS ON SECOND PERSON

I have before me the story of a bitterly divided brother and sister, forced together on the occasion of their grandmother's death, written using the second person limited point of view. In saying "you," the author appears to point to *me,* her reader; but since the narrator is evidently addressing Frank (the protagonist's brother), the strategy endows *me* with Frank's actions and traits, and its success depends upon this reader's willingness to be pressed into service as a participant in the story.

The chief advantage of second person is its novelty—although, since Jay McInerney used it in *Bright Lights, Big City* (his first novel and a huge commercial success), it has been worn to a frazzle.

Second-person narrative is most often used with humorous—or anyway, less-than-tragic—material. Lorrie Moore made heavy use of it in her short story collection, *Self-Help.*

> Meet in expensive beige raincoats, on a pea-soupy night. Like a detective movie. First, stand in front of Florsheim's Fifty-seventh Street window, press your face close to the glass, watch the fake velvet Hummels inside revolving around the wing tips; some white shoes, like your father wears, are propped up with garlands on a small mound of chemical snow. All the stores have closed. You can see your breath on the glass. Draw a peace sign. You are waiting for a bus.[56]

But there've been notable exceptions, including Nathaniel Hawthorne's "The Haunted Mind," one of the first short stories to use second person, and Faulkner's *Absalom, Absalom,* one of the first novels.

Still, to me there's something intrinsically funny about any narrative that casts me as its hero. Imagine yourself (if you can) cast in the role of Robert Jordan in Hemingway's *For Whom the Bell Tolls,* or as Humbert Humbert. Having never blown up bridges during the Spanish Civil War or committed statutory rape, you may feel similarly miscast.

But even when a narrator's role makes lesser demands on me, presented with a story in the second person I find myself crossing my arms defiantly as I read, "You hide your sister's cigarettes under the couch pillow," and saying under my breath, "No *I don't*. I don't

---

56 From "How to Be an Other Woman."

even smoke!" This defensiveness doesn't always make for a healthy reader/writer relationship, and may even lose you some readers.

Nuts & Bolts 1:
Generic vs. Authentic

119} GENERIC FARMHOUSES, PAINTINGS, WIDOWS, & WILDFLOWERS

The more a story trades on familiar settings and situations, the greater the author's burden to be specific and avoid the flood of generalizations and clichés that will certainly rush in to fill the vacuum left by an absence of specific details. In fiction the generic amounts to a vacuum.

"A farmhouse" is generic: It's a category, not a specific entity. Say that the farmhouse is a refurbished cider mill in Columbia County, and the farmhouse is no longer generic, but a genuine dwelling inhabitable by genuine people.

A graveyard is generic, as is an unspecified grave. What's needed are telling details, like the condition of the grass on the grave mound—does it still look fresh, two years after the funeral? Are the remains of last summer's roses still there—a few desiccated twigs in a Hellmann's mayonnaise jar? And what about that "group of mourners" nearby? The phrase assumes we know what mourners look like. We do: They look like a cliché. How are these mourners dressed? How does one know they're mourners and not out for a casual graveyard stroll? Suppose that, among the group of mourners, you inject a child who, behind their backs, plays with his yo-yo?

Like adjectives, nouns too ("mourners") can function as epithets or opinions—representing not solid things, but reductive labels *pasted on* solid things. What characterizes this particular set of mourners, we need to know. What sets them apart from generic mourners?

Another student describes a gallery opening:

> The gallery is awash in soft yellow light, with Walter's giant canvases hanging on different levels, making a universe of floating hues and textures. His paintings have texture. They are tangible and soothing, and the abstract scenes are an invitation to lose oneself in the fantastic world of imagination. Some of the paintings scream depression; others emanate warmth and comfort.

It's hard to describe paintings, especially abstract ones, and the attempt to do so here is laudable. But it fails by leaning on epithets and abstractions. We are told that the paintings "have texture," but we don't know, specifically, what that texture *is*. We learn that they are "tangible and soothing," but that tells us next to nothing: We can assume the first quality and we don't know what to make of the second. How, exactly, do some of the paintings "scream depression"? And what makes others warm and comfortable? In place of descriptions we are given adjectives, opinions.

Of course any description is interpretive, and therefore subjective: an *opinion*. But a concrete description does more than reflect what the interpreter sees; it helps, or even forces, us to see things as the interpreter (the narrator or point-of-view character) sees them, as the author does here:

> One of Walter's barn door sized canvasses looked like a bombed city rendered in melted American cheese and mud. The one next to it reminded Liz of the bicycle seat factory reject pile she and her pals played in back when she was a kid. And the one next to that, the one titled (not too ingeniously, she thought) "White on White," looked like an explosion in a Marshmallow Fluff factory.

In Ethan Canin's short story "Emperor of the Air," a retired high school biology teacher goes to extremes to prevent his neighbor from forcing him to cut down a two-hundred-year-old elm tree, a family heirloom, that is infested with "tiny red bugs" and threatens to fall on the neighbor's house. Does it matter that the teacher taught biology? That the tree is an elm, and not a maple? That the bugs are tiny and red? If the writer wants to avoid *genericism* and aims to endow the world of his story with specificity, then yes, these things do matter.

A recent widower's apartment, whose walls "hold only echoing footsteps and memories," remains generic: We *expect* a recent widower's apartment to hold those things. The author could specify a few items in the home and the memories they hold: a chair—one that the wife considered "an eyesore"—upholstered in slate-blue corduroy and filled with the fur and smell of Andy, their cocker spaniel.

The smallest parts of a story can offer opportunities for illumination. So, as writers, we have to be judicious in choosing which parts to specify and which to leave alone. As poet Robert Hogan said, "Sometimes a tree is just a tree." Sometimes a farmhouse is just a farmhouse, and an apartment is just an apartment. But bear in mind that, when readers are left to create their own trees or farmhouses out of generic materials, it won't be the same tree or farmhouse the author had in mind.

And specificity needn't take up lots of space. A line here and there is all that's required. Often it's not a matter of adding to existing descriptions, but of replacing them with concise, specific ones.

Which has more authority: a meadow of "wildflowers" or one of Queen Anne's lace and joe-pye weed?

120} A TREE GROWS IN THE BRONX: ON KNOWING THE NAMES OF THINGS

"The limits of my language are the limits of my mind."

—WITTGENSTEIN

Two tree surgeons are at work on a tree, one high on a limb, the other down in the street, holding the safety rope. Both wear hard hats and leather harnesses. As a writer passes by on the opposite side, the worker on the street yells to him, in a thick Eastern European accent, "Know what kind of a tree is this?"

The writer looks up at the tree—at least four stories high, with thin, pointy leaves. Not maple, that's all he knows. He takes a wild guess, "Elm?"

The tree surgeon shakes his head ruefully. "This is strongest of all tree, like iron. In old time they make axe handle from such tree."

"Chestnut?" the writer guesses again.

"Hickory," says the tree surgeon. "Ten year I live in this country. Ten year I'm asking peoples, 'What kind of tree is this?' Ten year and no one say right tree. One of ten peoples, maybe. Look—" He points to a tree on the other side of the road. "What is? I give clue. You breaks branch, comes strong sweet perfume. From this tree Indian make tea."

"Black birch," says the writer.

"No, not black birch. Sassafras."

"Oh, right. Sassafras."

All this time the tree surgeon has been holding the swinging rope, oblivious of his partner, still sawing at an overhead branch.

"And this?" the tree surgeon points to yet another tree, perfectly vertical.

"No idea," the writer tells him.

"Poplar. Is straight like arrow. Was used to make mast of ship, is so straight. When I'm come from, if you ask someone about tree, nine time out of ten they know. In America . . ." He purses his lips, squeezes his eyes shut, shakes his head again. Then his eyes pop open and he asks, "What you do?"

"I teach," says the writer, bashfully. "And I write."

"If writer, you should know all about tree," pronounced the tree surgeon.

The totemic power of words: We grasp things by their *names*. In Genesis, Adam is given the power to name all creatures on earth, symbolizing his dominion over them.

- Ferrule: the metal band on a pencil that holds the eraser.
- Philtrum: the midline groove running from top of upper lip to nose.
- Those little knobs forming the hull of a raspberry? Drupelets.
- Tittle: the dot over an i or j.
- Q: What do you call the plastic tip that binds the end of a shoelace? An: aglet.[57]

One can do worse than peruse dictionaries as a hobby, including Johnson's *Dictionary of the English Language,* where he describes a "blister" as "a pustule formed by raising the cuticle from the cutis, and filled with serous blood" and "network" as signifying "anything reticulated or decussated, at equal distances, with interstices between the intersections."

Nuts & Bolts 2: Dialogue

121} SELECTING DIALOGUE

Good dialogue bubbles up from our stories like methane gas from a swamp. If you have to second-guess what your characters might or would say, either you're not listening to them, or your characters aren't sufficiently motivated to speak. You should either respect their silence or provide them with the necessary motivation.

When good dialogue does bubble up, your job as author is not merely to record it but to select what your readers will hear; sum up the rest through narration, or *indirect dialogue*, dialogue that

---

57 One source for such exacting terms is a *picture dictionary.* Many writers refer to them.

tells of a conversation instead of replicating it. An example of indirect dialogue, from Clancy Sigal's *Going Away*:

> I explained to this garage man that he was one of a vanishing breed, and he surprised me by not disagreeing. He said the filling station was now to America what the one-family forty-acre farm used to be, the outpost of independence. I asked him how much independence he could have when he was mortgaged to the Eagle Petroleum Company, and he said plenty, everyone these days was mortgaged to somebody …

Indirect dialogue can capture the essence of a long exchange without taking up all that space. Furthermore, it has an authenticity born of *not* claiming, by way of quotation marks, that the conversation has been presented verbatim. It's left to the reader to imagine the fleshed-out conversation

We should aim to provide readers with only the most pertinent, illuminating, and entertaining parts of dialogue. Words like "Well," "Um," "Hey," "Oh," "Right," "Okay," "Yeah"—those "naturalistic" flourishes—can probably be ditched.

Two acquaintances meet at a bus stop. Here is an early draft of their exchange:

> "Hey, Joanna," said Ken. "I thought I might see you. How are you?"
> "I'm okay. Pretty good. I overslept. Glad I didn't miss the bus."
> "Sit next to me, why don't you?"
> "Okay." Joanna sat down. Ken looked at his watch.
> "The bus should be here soon. It's three minutes late already. So—how are you?"
> "You already asked me that. How are *you?*"
> "Oh, well. Not too bad, I guess. Considering."
> That's when she saw his cane. "Oh, my God. What's with the cane, Ken? What happened?"
> "I was wondering when you'd notice," said Ken, "I sprained my ankle yesterday on the way to Ben's Meat Market."

"How awful! Was it a bad sprain? I mean, did you, like, break any bones?"

"No, no broken bones. I mean it's bad enough, I guess, then again it could have been a lot worse. But no, no broken bone. Just a sprain."

"Are you sure? Did you see a doctor?"

"Yeah, sure, I saw a doctor. As a matter of fact I spent a grand total of seven boring hours at the emergency room. I got there at seven in the morning and left at four. Can you believe they kept me there that long?"

"Gee! What a drag! You must have been bored out of your mind!"

"Well, it wasn't all that bad, really. I took my students' stories with me and I got some work done, so the time went by pretty fast."

This exchange can be trimmed to:

They met at the bus stop.

"What's with the cane?" said Joanna.

"I sprained it yesterday on the way to Ben's Meat Market," Ken said. "I spent seven hours in the emergency room."

"What a drag!"

"It wasn't so bad. I took some of my students' stories with me and got some work done."

Hardly scintillating. But it wastes less time.

122} DOUBLING UP ON DIALOGUE

By doubling up on dialogue you blunt its effectiveness.

In the original draft:

"I mean, if you don't want to talk about it I understand," said Albert, turning back to the game. "I guess I was just sort of curious."

Shorter and better:

"I was just sort of curious," said Albert, returning to his game.

Or:

"If you don't want to talk about it, I understand," said Albert, turning back to the game.

And it would be nice if, once in a while, your characters didn't respond verbally to each other at all; their actions can speak *for* them.

> Albert turned back to the game.

Any of these choices are good. Combine them all, and the whole will be less than the sum of its parts.

123 } ASKED & ANSWERED: CALL & RESPONSE DIALOGUE

A student's dialogue suffers from being "tape-recorder" real. There's too much call-and-response, and too little subtext and surprise.

In spite of their "realistic" stammering, the characters appear to pay too close attention to each other. Although the writer has gone to great lengths to render dialogue naturalistic, he has overlooked the deeper fact that people seldom actually *listen* to each other. Because each speaker has her own agenda, dialogue doesn't always move neatly forward: It takes sharp curves, goes around detours, and stumbles over bumps and potholes, with each speaker taking part in a slightly different conversation.

In Cormac McCarthy's *Suttree,* an old railroader visits the title character in his shanty houseboat dwelling following a bar fight (I've edited out some stage directions):

> Hidy, said the old man.
> Come on in.
> Was you in bed?
> It's all right. Come on in.

> Cold in here. What happened to your head?
> [Poking the fire] I got hit with a floorbuffer.
> Say you did?
> What time is it?
> Could you not hear it comin?
> No. What time is it?

A writer friend of mine once suggested that the secret to writing great dialogue is never to have characters respond directly to each other. This takes it a bit too far, but I agree with the general notion: Too much dialogue is written *too directly*. (Note, by the way, that you needn't use quotation marks for a character's *thoughts*. Many authors do this, but it seems to suggest that people think in words and sentences.)

Another example, this one from George Axelrod's quirky screenplay for *The Manchurian Candidate* by Richard Condon. A nightmare-fraught Marco (Frank Sinatra) meets Rosie (Janet Leigh) aboard a train:

> MARCO: Do you mind if I smoke?
>
> ROSIE: Not at all. Please do.
>
> [Marco strikes a match to light a cigarette; it goes out. Embarrassed and frustrated, he stumbles through the car. He stops between cars and leans on a wall. The landscape rushes by. Rosie joins him. She taps him on the shoulder and offers him a cigarette.]
>
> ROSIE: Maryland's a beautiful state.
>
> MARCO: This is Delaware.
>
> ROSIE: I know. I was one of the original Chinese workmen who laid the track on this stretch. But, um, nonetheless, Maryland is a beautiful state. So is Ohio, for that matter.
>
> MARCO: I guess so. Columbus is a tremendous football town. You in the railroad business?

ROSIE: Not anymore. However, if you'll permit me to point out, when you ask that question, you really should say, "Are you in the railroad line?" (beat) Where's your home?

The chief virtue of this exchange (which departs significantly from Condon's novel) lies in its playful unpredictability. Instead of presenting us with a typical "boy meets girl" scene, Axelrod capitalizes on Leigh's flirtatiousness and Sinatra's delirium to produce a conversation so surreal it might have been penned by Ionesco or Sam Beckett.

Though Axelrod doesn't take my friend's advice, he does deal every third or fourth line of dialogue from, so to speak, the bottom of the deck, as if the characters aren't following a script, but improvising as they go.

Dialogue's chief function is to amuse. It does so chiefly by conveying character: by showing us how characters express themselves, by showcasing their spontaneous wit and charm. Now and then call-and-response dialogue may be unavoidable—as when the witness is grilled by a detective. But it seldom evokes character.

124 } I WOULDN'T SAY THAT: GENERALIZED DIALOGUE

Applied to dialogue, the conditional is troubling:

> "What's the matter, kid, you don't like bluestockings?" my father *would say.*
>
> "No," *I'd answer.* "And what's more I don't like stockings!"

The implication that the above exchange took place on several occasions—like some Abbott & Costello routine—is off-putting. By putting this conditional dialogue in quotation marks, the author inadvertently undermines confidence in his narrator's reliability.

Other key words to watch out for: "always," "whenever," "usually," "typically." Repeated use of such words is symptomatic of writing in *background* or *routine* mode, creating a pattern of predictable behavior against which, presumably, you intend to juxtapose exceptional events. But readers will tolerate only so much background before demanding that the tacit promise of a real story be fulfilled.

125} LOOK MA, NO QUOTATION MARKS

Joyce did away with them: He called them "eyesores" or "perverted commas" and used long (em) dashes instead. As seen in the example above, Cormac McCarthy does away with them—and the dashes—too.

I'm talking about quotation marks, those paired flea-specks that set off dialogue in most stories and novels. The fact is you *don't* need them, not if you make it otherwise clear who is speaking, and when. (It helps to have distinct-sounding characters.)

The fact that you *can* dispense with quotation marks doesn't mean that you should. Eliminating quotation marks from dialogue can lend a muted quality to your storytelling, as if the characters were speaking in a dream, their voices *seen* more than heard—like people paralyzed by sleep, unable to scream or shout.

Dialogue in quotation marks is "LOUDER!"

Nuts & Bolts 3: Sentences

126} BEST FOOT FORWARD: FIRST SENTENCES

You want your opening sentence to get directly to the heart of the matter, or at least to point the way there.

A story opens with: "Just after my twenty-eighth birthday, my boss in London asked me into his office." This could be the opening sentence of a story about:

(a) the protagonist's twenty-eighth birthday

(b) being promoted at or fired from her job

(c) a love affair with the boss

In fact, the story is about a woman experiencing culture shock as the result of a job transfer to New York City from London, her home.

Think of your opening sentence as the topic sentence of an essay. With that in mind, the above sentence might be rewritten as: "When my boss offered me a job at the New York bureau, I didn't hesitate." This points like an arrow to the heart of the story, and to the heart of its main character or narrator. As do these opening lines:

> By our second day at Camp Crescendo, the girls in my Brownie troop had decided to kick the asses of each and every girl in Brownie Troop 909.
>
> — Z.Z. PACKER, "BROWNIES"

> Of course, I had not always been a drunkard.
> — HANS FALLADA, *THE DRINKER*

> My father has asked me to be the fourth corner of the Joy Luck Club.
>
> —AMY TAN, *THE JOY LUCK CLUB*

> Jane's husband, Martin, works for the fire department.
> —RICHARD BAUSCH, "THE FIREMAN'S WIFE"

> First Lieutenant Jimmy Cross carried letters from a girl named Martha, a junior at Mt. Sebastian college in New Jersey.
> —TIM O'BRIEN, "THE THINGS THEY CARRIED"

Matters of Style

Uncas Metcalfe's Raleigh had been stolen.

—BETSEY OSBORNE, *THE NATURAL HISTORY*
OF UNCAS METCALFE

127 } MORE FIRST SENTENCES
        GOOD & BAD

When I read submissions for the journal *Alimentum,* what I look for in a first sentence isn't to be "grabbed by the throat," or to be shocked or dazzled by sensational imagery, action, or wordplay. Instead, I listen for the sound of a human voice—possibly (but not necessarily) a distinctive human voice.

Here is Kurt Vonnegut's voice, coming to me strong and clear (if a bit gruff from smoking all those Pall Malls) in the opening lines of his masterpiece, *Slaughterhouse-Five*:

> All this happened, more or less. The war parts, anyway, are pretty much true. One guy I knew really was shot in Dresden for taking a teapot that wasn't his. Another guy I knew really did threaten to have his personal enemies killed by hired gunman after the war. And so on. I've changed all the names.

Though this opening owes a debt to *Huckleberry Finn* ("That was a book by Mr. Mark Twain, and he told the truth, mainly"), the voice is unmistakably Vonnegut's; you can practically smell his breath reeking of cigarettes and bourbon.

Even if it's not so distinctive, still, a narrator's voice should be human. I want to feel that I'm in the presence not of a *writer* (I hear from *them* all the time), but of a person. Someone is reaching out from a piece of paper to talk to me.

Sometimes the simplest sentence carries the most humanity. Here are a few that kept me reading, all culled from the same issue of *Alimentum* in which they were published:

I am visiting a man on an island. [Simple, direct; provides information while raising questions: What man? Which island? Visiting for what reason?]

Lately Mrs. Jahangir had been waking in the middle of the night to wash her underclothes. [An opening that fairly whispers to the reader: Come a little closer; I have a story to tell you.]

The food ladies from the church went home hours ago. [Puts me right in the middle of things; in one sentence, the world of the story is not only created, but inhabited.]

At two minutes before seven A.M., I coast my bicycle into the Thermotech gravel parking lot, hop off, and wheel over to the red entry door. [The specificity of that "two minutes" tells me that this young worker—young, I assume, since he hops off his bicycle—punches a time clock at work. A lot of information packed into few words; the writer is clearly experienced.]

The first time I saw a chicken run around with its head cut off I was seven. [Direct, simple, doubtlessly true; I appreciate that the author has done without a comma after "off," to let those last three words to arrive with no pause. Here, too, I sense I'm in experienced hands.]

He came quick, running, and the birds scattered, the butterflies disbanded with a strong puff of air. [The sentence scatters too, organically, poetically.]

Each of the above sentences is inviting in its warmth and simplicity, its total lack of pretense, cleverness, sentiment, shock value, or overt poetic effect. Not that an opening sentence should never cash in on any of those qualities. But too many novices seem to feel that to gain an editor's attention they have to dazzle or shock, as if we editors have all been numbed by the mountains of submissions we get. But even assuming my brethren and I are all in deep comas, authors don't have to jolt us awake. Sometimes a gentle whisper will do.

Some less-than-inviting (for me) openers:

> Whoever dreamed up water torture might have appreciated Dot's agony as she watched Marlene eat her dinner that night. [Forced appeal to sensation, hyperbolic excess, cuteness.]

> The baby wasn't her baby. [First, why not just "The baby wasn't hers"? But in any case the sentence takes more than it gives, raising too many questions: Whose baby? What baby? Why wasn't it hers? Who said it was hers? The sentence begs to be unwritten, to be replaced by whatever it negates.]

> I sat at the white ceramic table and watched Florence put away the dishes she had just dried. [Though I appreciate specificity, in the author's first and most important sentence do we really need to know that the table is white and ceramic? Or, for that matter, that the narrator is sitting? Much of what the sentence states can be implied. The sentence could have read, "Florence put away the dishes."]

> I'm not psychic or anything like that, but I knew it would be just a matter of minutes before Washburn would ask his wife to excuse him so he could come into the cocktail lounge to see Claire and me. [Instead of striking a solid image, the sentence sends out tentacles in a dozen directions. It also violates P.O.V., since it describes actions the narrator can't be privy to.]

128} DUDS & MISFIRES: BACKWARD SENTENCES

Like the stories and novels we build from them, sentences have their own "plots"—beginnings and endings, development and resolution, setup and payoff. If the payoff comes before the setup, the sentence misfires.

I call them backward sentences.

EXAMPLE: "Anya flinched as Jack patted her on the head." The most important information comes too early and not where it should, as the resolution of a one-sentence story: As a result of having her head patted by a man named Jack, a woman named Anya flinches.

BETTER: "When Jack patted Anya's head she flinched." Or: "Jack patted Anya's head; she flinched." Now the actions occur in their proper sequence, and the resolution comes at the end, where it has some impact.

Other backward sentences:

> "Women weren't allowed to sit at the bar in the Bridge Tavern."

> "They would watch television when it was cold and rainy."

> "Elaine looked very self-righteous with her arms crossed."

> "We went to Applebee's that Friday night."

129 } BLUBBER & LARD: FLABBY SENTENCES

Even experienced and highly successful authors often create sentences that can be cut by a third, with no loss of music or meaning. Like this one from Jonathan Coe's *The Rain Before It Falls:*

> Whereas poor Gracie was not so fortunate.

The comparison is set up by the sentence as a whole, so "whereas" is already implied. And if we are told that Gracie was "not so fortunate," we don't need to have her labeled "poor." I also question the choice of "fortunate" over "lucky"—especially knowing the story is being dictated into a tape recorder by a dying old woman. (Why would she waste her breath on extra syllables?) The narrator would probably have said, "Gracie wasn't so lucky." Anyway, it's a better sentence.

"My ringing of the buzzer did not produce any answer." *Translation*: "I rang the buzzer." (The result will be obvious.)

130} PASSIVE SENTENCES SHOULD NOT EVER BE WRITTEN BY YOU

A passive sentence is one where the action is filched from the subject and given to the object. Or, to put it less passively: A passive sentence filches the action from its subject and gives it to its object. "Warren picked up his suitcase," becomes, passively, "The suitcase was picked up by Warren."

A less flagrant example:

"Daily the air had been filled with the snow of falling paper." That strikes a strong image. But because it involves us with no character, it feels gauzy and weightless, like a brush painting on rice paper. (Which, since the story is set in Japan, may be the author's intention.)

An *active* sentence would carry the image even more strongly:

"For six days Tsungai watched paper snow fall from the clouds."

Now we're caught up in the action—not of air or paper, but of a character.

131} SOME SENTENCE GEMS

1) (About a perfectionist chef): "When you sent out a cold *entrecote de veau* or fired a trout *meuniere* without clarified butter, you diminished his life's meaning." [Well done!]

2) "Sarah loved the windy path that wound down to the swimming rock, and the feel of soft needles under her feet as she ran down it." [The sentence has a Hemingway-like eloquence,

due in some measure to its artlessness, its earthy simplicity. We feel the wind and the pine needles.]

3) "Toby swallowed the three pills that looked like bits of colored chalk." [Captures the image perfectly from a child's point of view.]

4) "I was never not mostly afraid." [Though less simple and direct, this distinctive sentence (from "Where the Dark Ended" by William Tester) is better than "I was always afraid." "Never not mostly" conveys a weight of naive helplessness that would be lacking otherwise.]

For an example of a sentence that's "solid" and authentic I give you this one that I bumped into recently, while rereading Clancy Sigal's great but forgotten *Going Away* ("a report; a memoir"). If you're prudish you may want to skip this item.

> I had an erection so big I thought it would pick me up and throw me out the window.

Now *there's* a sentence you can't ignore, one that does its job far better than "I had a big erection"—yet there's nothing the least bit purple about it (the sentence, that is).

Nuts & Bolts 4: Words & Phrases

132} I KNOW NOT SHOULD: WHY THE CONDITIONAL KILLS

Routine can infect our stories unintentionally, through the words we choose and even our choice of tense (see Meditations # 15–17).

Look at this paragraph:

> Frank would never bother to knock, though Harriet would always complain that he *should* knock, that it was rude of him not to. "Family don't count," Frank would say to her, and Harriet was as good as family. And anyway he wouldn't just barge in. He would walk in gently and announce himself. As far as he was concerned Harriet could complain herself blue in the gills: His way was good manners enough.

At first glance there's nothing wrong with this. In fact it has its charms. Yet it's not all it could be. All those *woulds* and *coulds* suck the life from the passage.

A revision:

> Frank never knocked. "You damn well ought to," Harriet scolded. "It's rude not to."
>
> "Family don't count," Frank countered: Harriet was as good as family. Anyway he hadn't barged in; he'd entered gently, announcing himself. That was manners enough as far as he was concerned.

Here the *sense* of routine is preserved, but without the fly-in-amber fossilization that results from overuse of the conditional tense. The same scene, or one much like it, may have occurred often in the past, yet the reader experiences these events uniquely, as they occur *now*, with the authority and urgency of a present singular moment. The particular illustration merely proves the rule.

Often in student stories I'm told what a character "would" (generally) do. "Hal Conklin *would* sit out on the steps of the town hall with a bag over his head and both middle fingers held erect for all the world to see." This is less effective than, "That last week of October, all week long, Hal Conklin sat on the steps of the town hall with a shopping bag over his head and both middle fingers held erect for all the world to see."

When you find yourself leaning hard on "would," ask whether you may be stuck in routine mode. Dramatize a specific event and have that event stand for the routine.

133 } BRIGHT YELLOW FLUID: PERFUNCTORY MODIFIERS

Modifiers (adjectives and adverbs) should be used to add nuance or meaning that isn't already inferred or implied by the words they modify.

We already know tears wash *silently* down a person's face; no need to say so. But when a narrator tells us a character's shoes make "a light sticking sound on the linoleum," that supplies me with valuable sensory information.

Not all modifiers are perfunctory. Even piled on in machine-gun bursts, they can work well. "Yet sometimes it washes over me in *big fat sloshing* waves of sadness how much I miss her." Here, three adjectives are better than one or none.

But later in the same story, describing a catheter bag, the same narrator gives us "a pouch filled with a clear bright yellow fluid the color of a sugary summertime drink." The words "clear bright yellow fluid" are more than enough to evoke the image. "Bright yellow fluid" would suffice; so would "yellow fluid." So would "urine" or one of its less formal variants. By adding "sugary summer drink" the writer gilds his already golden lily.

134 } FLOATING BOWLING BALLS & FROZEN MAGGOTS: DEAD SIMILES

The battle fields of "creative" writing are littered with the corpses of dead similes. Among my favorite casualties:

> Her eyes were like two brown circles with big black dots in the center.

> The hailstones leaped from the street like maggots when fried in hot grease.

> He was as tall as a 6'3" tree.

The little boat gently drifted across the pond exactly the way a bowling ball wouldn't.

The brick wall was the color of a red-brick colored crayon.

She had a deep, throaty, genuine laugh, like that sound a dog makes just before it throws up.

The horizon swallowed the setting sun like a dog sucking an egg.

135} THE CASE AGAINST "SPIED": WRITERLY VERBS

We need to avoid writerly verbs, like "chortle," "utter," "opine" and "spy." I call them "writerly" since they're almost never used except by those who want to *sound like* writers—who believe that a writer's vocabulary must distinguish itself from that of mere laymen.

Writers are in fact humans who speak in human tongues. Whatever words they use, good writers come by them honestly, through their characters and settings and the stories they have to tell about them.

Yet even practiced writers can slip into "writerly" language, using the verb to "place" as a synonym for "put": "She *placed* her suitcase on the floor"; "He *placed* his arm around her waist." We should avoid anything that calls attention away from our stories to the web of words they're made of—and pay attention to the choice between "put" and "placed."

On the same note I can almost always live without "acquire" or "purchase" as synonyms for "buy." And why, in fiction, do people always "glance" and never simply "look" at things?

As for verbs like "spy," "spot," "utter," and "chortle," they are in effect one-word clichés. Who ever "spies" "or "spots" anything, except in works of fiction? Unless your characters happen to be espionage agents, stick to "saw" or "noticed."

136 } EVITARE POLYSYLLABIC MERDA: ESCHEW LATINISMS

Judges, scientists, and academics tend to favor Latin. *Discourse, excavate, expectorate, elevate, illuminate, indicate, liberate, concatenate, incarcerate, masticate, copulate*—these are a few of the Latin-based baubles that some of us can't resist rolling around in our mouths.

Yet each of these words has a fine, blunt, Anglo-Saxon equivalent: *talk, dig, spit, raise, light, point, free, jail, chew, fuck.* Their Latin cousins are more intent on talk than action.

Anglo-Saxon derived words are the kind we use most among our friends. They are the words of *spoken* or informal, as opposed to written or formal, English. This is exactly why, as *good* writers, we should lean on them, since good writing is writing that's vivid and earthy and gets its point across in as few syllables as possible.[58]

137 } HEDGES, WIND, & CHATTER: MORE CRAP WORDS & PHRASES

Our language is riddled with commonly accepted words and phrases that don't withstand scrutiny.

The phrase "proceeded to" should, most of the time, be followed by something other than a verb: "He proceeded to the principal's office." Otherwise it's an empty phrase: "Gaylord proceeded to cry"; "The wind proceeded to howl." It's an emperor with no clothes, since all actions implicitly "proceed" from other actions. "The majority of" is another crap phrase. Just say, "most."

---

58 Depending, of course, on the desired *tone.* The story Nabokov tells in *Lolita* could be summarized in a half-dozen pages, but the language of its telling is part of the story; to that end every syllable counts. The same can be said of any masterpiece.

I don't mean to give offense, but I do mean to provoke you—into thinking more about such phrases before putting them on paper.

We need to be suspicious of choices that are usually taken for granted. For instance, why write, "He began to reel in the fishing line"? The beginning of any action is implied by the action. Similarly: "He started to run after her"; or "Sally turned around and started laughing in his face." Better say, "Sally laughed in his face"—unless the way she turns has some specific gravity: "She spun around and ..."

Avoid the toxic conditional: "Jim *could see* Jill coming toward him." Unless he was blind a sentence ago, the point isn't that Jim *can* see, but that he *sees* Jill.

Through this sort of detailed questioning we evolve the principles (and prejudices) that define our personal aesthetic; we arrive at the right stylistic choices *for ourselves*. We also heighten our sensitivity to, and appreciation for, language itself. By questioning words, we show our respect[59] for them.

Some other words and phrases to hold suspect:

> WORDS:
> almost / seemed / somewhat / anyway / suddenly / really / actually / quickly / literally [and most other adverbs]

These words fall into two categories: hedging words (like "somewhat") indicate an author's unwillingness to commit fully to the truth of a statement; superfluous adverbs (like "actually") do nothing but take up space.

> PHRASES:
> for example / for instance / of course / seemed to / in this case / such as it was [or is] / little did [fill in the blank] know / at this [or that] point in time / as a matter of fact / for that matter / without

---

59 I almost wrote—in fact I *did* write—"utmost respect." Why? Because the phrase exists readymade like sauce in a jar; just heat and serve.

a doubt / some kind of / unbeknownst to [whomever] / pretty
much / I can honestly say / to say the least / disappear or vanish
from sight or view / happens to be / be that as it may

All of these phrases add nothing but wind and chatter.

138 } SCISSORS & RAZOR BLADES: CUT, CUT, CUT

An editor at *The New Yorker* has just telephoned to say how much
she enjoyed your story. It's nearly perfect, she says, and she'd like
to publish it. There's just one thing. It needs a little ... um ... trimming. Say—by a third. Meaning, since the story runs 9,000 words,
you've got to cut 3,000.

The New Yorker pays two dollars per published word. Think
you can make those cuts? You'd better believe it!

Whether *The New Yorker* calls or not, if you can possibly cut
3,000 words from a story, you should probably cut them. If you
don't cut every extra word from your work, odds are no editors
will be calling.

You'd be amazed at what you can cut when you have to. You
may use too many modifiers, or "double-dip" your dialogue,
which is also flabby with "naturalisms" like "oh" and "well." You
state what's implied and explain what's already shown. You paint
every leaf on every tree, instead of letting your readers' imaginations do some painting themselves.

How to go about cutting?

- Read your stuff out loud, pencil in hand.

- If you can't cut entire pages, cut paragraphs; if you can't cut
  paragraphs, cut sentences; if you can't cut sentences, cut
  phrases; if you can't cut phrases, cut words.

- If you can't cut words, go after syllables.

- Avoid the passive voice, progressive tense, and dead verbs.

In this story about a teenager botching a burglary, the excess words slow the action.

> I run through the next-door neighbor's backyard, running, legs flying, heart beating, thudding in my chest. I climb a fence, the chain links rattling, flip over the top and land with a hard thud, stop, look around, my breath catching in my throat. I'm in some sort of alley now, surrounded by sleeping apartment buildings. There's someone's swimming pool to my left with a four-foot fence between it and me. What should I do? There's nowhere to run. I dash, leap, climb up the fence, cut my arm on something, hear a crash of metal on metal behind me somewhere, the sound of gun-metal banging against the chain-links. I run around the pool, dart across slippery pool tiles, feeling like Jesus running on water. Then up and over the next chain-link fence, onto a strip of grass. I hear a voice or voices shouting above me. There's a gate opening into another yard. I come to a glass door …

The style aimed for here is machine-gun prose that wastes no words, every syllable a bullet. But it needs cutting:

> I run through the backyard, hop a fence, stop, look. In some sort of alley now, between apartment buildings. A swimming pool to my left. A four-foot fence between it and me. Nowhere to run. I dash, leap, cut my arm. A crash behind me—metal meets chain-link. Keep running. Dart across slippery pool tiles, Jesus running on water. Another fence, another strip of grass. Shouting above me. A gate opens into another yard. I come to a glass door, slide it open, slither into darkness. Kitchen smells—coffee, tea bags, dishwater, dog food. Refrigerator hum. I lie on my back under the table tasting my bloody fucking arm …

Even when not writing machine-gun prose, you want to make every bullet count. Pretend there's a gun to your head and just *do it*.

But when cutting and trimming remember, too, that conveying mere information in the proper order isn't enough: Your narrator should have a distinct voice, whose rhythms and syntax should be respected even as cuts are made.

So, cut by all means. Forget the tweezers. Cut with a chainsaw, a hatchet, a scalpel, or a razor blade. But try not to slit your narrator's throat.

139 } WHITE SPACE: A WRITER'S BEST FRIEND

What about all those transitions you've labored over, making the material between scenes interesting so it doesn't read like mortar between bricks? Consider doing away with them completely. Who needs mortar, if you can build a story out of pure bricks, held together by gravity and air?

As writer Mary Gordon has said, "Honor the white space."

White space: That thin slice of empty narrative real estate, achieved by hitting an extra hard return between paragraphs.

White space signals a transition, and creates it. The transition may be temporal—a switch to another location or time—or it may be to another character's point of view, or it may be a transition in tone or style.

Or it may be all of these things.

> She never wanted to go back to the men's apartments. After a two hundred dollar meal, men sometimes expected it. Even if it was expense account. Things seemed drab after the restaurant. The glow of good eating was gone. She preferred making love first, then eating. Anticipating dinner afterwards made the end of sex less lonely.

> She had met Edward on her lunch hour at the stand-up coffee bar at Bloomingdales …

Matters of Style

Author Joanna Torrey inserts a break in her short story "Hungry" to emphasize the distinction between her heroines' past dating experiences and her present love affair—a distinction that (we sense) may be more apparent than real.

Sometimes my students use white spaces capriciously or without sufficient reason; more often, they neglect to use them. The beauty of white spaces is that they throw the transition ball into the reader's court, letting him fill in the gap. Should the transition be written poorly, the reader has no one to blame but himself.

Another way to think of white space: As a serving of green tea sorbet, to cleanse the palette between courses in a meal.

Other Stylistic Odds & Ends

140} RETYPE FROM SCRATCH

When revising, I suggest retyping (or "rekeyboarding," if you insist) from scratch, using the previous draft as a guide only. Make each sentence ring like a bell. Apply notes and suggestions by others, bearing in mind that they are just suggestions.

Ask of every word, is it essential? If not, don't let it stand. Your allegiance should be to the story and only to the story, not to the words you've already written.

If nothing else, your typing skills will improve.

141} ITALICS & OTHER EYESORES

I've already mentioned Joyce and his aversion to quotation marks, which he called "eyesores."

Italics—especially when deployed over long passages—similarly rub many people the wrong way. And no wonder: Italics are hard on the eyes. Italics are often used to set apart a prologue—as if the word "prologue" at the top of the section (coming just before "Chapter 1") isn't a big enough hint.

Joyce had it right: Unless absolutely necessary, punctuation marks and typographical embellishments are eyesores. They're best reserved for novels, which have more room for them.

Whenever possible, revert to plain roman type.

142} ! ! ! ! !

"Exclamation marks—like laughing at your own jokes."

— F. Scott Fitzgerald

Frank Conroy, the fabled former director of the Iowa Writer's Workshop, had a rule about exclamation points: "One per three pages," he used to say.

I'm more generous; I say two. But use them sparingly, or your prose will look like the living room rug after you drag the Christmas tree away.

The overuse of exclamation marks indicates an author's lack of faith in his story or his readers, or both. When a line of dialogue or even a remark made by your narrator is exclamatory, the exclamation mark is implied.

143} SIMILAR CHARACTER NAMES

Felicity and Filomena are too similar. So are Mildred and Myra. So are Inga and Igor.

Unless meant to suggest that your characters are as interchangeable as Tweedledum and Tweedledee, pick names that help us distinguish them.

144 } THE WAR AGAINST "WAS": THE DEADEST OF VERBS

In all of its conjugations, the verb "to be" is one of the two deadest verbs in English; "to have" is the other. Since verbs are the most powerful of all parts of speech, by using "was" you defeat yourself doubly.

Try replacing conjugations of "to be" with more exact, interesting verbs ("The vase is on the table" becomes: "The vase stands on the table"). Or recast your sentences entirely ("The horse with the white spots was an appaloosa" becomes: "He rode a horse with white spots, an appaloosa").

I also avoid the past progressive. "She was clinging" becomes "she clung." Instead of "Harold was wearing a yellow raincoat," write, "He wore a yellow raincoat." Save the past progressive for moments when it truly applies: "Stuart was getting out of his car when he saw the dead rabbit lying next to the driveway."

145 } "IT WAS" & OTHER DEAD WORDPAIRS

"It was": the lamest word-pair in the English language, and a dreary way to begin a sentence, let alone a story or a novel. "It was a dark and stormy night." Perhaps it was, but find another way to say so. How about, "Night fell dark and stormy"? Or "The night lumbered by in darkness and storms"—anything to get rid of that deadly duo.

Used portentously, the phrase is even deadlier: "It was then that … " "It was so-and-so who … "

Other dead word pairs: "The man ~~who was~~ standing by the door." "An essay ~~which was~~ published in ... "

That was, which were, who is, which was: all get the editor's ax.

146} PUT THE ADJECTIVE AFTER THE NOUN

This is one of my former mentor Don's good ideas. By putting our modifiers after the nouns they modify, we charge them with the actions of verbs so they feel less passive.

"Scalding tears fell from her eyes," becomes "Tears fell scalding from her eyes." Similarly, "A dark, heavy rain fell over the city," becomes "The rain fell dark and heavy over the city."

And this pungent example from Adam Day's poem "Braunvieh":

> *... Outside*
> *a cow has dropped green dung*
> *wet over a bucket of cherries*

Matters of Style

Q. CAN YOU LAY OUT SOME DOS AND DON'TS FOR A GOOD STYLE?

A. Sure. First, make your primary goal in writing is not artistic expression, but clear communication. Never try to sound like a writer; if you end up sounding like one that's all right, provided the writer is you; but do your best not to try. To that end, eschew "writerly" language and constructions ("unbeknownst to her").

Don't force metaphors and similes. Remember that these are tools, and that tools should be used only when necessary, and not for pleasure (if you can pry a nail loose with your fingers you don't use a crowbar).

When brooding on the choice between two words, use the shorter (for instance: I opened my answer to this question by saying, "Sure." I might have said, "Certainly." I didn't. That's the stylist in me at work.).

Clarity and concision should be your main aims. No effect for its own sake, ever.

When describing violent actions or emotions, use restrained, even clinically dry, language.

Let language carry, rather than create, humor, which should arise from situation. Humor derived strictly from linguistic high jinks is called literary humor and belongs to the last century, which can keep it.

Specify! Don't just say "a box of matches," say, "a box of Ohio blue-tipped safety matches." Why? Because specificity is the solvent that dissolves cliché and genericism. Unlike literary humor, it adds authenticity to what is already there, concretely, in our stories, rather than inflating them artificially with language.

Don't report dull dialogue; if you must, do so indirectly to sum up a long or dry exchange.

When they have something interesting to say, or an interesting way to say it, by all means let characters speak. If not, let their actions or their silences speak for them.

Don't be afraid of adjectives and adverbs, but do question them. If a modifier doesn't do something for the word it modifies that the word itself can't do, then strike it. Then again, certain modifiers—quickly, quietly, cautiously, carefully, certainly—rarely earn their keep. If you can cut it, do.

When making transitions, do what Mary Gordon calls "honoring the white space." Why drag your readers through a transitional paragraph or even a sentence when you can treat them to a nice blank spot on the page?

If you must overwrite, fine. Then go back through and cut every other word. When it comes to cutting, be ruthless. As my friend says, "Use an axe, not tweezers."

Achieve poetry, but don't try for it. To try is almost certainly to fail. Try for clarity, for specificity, for economy, for authenticity. And poetry may just come.

Avoid backward sentences. "He stabbed his sister-in-law in the back shortly after arriving home from work at the Piggly Wiggly." The bullet should come out at the end of the sentence.

Don't overuse exclamation marks. Three per story, says Frank Conroy. And unless you want your narrators to be airheads don't bundle up on them!!!!

Matters of
Soul

Water Cannot Rise
Above Its Source

Why should storytelling be in any way, by any measure, "hard"? Why, when we tell stories all the time, when storytelling is as much a part of everyday social intercourse as eating, joking, or sex? Why, when most of us tell stories naturally enough in person, does storytelling on paper not come naturally?

147 } ALL OF OUR STORIES LIVE INSIDE US: THE TALE OF THE TAXI DRIVER

Riding a taxi to the airport, I asked the driver what I thought was an innocuous question—something along the lines of "How are you?"

Instead of answering, "Fine. And you?" the driver launched into his life story. But in place of the usual tale of immigration and struggle, he described to me a day in his life, beginning with the moment his alarm went off at six o'clock in the morning, and how he made breakfast for himself and his two children and got them ready for school. As he launched into this blow-by-blow description of his day, I gripped the passenger strap—bracing myself for a collision not with an oncoming car, but with this man's entire existence.

As he went on speaking, describing his method of preparing oatmeal by microwave and how, before leaving them to catch the school bus, he would stoop forward to kiss his children on their foreheads, something strange happened. In place of the boredom I'd girded myself for, I found myself gripped by his tale. For an hour and forty minutes, the length of the taxi ride to the airport, I listened, rapt, to this man's "story"—which was not a story so much as a thorough description of the process of *being him*—i.e., a precise and detailed answer to my question, "How are you?"

In her essay *Writing Short Stories,* Flannery O'Connor recalls how a woman living down the road from her, having read some of her stories, remarked, "Well, them stories just gone and shown you how some folks would do." The remark impressed O'Connor, who goes on to say, "When you write stories, you have to be content to start exactly there—showing how some specific folks will do, will do in spite of everything."

O'Connor's notion was exemplified in my taxi driver's tale. O'Connor goes on to observe:

> This is a very humble level to have to begin on, and most people who think they want to write stories are not willing to start there. They want to write about problems, not people; or about abstract issues, not concrete situations. They have an idea, or a feeling, or an overflowing ego, or they want to Be A Writer, or they want to give their wisdom to the world in a simple-enough way for the world to be able to absorb it. In any case, they don't have a story and they wouldn't be willing to write it if they did; and in the absence of a story, they set out to find a theory or a formula or a technique.

My cab driver had no theories to espouse, no formulas or techniques to illustrate, no abstract themes or problems to hunt down or resolve, and no sensational tale to tell. He had been asked a question, and he answered it: concretely, specifically, honestly, with feeling. And I listened, enthralled. He was a storyteller.

Starved Egos &
Self-Consciousness

Of the hundred or so stories that I may read in a semester of workshops, all but a very few will at first fail—fail to engage me as a reader, fail to find a publisher. Writing stories may be among the most self-conscious of undertakings. The materials we work from are personal: *our* memories, *our* experiences, *our* fears and fantasies.

If writing stories should be a natural process, why do we writers struggle—and, more importantly, fail?

Most of the pitfalls we face as writers are internal, and especially hard to distinguish and avoid. All of our stories live inside us. And so do many of the problems that keep us from writing successful ones.

148} ATTACK OF THE DEFENSIVE EGO: SELF-CONSCIOUSNESS

I reach into my shoulder satchel, pull out a story. Halfway down page one I read:

> ...Vivid images of dreamful places lie scattered about on library shelves in the castle walls of his mind. He feels immediately lost among the memories and hopes scribbled on the walls and the veritable vaults of past thoughts and future dreams that will never come true. He passes through the traumatizing memories room but not without turning his head to say hello to the last happy image of his dear departed wife. After a wave hello he runs on through skipping along hallways of time past and present not knowing what he's looking for. A picture of a chapel suddenly fills the screen of his mind's eye and the wedding scene with his friends and family replays like a reel-to-reel slideshow, his memories of those better days bright and illuminated. Suddenly the cocoons that filled his stomach before are the butterflies that fly there now, with his thoughts placed like subtitles under his subconscious movie ...

I lower the page with a sigh.

Some beginning writers operate under a false assumption: They assume that stories are about *language*. But language is merely the medium in which stories are created.

Here, that false assumption is hard at work. In that blizzard of mixed metaphors (castles and libraries, slideshows and movie screens), what is being evoked? Little beyond a flurry of words—words that remain dreamy abstractions ("traumatizing memories," "bright and illuminated"). Where is the *world* of the story? Who are the people? *Is* there a story?

With rare exceptions *(Ulysses, Lolita),* stories are never about language, or never *exclusively* about language. Yet the above passage gives me nothing else. It is, essentially, a piece of writing turned inward against itself. The subject of the passage, in fact, is the way in which it has been written. It was written to call attention to itself, to writing as a self-conscious process, and thus to the writer himself.

But good writing doesn't bring attention to us as creators; it directs the reader's attention to a created world. We do that by *losing* ourselves in telling a good story—making discoveries that we invite others to enter into with us. New writers don't do this, often because they don't understand that they're *supposed* to do it.

Did my student intend to draw attention to himself? Knowing him, I would answer, No. In fact he's a shy, self-effacing person. Raising the question: How does a shy, self-effacing person end up creating the rhetorical equivalent of a billboard that shouts LOOK AT ME!?

Self-consciousness (not to be confused with self-awareness) inevitably impairs our capacity for empathy and understanding, substituting a competitiveness and overcompensation bred of our own insecurities. On behalf of our starved egos we show off, drawing unflattering attention to our work and to ourselves.

All of which happens unconsciously.

Except for clowns and sitcom stars, no one really wants to make a fool of himself. But the ego has its own agenda. That is why egos can't write. They can string words together, but every word that they string is informed (and corrupted) by the desire to impress others—a desire fed not by strength, but by weakness, by self-consciousness.

Not that there haven't been egotistical authors, including some great ones. The headline of Norman Mailer's obituary in the *Times* read, "Towering Writer With a Matching Ego Dies at 84." Some "towering egos" manifest in the scale and sweep of their owner's ambitions (Balzac, Ayn Rand), others through the flamboyance of their public personas (Wilde, Hemingway). Mailer did both. Jean Cocteau famously remarked, "Victor Hugo was a madman who believed he was Victor Hugo."

Then there are artistic egos that express themselves *defensively.* For Tennessee Williams, every bad review was an obituary that would plunge him into an alcohol- and pill-supplemented isolation. So protective was Saul Bellow of his ego, he wouldn't tolerate criticism of his work from even his closest friends; no sooner did they criticize him than the friendship ceased. Even a Nobel Prize failed to thicken Bellow's skin. Ernesto Sabato[60] reminds us, "Only a thick skin can defend itself, and the characteristic of an artist is an extremely thick skin."

149 } BRANDO BLOWS HIS LINES: ON WANTING TO BE "A WRITER"

Not long ago I watched a video of Marlon Brando being interviewed by Larry King. It was an old interview, obviously, done some years before Marlon died in 2004, at age 80. Marlon is a hero of mine, the greatest male actor in my opinion. But the same man who exuded musk in *Streetcar,* mumbled and scratched his way to a (snubbed) Oscar in *The Godfather,* and broke Maria Schneider's heart (and took liberties with other body parts) in *Last Tango in Paris,* could be obnoxious in person. No celebrity has gone to greater lengths to thumb his nose at his public. He also denigrated the acting profession, in this case by denying it altogether:

> Everybody here in this room is an actor. . . . The best performances I've ever seen is when the director says cut and the

60 Argentinean author, painter, physicist, and pedagogue. The quote is from *Entre la Letra y la Sangre.*

director says that was great. That was wonderful. That was good ... When you say how do you do, how are you, you look fine, you're doing two things at once. You're reading the person's real intention. You're trying to feel who he is and making an assessment and trying to ignore the mythology.

King might have pointed out that, while everyone may be an actor offstage, the instant you point a camera at them most people either freeze or turn into lousy actors.

This is what happens to writers much of the time. Call it performance anxiety. The greater our desire to *be* writers, to be seen and admired and judged as writers, the more vulnerable we are to this syndrome. The mere act of thinking of oneself as *a writer* and not as a storyteller (or better, *as someone who happens to tell stories*) is an act of self-consciousness—and an act of self-sabotage.

Attached to this notion of being "a writer" is a legacy of misunderstandings and misconceptions, undermining the qualities that truly equip us to write stories. Writers are "supposed" to be romantic, exotic, quixotic; dashing dandies in spanking white linen suits; heroic outdoorsmen—Teddy Roosevelt with a typewriter. (There are stereotypes for women writers, too: the suicidal modernist, the gifted young poetess, the proto-feminist.)

But, first and foremost, a storyteller must be a *human being*— and not necessarily an extraordinary human being. A writer's ordinariness, combined with empathic power and an urge to tell stories about other ordinary people, is what makes a writer good or even great. In embracing the label "writer," with its blinding twinkle and flash, we shun our essential ordinariness.

150 } "TALENT" & "GENIUS": THE EGO'S FALSE GODS

Self-conscious writers suffer especially from misunderstandings connected with the words *talent* and *genius.*

Nietzsche questioned whether these "gifts" are merely a result of other traits:

> Don't talk about giftedness, inborn talents! One can name all kinds of great men who were not very gifted. They *acquired* greatness, became 'geniuses' (as we put it) through [other] qualities . . .: all of them had that diligent seriousness of a craftsman, learning first to construct the parts properly before daring to make a great whole. They allowed themselves time for it, because they took more pleasure in making the little, secondary things well than in the effect of a dazzling whole.

In the play *A Streetcar Named Desire,* the brute Stanley Kowalski says, "Luck is believing you're lucky." He might have said something similar about talent: Among other things, talent is believing you're talented.

The principal difference between people who can sing and those who can't hold a tune is that the former were *told* that they could sing. Or anyway they weren't told that they couldn't. Once, when I presented her a crayon drawing of the Empire State Building, my kindergarten teacher—Mrs. Decker—kissed my cheek. An artist was born. Was the drawing any good? Who knows? It was good enough for Mrs. Decker.

Does this account for what I'll call freakish talent, the sort of talent one associates with Mozart, or any prodigy? No. But it accounts for most of the rest. And freakish talent isn't the subject here. Freakish talent gets its own book by someone who knows something about it. Which lets me off the hook.

Talent lifts us out of self-consciousness and, depending on how talented we think we are, propels us up into the cloudless, fearless heights. But like any catalyst, lubricant, or impetus, to work talent needs to be applied to something. It needs to be applied to industry, to practice, performance, to discipline. Like luck, it exists only to the extent that some goal or process is touched by it.

But like luck, talent can be fickle. It's easier for the young and inexperienced to be "talented": Their faith in themselves hasn't yet been tainted by things like rejection and criticism, by the voices whispering no in our ears.

151} FAITH & ENDURANCE: MORE VITAL THAN TALENT

According to Nietzsche (who was among other things a frustrated poet and novelist), the blame for an author's inability to produce a masterpiece owed less to lack of genius or talent than to lack of faith and endurance. The "recipe" for writing a great novel was, according to him, simple enough. But—

> ... to carry it out presupposes qualities one is accustomed to overlook when one says 'I do not have enough talent.' One has only to make a hundred or so sketches for novels, none longer than two pages but of such distinctness that every word in them is necessary; one should write down anecdotes every day until one has learned how to give them the most pregnant and effective form; one should be tireless in collecting and describing human types and characters; one should above all relate things to others and listen to others relate, keeping one's eyes and ears open for the effect produced on those present, one should travel like a landscape painter or costume designer ... one should, finally, reflect on the motives of human actions, disdain no signpost for instruction about them and be a collector of these things by day and night. One should continue in this many-sided exercise for some ten years; what is then created in the workshop ... will be fit to go out into the world.

Talent fades; skill and perseverance endure and even increase. This explains why, at nearly eighty, John Updike was arguably as good or better a writer than he was at twenty-five. If he seemed less "talented," it may have been because we'd come to expect great things of him.

152} A GENIUS KNOWS HIS LIMITS: THE ART OF WAR

"Artistic genius is knowing and working well *within your limits*. In his sixth-century B.C.E. treatise on military strategy, *The Art of War*, Sun Tzu declares:

> One who knows the enemy and knows himself will not be in danger in a hundred battles.
>
> One who does not know the enemy but knows himself will sometimes win, sometimes lose.
>
> One who does not know the enemy and does not know himself will be in danger in every battle.

The wisdom of *The Art of War* has by now been applied to business, politics, sports, and other competitive undertakings. I see no reason why it shouldn't apply to the art of fiction writing. In knowing themselves, fiction writers, too, may avert the dangers of "a hundred battles." And a big part of knowing oneself is knowing one's limitations.

I don't mean to imply that great artists don't challenge themselves. But every great or successful artist knows the difference between practice and performance, between experiment and success.

Amateur writers, on the other hand, are always exceeding their limits. They use techniques that they haven't yet understood, let alone mastered, flinging freshly discovered words that reek of the thesaurus. In their anxiety to be "original," like the Starship *Enterprise* they boldly go where no one has ever gone before. But in their case the voyage may be bound for disaster.

To invite failure via experimentation isn't a bad thing; it's good and necessary from time to time. But when invited, the odds are that failure will indeed show up.

Matters of Soul

There's another kind of genius, though, immeasurable and mysterious, that can't be willed or saddled or forced, that rises from the depths of our egoless souls, and that seems not to belong to but to be *using* us, laying claim to our bodies and brains as aliens do to their victims in horror movies. But artistic genius is a *benevolent* force, one that seizes only a few select souls that volunteer themselves—and even then genius may not strike. This type of genius isn't a product of drudgery and has little to do with intellect; intellect may even be antithetical to it. But it has plenty to do with patience, courage, generosity, and faith: faith that the mystery will present itself; patience to wait as long as it takes; courage so if and when it does we may look it boldly in the eyes; and generosity to share with others what we have seen.

The best writing, however, happens when we somehow break through the wall of common knowledge and perceptions and enter into a different world, the realm of the sublime. Some call it "writing from the gut" or "seeing with the third (or inner) eye." Jung spoke of the *collective unconscious*.

As Lewis Hyde tells us in his marvelous book, *The Gift*, the "gift" of artistic genius belongs first and foremost to those who are most prepared and inclined to give it away:

> We also rightly speak of intuition or inspiration as a gift. As the artist works, some portion of his creation is bestowed upon him. An idea pops into his head, a tune begins to play, a phrase comes to mind, a color falls in place on the canvas. Usually, in fact, the artist does not find himself engaged or exhilarated by the work, nor does it seem authentic, until this gratuitous element has appeared, so that along with any true creation comes the uncanny sense that "I," the artist, did not make the work. "Not I, not I, but the wind that blows through me," says D.H. Lawrence. Not all artists emphasize "the gift" phase of their creations to the degree that Lawrence does, but all artists feel it.

Technical Shortcomings

153} FAMILIARITY WITH FORM

If genius calls for enlightenment, how do we prepare ourselves? By mastering technique.

To young Alexander Pope, William Walsh, a country gentleman and dabbler in poetry, gave this advice: "Be correct." By this Walsh meant master existing forms: couplets, sestina, villanelle, sonnet, terza rima, so on.

For fiction we may apply "form" to things prosaic: chapters, scenes, paragraphs, sentences.

The short story as a whole is a form to which *principles* apply. It should have a beginning, a middle, an end. It promises certain things and it delivers on those promises. It has a theme or even several themes, but usually one grand or inclusive theme that can be expressed in just a few words (or even one). It leaves us satisfied, but also surprised—wanting nothing more or less.

The form of the novel is similar in that it, too, has a theme or themes as well as a beginning, a middle, and an end. It differs in being much longer, less constrained, containing chapters that may weave together several plots.

There are two ways to master form: through *absorption* and through *imitation.*

By "absorption" I mean simply by reading, by taking stories into our blood through our eyes and our "ears"—the mind's ear, the one that "hears" the sounds of words written on paper. In some this mental ear is well developed and acutely sensitive; in others it has to be cultivated.

154 } MASTERY THROUGH ABSORPTION: EXPERT READERS

Those who read with an eye toward mastering form may never again enjoy reading entirely for its own sake, as pure entertainment. "How Nellie Lost Her Knickers" no longer matters to us nearly as much as how Nellie's creator makes us care whether, and how, she loses them. Reading for mastery means reading for *technique*. It means being aware of plot, scenes, paragraphs, sentences, words, punctuation—the very things that, as regular "civilian" readers, we happily surrender our awareness of when immersed in a story.

The expert reader is aware of both the effect and how it's achieved—the ropes and pulleys and switches that move the scenery, the stage manager and the cues. She gets two performances for the price of one: the one on stage and the one in the wings.

I'm always amazed at beginning writers, young and old, who don't read much, let alone voraciously—let alone to master form. This explains why, among other things, they don't know how to format dialogue: either they've rarely seen it, or they haven't noticed it. To read with an eye for technique and form is to access the greatest writing instructors of all time. Want to study with Shakespeare? James Joyce? Virginia Woolf? Just open up a book.

155 } CONTEMPT OF COMMA: LACK OF RUDIMENTARY TECHNICAL SKILLS

To write fiction—to write anything, for that matter—you have to be able to spell, to punctuate, to conjugate, to identify the parts of a sentence. That should go without saying, but it doesn't. To some writing students, a sentence is anything that starts with a capital letter and ends with a period—and those are the ones with high standards. Others have been taught never to use a one-syllable word when a three- or four-syllable one is available—preferably one whose meaning is obscure to them.

To be clear is dull; to be grammatical is square. And all that technical stuff is too much of a bother—and interferes with their creativity.

More than a few of my undergraduate students don't know what a paragraph is, let alone a paragraph break, or (heaven forbid) an indent. I've considered petitioning for an official holiday, NATIONAL PARAGRAPH INDENT DAY, when all good citizens take a moment to reflect upon the humble beauty of that blank white space that heralds the inception of every paragraph—or used to, before e-mail and the Internet and technospeak did away with such niceties.

But the things that govern form and keep it from falling into chaos are grammar, spelling, and punctuation. Without them (as Yeats wrote):

> *the center cannot hold*
> *mere anarchy is loosed upon the world.*

If you can't see the beauty of a genuine paragraph, if you don't experience the thrill of a well-placed comma, then you need to develop your visual "ear": You need to learn to hear *with your eyes.*

156} MASTERY THROUGH EMULATION: IMITATIONS GOOD & BAD

Beyond reading, another way to master form is to imitate it.

Imitation, as we know, is the highest form of flattery. It is emulation. And emulation is appreciation. And to appreciate something is to take it to heart. It's a first step toward making something one's own.

One writing exercise (now seldom used) has students take the first pages of a book or story by a favorite author and type them verbatim. In doing so, the student gets to "feel" the words as if he wrote them himself. This goes a step beyond just hearing the words with our mental ears, to actually feeling them with our fingers as we type—possibly even breathing to the rhythms of these masterful sentences. We absorb those sentences: They permeate us. We exercise our mental ears. We soak ourselves in a favorite author's style.

Having imitated, we can *emulate*, setting our own stories (in our own words) to borrowed "music." We write a story or a passage that sounds like—has the shape and feel of—a passage of Toni Morrison, or Chuck Palahniuk, or the Bible. In time we outgrow the authors we emulate: Our contents no longer fit their forms. Some call it rebellion. I prefer to think of it as simply moving on.

Imitate form, not content. To imitate form is fine. To imitate content is not. Students often get it backwards. They contrive new and elaborate forms and then fill them with anything at hand— imitating plots or character "types" or even strings of words.

The tendency to imitate form *and not content* seems to relate directly to talent. It may even determine it.

157} VOCABULARY: AN INFLATED IDEAL

The one "asset" beginners tend to value most is in fact the most dubious: a fat vocabulary. People who in daily life would never use words like "associative" or "essentially" sprinkle them in their prose.

Somewhere along the line, most of us have been taught to use formal diction when writing. Students gussy up their prose to make whatever they have to say *look* important, whether or not it is.

What good teachers want from their students isn't pomp or pretension. What they want is communication, *clarity*—the humble truth expressed as simply and directly as possible. Use the best words, not the biggest. The most elegant sentences, not the most convoluted. By elegant I don't mean *formal*. To be elegant means to act or perform a task with "skill, ease, and grace."

Unfortunately, for most people it is harder to write clearly and simply than to write pretentiously, obscurely. Pretension and obscurity can hide the fact that we have little to say. They serve another fine purpose, too. They impress fools. To be easily understood, in some circles, is taken as a sign of shallowness.

By the time they become graduate students, many have embraced this particular bit of false wisdom.

Bad Taste & Where It Comes From

158} M^cFICTION: BAD TASTE AND WHERE IT COMES FROM

From an unpublished story:

> The world stood witness; some fainted, others cried, a few wet themselves, some fell dead in sheer terror; but most were cemented in place, struck with wonder, mouths agape, heads tilted back, looking upward in unison as the ball of fire molded itself into a silhouetted face. The flickering flames danced themselves into details of the most sinister creature imaginable. Gracefully did the flames form as the eyes lit up with fury and the mouth yawned open.
>
> "Seven days," uttered a near-deafening voice, its echoes shaking the ground. "You have seven days to bring me the Sword of Doom, or it shall be your demise!"

I know of three things that cause bad taste: a diet of literary junk food; weak or nonexistent powers of judgment; and emotional detachment. Typically, the three go hand in hand.

When I say "literary junk food," I mean shoddy fantasies, thrillers, and romance pulps unleavened by anything remotely challenging or nutritious—like a diet of potato chips and jelly beans. "Emotional detachment" means that the writer's feelings are operating on automatic pilot—responding by rote rather than directly, conforming to what he believes (or has been taught) his response *ought to* be. As writers—as artists—we need to risk forming our own judgments, even at the risk of violating the aesthetics of others.

Bad taste and cliché are really the same thing. Our bestsellers are rarely the best books; they've been vaulted to the top of the best-seller list by honest readers, sure, but by even more people who, instead of exercising their own critical judgment, have bought into the received wisdom of others. Most people read what they read because everyone else is reading it (see Meditation # 32).

Many popular things, especially those that qualify as trendy, are popular by default, meaning that the mass or conglomerate will has lacked the force to resist them.

When one has never exercised one's critical judgment; when one's aesthetic sensibilities have been formed in the vacuum of mindless consumerism; when one can no longer tell wine from soda pop ... guess what gets guzzled?

159 } TEND YOUR GARDEN, SAVE YOUR SOUL

Bad taste is what happens when individual sensibilities succumb, through inertia, to public propaganda and mass opinion.

How to tend our sensibilities and keep them from succumbing?

First, resist mass opinion. Resist it with all your heart and soul. Resist it for your artistic good and for the good of society. Distrust all forms of advertising. Resist prepackaged ideas and bubble-wrapped opinions as you would the sermons of a soapbox preacher or the prescriptions of a quack.

This may render you unpopular with those who have cheerily surrendered their best instincts. You have several options: (a) find a new set of friends who, like you, wish to preserve their souls, (b) keep your opinions to yourself (and pretend to enjoy mass-consumption media), and (c) enjoy the occasional stupid movie (etc.), aware that you have temporarily suspended your critical judgment and are slumming.

Heck, even a snob can enjoy Cheez Doodles once in a while.

Discipline: Two Kinds

160} ARTIFICIAL DISCIPLINE VS. INNER DRIVE

At the start of every writing workshop I always ask my students: *What are you here for? What do you want from this class?* Three out of four say "discipline."

In an age of convenience, discipline is a scarce commodity.

Of all pursuits, writing fiction may be the least practical. As a means to get rich, it must be among the hardest. Nor is writing likely to increase your popularity, decrease your waistline, or furnish the key to happiness. It will more likely aggravate your sciatica and make you introspective and gloomy. And as Saul Bellow quipped, "The unexamined life may not be worth living, but the examined life makes you want to kill yourself." That's an exaggeration. But if unqualified happiness is your goal, writing fiction may not be the best way to achieve it.

What writing gives you, or can give you, is satisfaction: the satisfaction of knowing that you've made something, a satisfaction not unlike the satisfaction of a cabinetmaker who turns raw material into functional beauty, only instead of wood, glue, nails, stain, and varnish, you work with thoughts, dreams, imagination, experience.

When a writer goes to work, he isn't always sure where the next thought or inspiration will come from, or if it will come at all. He sits down at his computer, or in front of a blank sheet of paper. Maybe he does research; maybe he writes a few letters to warm himself up. Maybe he meditates, or paces, or prays. Or maybe he just sits there and waits, pencil in hand, keyboard under his fingers, patient as Job. Or he drags himself to his task with grim determination, gritting his teeth, putting down sentence after sentence that he subsequently deletes with as much bilious fury as went into their composition. One way or another, calmly or anxiously, slowly or quickly, gently or stormily, he gets down to work.

When students come to classes seeking discipline, they're looking *outside* themselves for something that exists *inside*. The discipline of attending a class every Tuesday night is a different discipline than that of working alone in a studio, without an audience, witnesses, or comrades. Teachers and workshop leaders may give assignments and set deadlines to spur productivity, but they can't kindle a writer's *inner drive*.

But this is precisely the sort of discipline that student writers seek: the self-generating kind, the kind that can't find satisfaction without its work—the *particular* work of writing. When students ask for discipline, what they're really asking for, hoping for, is to become the sort of person who, if she misses a day in the studio, turns grumpy. Seeking the real thing, most students have to settle, meanwhile, for an artificial, substitute form of discipline—that of the classroom or workshop.

The inward drive, if it exists at all, *must* be satisfied. A writer is not someone who needs to have written, but someone who needs *to be writing,* in order to feel alive and, more or less, content.

161 } REAL DISCIPLINE: AN INVITATION TO BLISS

There's another side to discipline that's less arduous, that's even blissful. I'm talking about *concentration*—that very special place where the mind arrives if it is sufficiently focused on the task at hand, willing to put up with almost any discomfort and pain to reach its goal. Past and future cease to exist; there are no goals beyond the present goal. For the writer the goal may be choosing a single word. However long it takes, the writer is willing to take that time—because there's no such thing as time.

I think most writers—and all creative people—live for the divine bliss of concentration. I know I do. To enter the world of concentration is to abandon the material world, including our own bodies and the pain that comes with them. We become pure spirit, or as close to it as we can come while still living and breathing.

When we ask for discipline we're really asking for a pure, heavenly slice of our own weightless souls, for the benefits of eternity without the drawbacks of death.

162 } A DICTIONARY NAMED DESIRE: AN ARTIST'S GLOSSARY

1. DESIRE: The first ingredient. Far more crucial than talent, the basis of human striving and accomplishment.

2. TASTE: Acquired through time, learned. Subjective yet indispensable.

3. DISCIPLINE: Accompanies desire: Where desire is sufficiently strong, discipline follows.

4. TECHNIQUE: Learned academically or through experiment.

5. IMAGINATION: Cannot be taught, except possibly by example. You can't teach someone to dream.

6. TALENT: A by-product of # 1–5; unnecessary if you have the others.

7. DEXTERITY: Facility, acute vision—not mandatory for the creation of beauty and order. (Secondary to imagination and desire.)

Matters of Soul

A writer is someone who writes: someone who makes a habit of writing, but also of reading and thinking like a writer. Putting words on paper (or on a computer screen) is merely one result of these habits, a result of cultivating that character.

Style was not put on this earth to feed writers' starved egos, but to humbly serve precision and truth.

Sensibility aligns itself with the soul, identity with ego, thus:

$$\text{IDENTITY} = \text{EGO}$$
$$\text{SENSIBILITY} = \text{SOUL}$$

The fiction writer's job is to convey experience, to do so in a spirit of generosity and by the grace of concentration, which can be had only through discipline.

Q. HOW DO I GET PAST SELF-CONSCIOUSNESS?

A. By focusing on what you have to say, and how to best say it, rather than how it will be experienced or admired by the reader. Your duty is to the story; your goal is to make that story clear. If you win praise, it should be for having done so. If you are censured, it will or should be only for failure to have done so. In either case, it's not about you, it's about the story; you are merely a conduit.

Easier said than done, you say.

Yes, self-consciousness, once it's got hold of us, isn't so easily gotten rid of. But where eliminating self-consciousness is a negative, and hence, a weak goal, telling a story clearly, concisely, authentically are all positive, challenging goals, goals before which we as writers stand humbly in awe, for we know that to be clear and concise isn't easy; we know it takes great rigor and discipline.

And we know, too, that in trying to tell authentic stories we are up against two powerful enemies, cliché and stereotype. "All good writing," Martin Amis tells us, "is a war against cliché." If he's right, then we are all soldiers on the good side of that war. And a soldier doesn't worry about himself; he worries about his fellow soldiers and about winning the battle.

Q. WHEN SHOULD I REACH BEYOND MY LIMITS?

A. When reading, always; when writing, only when you can afford to fail. As a writer, the things that you read expand the limits of your ambitions. That's why it's important to read difficult works: They stretch your brain. But as soon as we reach beyond our natural limits we are all but certain to produce failures. This is why hack authors are always so successful: They never reach beyond their limits; in fact they always aim lower. To do otherwise takes two things: time and courage. It may cost you money, too.

Q. HOW MUCH TIME SHOULD I SPEND READING VS. WRITING?

A. That is a choice almost as terrible as Sophie's. But if you must choose, then I would say read more. Especially if you don't consider yourself well-read, you should catch up on your reading. But rather than read as most people do, for entertainment, read to learn how books and stories are written, to study technique, to learn, for instance, what a semicolon can do when used judiciously, or how to transition from one scene to another, or how to seamlessly shift viewpoints within a scene. In this way, while reading you are actually working your muscles as a writer.

Q. WHAT SHOULD I READ?

A. Read promiscuously—that's my advice. Read high and low, everything from airport thrillers to Proust. But maybe the best piece of advice I can give you is to discover your own, unknown—or at least unfamiliar—authors. The place to do so is in the stacks of libraries and in used bookstores. Browse the dusty lower shelves. Pull out books at random, blow the dust from their spines, open to Page 1 and read just a paragraph or two.

By this method I discovered many if not all of the writers who have influenced me the most. If I tell you their names odds are you will recognize few if any of them (Emmanuel Bove? Alexander Trocchi? Xavier Domingo?).

That's the point, part of the point: to discover your own, unique influences: to drink from your own and not everyone's else's well.

Unless you yearn to be like everyone else. But then why write?

And damn the best-seller lists.

Q. WHAT IS THE BEST WAY TO CULTIVATE DISCIPLINE?

A. "Applying the seat of the pants to the seat of the chair." That, according to Mary Heaton Vorse, is one form of discipline. But there are other forms that can be practiced standing up, like getting into the habit of close, careful observation—with a special eye peeled always for the "telling" or "authenticating" detail. And then there's also the habit of close reading to get into.

Within the act of writing itself, there are other disciplines to practice. The discipline of being on one's guard against clichés, for one, and the discipline that makes us resist long, fancy words when short, simple ones will do, and the discipline that has us strike a supremely clever phrase or sentence that draws the readers' attention away from the story being told and to the teller.

One bit of good news about discipline is that it does come easier with age, maybe because the things that distract us from a disciplined routine—bars, parties, movies, and other social and recreational activities—hold less and less appeal as time goes on; at least for me they do. Nowadays, I feel the way most writers do about socializing: That it's an obligation and (usually) a bore. I'd rather be writing.

Q. CAN'T YOU PROVIDE MORE CONCRETE, SPECIFIC WAYS TO OBTAIN DISCIPLINE?

A. Okay, write 500 words a day, every day. The 500 words needn't be beautiful or wonderful or poetic or sublime; the only standards they should meet are those of sincerity and authenticity: Mean what you say, and aim for clarity of communication.

When working, do not hurry, but do not pause. As long as you are sitting there working, even if you produce only one sentence in an hour, that counts as discipline. But if you get up and run to the refrigerator, or watch YouTube videos, that doesn't.

Other
Matters

Getting Personal

Writing isn't like other jobs. You can talk a good game about being professional, about putting your ego aside and not taking things personally. But let's be honest: Writing, especially writing fiction, *is* personal.

When we dig into the unconscious, into our obsessions and dreams, or when we appeal to our imaginations, those things give us only what was there to begin with. We may not recognize half the things that we come up with, but they're ours: They belong to us. Some of it's painful; a lot of it is embarrassing. The very best things we write are a bit of both.

And that's the *good* news.

After we've put our deepest selves on paper—dredged up all that dark, frightening, embarrassing matter—then, unless we are already hugely successful, we must submit ourselves to the slap in the face that is rejection.

For this we bare our souls?

No, not exactly. But we write to have our words read by other people, and that usually means to be published. Which means rejection, since, though the world badly needs many things, your writing (mine, too) isn't one of them.

In a sense, every good writer has to be his own full-time therapist. And every good writing teacher should have a grasp not only of psychology, but of group dynamics, and must be prepared to salve bruised egos.

In this business, egos are bound to get bruised.

But before dealing with rejection and other matters unpleasant, I want to say a few words about the two things I love most in writing: setting and atmosphere.

Setting & Atmosphere

163} DUELING LANDSCAPES: SOME FIELD NOTES ON SETTING

I'm writing this at a café in the Piazza del Pantheon, Rome, on a dreary winter's day. Clouds hang low over Marcus Agrippa's temple to the Gods, that ancient concrete and granite eyeball open to the skies.

No wine without the glass, they say. And no story without a setting.

I've planted myself here with the resoluteness of a weed: You can do that in Roman cafés. I've come here to write. I may write about the rotting, ruined hat factories in the Connecticut town where I grew up, or about the courtyards of Piacenza, where my mother once lived. Whatever I write, it will be informed by the slightly wobbly table with its blue and yellow linens, by the lingering sweetness of the coffee, by the Pantheon's blackened columns, and by the fountain whose waters, on this grim, damp day, feel redundant. I write with the sense that I've been here and will be here forever, as fixed to this spot on the earth as the columns of the Pantheon.

I grew up in two countries: the Europe inside my parents' home, and the America outside. Inside were books in foreign languages crammed onto shelves, along with my father's sloppy but solid paintings of fountains and statues. Outside were baseball diamonds, white picket fences, and woods. Inside was the must of the Old World, outside were five-and-dime stores and the ruins of hat factories. (The phrase itself is quaint: Men once bought hats, and wore them.)

I was eight when we crossed the Atlantic by ocean liner and finally got to see that other world. Though too young to appreciate very much beyond *gelato nocciola,* still, I did stand transfixed before the courtyards of Piacenza, gazing through the locked iron gates at weeping willow trees and marble Venus statues. In Italy, every surface was cracked and pitted or burnished smooth. Voices bounced off the broken walls like organ notes in a cathedral. Even the pigeons sounded different, cooing in Italian, saying, *"Ma basta, ma basta"* (translation: Cut it out!). Birds, trees, flowers, bricks, pigeons—all seemed happier here. And I loved that everything was ancient and dusty.

Back home, environment exerted its own influences. The house I grew up in sat on a Connecticut hill with its back to the woods. I spent lots of time in those woods—dark and Dantesque, but also my best friend, always willing to play with me. I'd hike up to the bald patch of rocks we called Eagle's Nest. From there you could see the whole town, a valley packed with abandoned hat factories, their smokestacks pointing like brick fingers into the sky. I'd take a deep breath and run fast as I could down the hill, leaping over rocks and fallen trees (it's a miracle I didn't break my neck). Those woods were my real home, as was the Italy that lived in our house.

Setting. I think of Saul Bellow's New York and Chicago, of the skyscrapers he once described as "monuments to (men's) mysteries," of his transit buses spewing poisonous bouquets of vapors. No writer has done more justice to America's cities than Bellow, faithfully translating their magnificence and meanness, their generosity and cruelty. Here is a Chicago morning from *Dangling Man,* his second novel:

> In the upper light there were small fair heads of cloud turning. The streets, in contrast, looked burnt-out; the chimneys pointed heavenward in openmouthed exhaustion. The turf, intersected by sidewalk, was bedraggled with the whole winter's deposit of deadwood, match cards, cigarettes, dogmire, rubble.

> The grass behind the palings and wrought iron frills was still yellow, although in many places the sun had already succeeded in shaking it into a livelier green. And the houses, their doors and windows open, drawing in the freshness, were like old drunkards or consumptives taking a cure.

In Bellow's hands, the opened windows of a tenement yawn in great gulps of tainted air. A clump of weeds rising from a rubbled lot invites as much pity as any foundling in Dickens. In most great descriptions, the pathetic fallacy is at least courted—or even engaged outright.

A sign flashing *Blatz* in a bar window draws sympathy from Nelson Algren. For Algren even shadows and air have feelings:

> There through the starless night or the thunderous noon, sunlight or rain or windless cold, she would sit till the tenement's long shadows moved all the way down from the fourth floor rear, slid silently under her door and drifted across her lap, to tremble one moment at still finding her there and then lie comforted and still. While all the air hung wearily.

Sometimes interior and exterior landscapes are so inextricably linked it's hard to say which is more real. Is the Mexico in Lowry's *Under the Volcano* the *setting* of the drunken consul's deliriums, or their result? In Joyce's *Ulysses*, the characters seem to live in cities of thought, with the map of Dublin identical to that of Leopold Bloom's brain. The plot of that novel couldn't be simpler: Two men, crossing a city in opposite directions, meet along the way. Yet the inventory of sensual phenomena borne by their dual streams of consciousness couldn't be more exhaustive. Joyce didn't plot his masterpiece so much as he connived it as a way of recovering the Dublin he'd abandoned as a young man, and which he spent much of the rest of his life reconstructing—pub by paving stone—out of words. With the possible exception of Faulkner and his Yoknapatawpha County, no author ever made a setting more completely his own.

Other Matters

Compare Joyce to Dostoyevsky, whose novels are so wanting for atmosphere one searches in vain for a piece of furniture to sit on while his characters beat each other's Slavic brows. With Dostoyevsky talk isn't cheap, but it is in infinite supply, and readers in search of a breeze or a sofa may as well search for oxygen on Mars.

The same atmospheric stinginess serves to enhance the effect of setting in Hemingway's stories and novels. The less lush his descriptions, the greater their impact. How does Papa do it? If he washes a trout in a clear, rushing stream, you feel the water so cold against your fingertips they grow numb. When, at the Select (his favorite Parisian café), he drinks down oysters with cold wine, you feel that cold against the back of your throat:

> As I ate the oysters with their strong taste of the sea and their faint metallic taste that the cold wine washed away, leaving only the sea taste and the succulent texture, and as I drank their cold liquid from each shell and washed it down with the crisp taste of the wine, I lost the empty feeling and began to be happy and make plans.

In this passage from *A Moveable Feast,* atmosphere is so well evoked it gives you an ice cream headache. Yet there's nothing purple here; the feelings are evoked by things themselves, not by the author's wish to sanctify or glorify them.

Then there are minimalists like Camus, for whom all of Paris "with its black pigeons and sooty courtyards" is dispatched with a single phrase. From then on in *The Stranger,* except for that blinding burst of sunlight on the Algerian shore, setting will take a back seat to thought. But note how the glare of sunlight in that fateful scene contrasts with the blackness of the city, as if civilization were an inkblot on a sunny landscape.

Great stories are joined to their settings: the fogged-in London of *Bleak House,* Kinnan Rawlings's creeks and bayous, the Marabar Caves in *A Passage to India,* the coffin-shaped gondolas in *Death in Venice,* the bureaucratic metropolis of Kafka's unfinished *The Trial* (where men's souls are jammed like punch cards through a monumental computer). The desolate moors of Yorkshire give rise to the characters in Emily Brontë's *Wuthering Heights.* Her bad-tempered, vengeful antagonist is named "Heathcliff," evoking the windy bluff on which perches the dark, foreboding house he grew up in. In Mary Shelley's *Frankenstein,* the doctor's country home near Geneva is also isolated, hemmed in by snowcapped mountains, brooding over a still, dark lake, cut off from society. These are landscapes perfectly suited to characters struggling by sheer willpower against forces and fates over which they have no control.

With civilization wedging itself into every nook and cranny on the globe, such "raw," "brooding" landscapes have grown increasingly rare. From the taming effects of human intervention even the oceans and heavens aren't safe. Now that we've torn the lids off of inner and outer space, what sort of settings would Jules Verne choose for his speculative fictions?

Settings are an endangered species: forests burn; glaciers melt. Aside from its tattoo and pizza parlors, small town America is gone, replaced by one big mall (the setting of Nicholson Baker's *The Fermata,* where several hundred pages are devoted to a voyage up an escalator). The last few decades have served up a slew of minimalist fictions exploring nihilism and ennui, fiction in which settings are distilled down to and codified by brand names of clothing and burger franchises. It's not the writing that's turned generic, but the world: McSetting. In such sandy soil can stories survive, let alone thrive?

The streets of my hometown were equal parts dangerous and drowsy, heavy with boredom, suspicions and conformity. My brother and I pedaled our bikes endlessly, ducking into the Town Hall to slurp from the freezing water fountain. Or we sat atop May Hill, the limestone cliff overlooking a one-time hat factory converted into a bicycle seat company, breaking off chunks of cheesy stone and hurling them onto the corrugated tin roof of the reject shed. God, were we bored! We longed for an apocalypse, for the fuel oil tanks by the railroad to explode and suck the town into a fireball. Sometimes we'd set imaginary plastic explosives along the railroad tracks and do the job ourselves—like Burt Lancaster in *The Train*. My hometown's landscape of violence-inducing boredom stood in sharp contrast to the promise of heaven held out by those dreamy Italian courtyards: the dual landscapes of a divided human nature—destructive and contemplative, deadly and dreamy.

In her essay, "The Nature and Aim of Fiction," Flannery O'Connor writes, "The writer operates at a peculiar crossroads where time and place and eternity somehow meet. His problem is to find the location." Where and when would my dueling landscapes find their one home?

Whether we're writers or not, each of us, in her own way, is searching for that ultimate setting—not just for our stories, but for ourselves, for our souls, for a place to hang our emotional hats. Maybe that crossroads doesn't exist, at least not in physical time and space. Maybe it can't be pinned down by longitude and latitude. Maybe it only exists on paper.

It may be, too, that as fiction writers the only place we can ever safely call home is the one where dreams and ideas meet, where thoughts turn into words, sentences, and scenes, where moods, inspirations, and feelings are nailed down, as fixed on the page as the stars in the night sky: a sheet of paper.

The ultimate setting for all of our stories.

164 } RAGING & BLOWING: WHIPPING UP A STORM

Weather can add atmosphere and even psychology to our stories. Temperature is pain or pleasure; humidity is mood; barometric pressure is destiny (in terms of weather, but also in terms of human nature).

> There is something uneasy in the Los Angeles air this afternoon, some unnatural stillness, some tension. What it means is that tonight a Santa Ana will begin to blow, a hot wind from the northeast whining down through the Cajon and San Gorgonio Passes, blowing up sand storms out along Route 66, drying the hills and the nerves to flash point. For a few days now we will see smoke back in the canyons, and hear sirens in the night. I have neither heard nor read that a Santa Ana is due, but I know it, and almost everyone I have seen today knows it too. We know it because we feel it. The baby frets. The maid sulks. I rekindle a waning argument with the telephone company, then cut my losses and lie down, given over to whatever it is in the air. To live with the Santa Ana is to accept, consciously or unconsciously, a deeply mechanistic view of human behavior.

In Joan Didion's essay, "Los Angeles Notebook," the Santa Ana winds function as both setting and character, heralding but also instigating the narrator's deep depression. Similarly the fog that sets the stage in Dickens's *Bleak House* hangs metaphorically over the rest of his nine-hundred-page novel. The forest fire that provides the climax for Roxanna Robinson's novel *Sweetwater* grows organically—not just out of the drought-afflicted Adirondack landscape, but out of the smoldering relationships between characters. And of course there's the great storm on the heath in Act Three of *King Lear*, which rages as much within the baffled and buffeted monarch as without.

Another storm scene ends a student's novel-in-outline: A lot will depend on how it is set up. Is the hurricane an inevitable occurrence, or just an authorial convenience? Is it properly foreshadowed? Does it function metaphorically or symbolically, or is it merely there to make something happen in a story that otherwise would have been static? Is it part of the plot, or a substitute for the lack of one? If the plot hinges entirely on the hurricane, then the action has been taken out of the characters' hands and turned over to Mother Nature. The result would be a *deus ex machina* ("god in his machine"), an ending that doesn't function organically.

On the other hand, as in Didion's essay, the weather may play a central role in the drama—but that intention should be clear, or at least hinted at, from the start. A storm scene in a novel or story shouldn't be a random climactic act, but one ordained by and intrinsic to the story, that complicates or resolves a drama that is already stormy.

165} NOT IN MY BACKYARD: RESEARCH SETTINGS

When writing about a real place, it pays to research your setting. One can't arrive at Rockefeller Plaza via Madison Avenue, though a character in a story does just that. And I can't remember the last time I saw a "No Loitering" sign anywhere in Manhattan, let alone in Times Square, where the same character finds one. Furthermore one usually can't access restrooms in office buildings without a key or a visitor's pass; but this same lucky fellow does so. Quibbles, I know, but New York City is too well known to get details like that wrong.

We owe it not only to our readers but to ourselves to believe every word that we write. And though we're writing fiction, when that fiction is set in a real place—especially a famous real place— we should try to be as accurate and authentic as possible.

Readers want to believe. Why make it any harder for them than necessary?

Writing Books, Workshops, & Feedback

166} CAN WRITING (ESPECIALLY "CREATIVE" WRITING) BE TAUGHT?

I've been teaching for a dozen years and have written two books on the subject. Still, I wonder sometimes whether teaching writing is a waste of time. And worse: if my foolhardy attempts to teach writing create bad writers and worse writing.

Then I remember how much I've learned as a writer over the past thirty years. And if something can be learned it can be taught. Indeed, writing *must* be taught, because it must be learned. A born writer is as mythical a beast as the unicorn.

How do we learn? By trial and error, by imitation, by example, by osmosis, by prescription. We learn consciously and unconsciously, intellectually and instinctively. We learn through pain and through pleasure. We learn from our mistakes and from our triumphs. And we learn from the triumphs and mistakes of others.

The hardest lessons to learn are those that threaten our own self-preserving egos. The student who brings to class the conviction that he has already perfected his style and is just waiting to be discovered won't learn much from me—or from anyone; Tolstoy couldn't teach him anything.

Some say the only way to learn to write is to read. I agree. Teaching writing is, at best, a form of guided, annotated reading. We read the works of masters and we read the work of our peers, to say nothing of our own works, and we do so with an eye to craft and the technical issues raised and solved by craft.

What about inspiration? And intuition? Doesn't so much emphasis on "craft" impair those elements?

It can. An obsession with craft must not sweep away inspiration. That's why I tell my students that their first drafts are none of my business, nor the business of anyone else in the class; their first drafts are between them and their private muses. Similarly, I tend to give writing exercises only on demand, since they may circumscribe a writer's first and best instincts and steer him away from authenticity.

True, teachers have been known to inspire their students. But the mechanics of inspiration are at best murky. What inspires one may discourage another.

The key to teaching any form of art is to achieve a balance between instinct and technique. The relationship between will-power and art has always been heavily debated, with intuitive writers like Kerouac and Whitman at one end of the argument and formalists like Eliot and Pound at the other. Of that relationship Lewis Hyde says:

> There are at least two phases in the completion of a work of art, one in which the will is suspended and another in which it is active. The suspension is primary. It is when the will is slack that we feel moved or we are struck by an event, intuition, or image. The *material* must begin to flow before it can begin to be worked, and not only is the will powerless to initiate that flow, but it actually seems to interfere, for artists have traditionally used devices—drugs, fasting, trances, sleep deprivation, dancing—to suspend the will so that something "other" will come forward. When the material finally appears, it is usually in a jumble, personally moving, perhaps, but not much use to anyone else—not, at any rate, a work of art. There are exceptions, but the initial formulation of a work is rarely satisfactory … like a person who must struggle to say what he means, the imagination stutters toward the clear articulation of its feeling. The will has the power to carry the material back to the imagination and contain it there while it is re-formed. [It pro-

vides] the energy and the direct attention called for by a dialogue with the imagination.

As the muscles are exercised on playing fields and in gymnasiums, the creative will is exercised in classrooms and writing workshops.

167 } SLEEPING PILLS & LAXATIVES: BOOKS ON WRITING

And what of books about writing—like this one? Can we really expect to learn anything from them?

Like sleeping pills and laxatives, books about writing work best for those who need them least.

By working "best," what do I mean? I guess I mean they're best enjoyed by those who don't expect too much from them— those who don't expect to be taught "how to" write and who have already evolved certain aesthetic opinions and principles. For experienced writers, books about writing are like walking into a study and finding another author there, and settling in for a few hours of cozy shoptalk. The conversation may be one-sided, but it doesn't have to be: that's what pens and margins are for. I personally love to read writing books, if only to disagree with them, or just to see where and how my ideas differ or coincide with others'.

I'm not alone. Many of my writer acquaintances, some very successful, love to read books about writing: They find them relaxing, comforting, and even, at times, inspiring and edifying. A few even admit that they've learned things from them.

And what about beginners? Are writing books good for them?

I think so. I think books on writing can spare novices a lot of time and misunderstanding. They can point toward examples that may help them in their choices, open up possibilities that they might not have seen or considered, encourage them to delve into literature they've overlooked.

At the very least a book like this can make you think more and more deeply about what you, as a writer, have done and are doing.

What books on writing give us is *a little knowledge.* To get the rest you need to read stories and novels, all kinds of stories and novels, and lots of them.

And of course you need to write. Start with 500 words a day. Aim for a million words. They don't have to be the greatest words ever written, or great by any means, or even all that good. As long as you write sincerely, and keep writing.

Get through the first million words.

Then pat yourself on the back and write the next million.

But yes, except as a form of amusement, and to supplement the reading and writing by which you exercise your craft, books like this are mostly a waste of time.

168 } TOUGH LOVE: CONROY CUTS ME ONE

Like gymnasiums, workshops can be places of pain.

I speak from experience. Years ago, it was my privilege to participate in a workshop led by the late Frank Conroy, then director of the Iowa Writer's Workshop, whose memoir *Stop-Time* was one of my ten favorite books.

By the time I studied with him, Conroy had been leading workshops for thirty years—possibly too long: He seemed a bit tired, a bit jaded. Yet his first critique of my work (each student had two turns at bat) was, if anything, generous: He had only praise for the novel chapter I submitted. I had been forewarned that, if I was any good at all, Conroy would "cut me a new asshole," and so I wondered if I'd fallen short.

I didn't have to wonder long. My next time up, Conroy did indeed cut me a supplementary orifice. He read the first sentences of my new chapter out loud until he arrived at the word *preponder-*

ance. "At that point, I stopped reading," Conroy said, and by way of illustration flung my manuscript over his shoulders. The pages fluttered to the floor like the wings of a freshly beheaded chicken.

I waited for the burlesque to end and for Conroy to say something more. But there *was* nothing more; he *hadn't* read any more of that chapter. It was the harshest criticism I have ever gotten, yet it made the point: Don't show off.

As writer Robert Stone said, speaking of his own apprenticeship: "I never learned anything as a writer that didn't break my heart."

169} GIVING WRITERS THE BENEFIT OF THE DOUBT

There have been times when, as a teacher, I've wondered if I should ignore my own responses and give a student the benefit of that doubt. Have I been guilty of not granting my students the authority of their own words?

With experience, you can distinguish between writing that generates its own authority and writing that doesn't. And no: The difference *is not* obscured by poor grammar or mechanical difficulties (as demonstrated by a Chinese student of mine, whose English grammar was poor but whose stories shone with authority).

It's up to our stories to seduce their readers, and not up to our readers to give us the benefit of anything. In the artificial environment of the writers' workshop, classmates rarely surrender their authority to the writer. That's as it should be, since in real life that authority is surrendered *only when the work has been so well and deeply imagined* that it no longer needs to satisfy any terms other than those it has established for itself.

We write for an ideal reader: intelligent, sensitive, discriminating; immune to hype, free of prejudices, whose only loyalty is to good writing, and whose taste in such matters is ironclad. When people urge us to "give the writer the benefit of the doubt," they want to entrust him to a less-than-ideal reader, to someone less discerning, someone less demanding, someone more easily duped. We may as well throw his work out the window. Or just tell him it's wonderful (which may amount to the same thing).

Love the writer; respect the writer; honor the writer. But when there's a doubt, give the author its benefit by expressing your concerns, feelings, and criticisms, and let the author choose whether or not to reject them.

170} NO SOFT HITS FOR HARD WRITERS: WORKSHOP WOES

A student writes me a note:

> I was disappointed by the comments I got for my work. My piece was a first draft, yet no one bothered to ask what I was trying to do, or to consider that I might be up to something different from what they had in mind or are used to. My draft manuscript was returned to me marked up as if I were a complete novice, and not someone who has been writing for years.

I'm glad my student wrote this note to me; I wouldn't have guessed his feelings. Responding to it, I said first that I hoped my own comments had registered with him, since I remembered having praised the work highly. Then I went on:

> People in the class focused on the structural issue raised by your piece, the two sections not fulfilling each other, forming an incomplete and unsatisfying whole. You may need to accept that this may be true. It takes nothing away from your virtuosity as a writer, your solid gifts. Is the story perfect as written? You know it isn't. Did the class appreciate what you were trying to do, the risks you took? Probably not; that's asking too much of any workshop.
>
> Typically, the most accomplished work gets or seems to get the toughest criticism. The playing field is not even: Every story

sets up its own level of response and critique. The more accomplished the work, the higher the standards applied to it. It may well be that your work has run afoul of this formula. If you were thinking that, being a major-league hitter, it would be fun to slum with the minors, whack a few out of the ball park before their wondrous eyes, forget it. As a friend of mine once said (*a propos* tennis, not softball): You hit hard, I hit back harder. That's how it works in life, that's how it works in writing workshops. Few 'soft hits' for hard writers.

And why should you want them? I think the cruelest thing one writer can do to another is mislead them into thinking their work succeeds when it doesn't, or is ready to submit when it isn't.

One last thought re: people asking about your intentions. Those kinds of discussions are usually fruitless. I don't want people asking authors what they were 'trying' to do, or authors having to answer. Doing so degrades writers and authors; it backs them into defensive corners. And anyway explanations as to intentions are irrelevant; the work must speak for itself.

Suggestion: Latch on to the one or two people in the group whose comments you find valuable. Ignore the others. Including, if necessary, me.

171 } CARVED IN STONE: REFUSAL TO REVISE

I've now read three pieces by one of my students and frankly I'm starting to worry. He may well be the most intelligent and imaginative student I've taught, and certainly he's got talent and the energy to produce vast quantities of work.

But this won't do. Though he's added a sentence here and there, and expanded the material, he refuses to revise.

When I begin my fiction classes, I point out the two loves a person should have to be a writer: love of words and love of truth. Love of words: because to a writer they must be treated as gold,

Other Matters

weighed and measured and never wasted. Love of truth: because lies are everywhere, emotional lies as well as factual lies, and only fiction can dare to tell us the truth about how we behave, how we live. To convince us, things have to feel just right, with each word carrying more than its own weight and no room for the gratuitous. (Even mediocre work requires a certain regard for the truth—that is, if it is mediocre *and publishable*.)

What this student has in spades is a love of knowledge and ideas. But those two loves can only serve a writer in conjunction with the other two.

Practically everyone has ideas. Some have both ideas and the energy to put them on paper. But only those who take the next step can rightly call themselves authors.

And the next step is *to revise*, to get down to the painstaking task of sculpting truth with words.

172} FROM INFRARED PROPAGANDA TO ULTRAVIOLET SELF-INDULGENCE

In his workshop Frank Conroy spoke of the "reader/writer rainbow," the continuum between *private* writing—writing as an act of pure self-expression—and *public* writing—writing done to influence others, i.e., propaganda. These two extremes form the infrared and ultraviolet of Conroy's symbolic "rainbow."

The author's challenge, according to Conroy, is to achieve a balance between those extremes, so that our words communicate to the reader without either pandering or badgering. Public writing tells us what we *ought to* think and feel; private writing is the writer talking to herself. Near the center of the rainbow is the place where both extremes meet, where communication without didacticism is possible, where writer's words and reader's imagination engage in a healthy collaboration. And where, according to Conroy, all good writing happens.

In student stories, much of the writing falls on one end of the spectrum or the other, the private (ultraviolet), or the propagandistic (infrared). Things are vague, cryptic, or formless, or they are too directly stated or otherwise overdetermined. The reader is told too much, or too little.

To move them toward the center of the rainbow, to where writer and reader meet each other halfway, *that's* the writing teacher's main function.

Self-Confidence & What It Takes

173} IDENTITY CRISIS: THE WRITE STUFF

A student asks me, "Have I got what it takes to really be a writer? Will I succeed?" Confronted with similar questions, another writing teacher I know would tell his students, "Probably not." Those who didn't accept the verdict had "what it takes."

My response is different and depends on how one defines success. Publication, fortune, fame, rave reviews—all of the above? Do we measure our success based on the evaluations of others, or on our own? Does growth count, or only results? What's more important, the work we did yesterday or today, or the work we'll do tomorrow?

Here's what I believe: Every hour you spend at your writing, you leave the desk a better writer than when you started. If I didn't believe that, I'd quit myself. If I thought worldly success is all that matters, I'd die of despair.

I measure success according to where I've come from, and how far I've come, and what I've managed to do given my humble origins. Do I want worldly success? Sure. Do I crave and yearn for it?

Not so much anymore. Will I kill myself if I don't get it? Certainly not. If every day (or every other day) I can say to myself, "You've done your best and you're getting better," then that's enough for me to justify my existence.

I say write not to "succeed," but to improve. And you will.

And you'll publish. Though it will take time and—let's face it—some luck.

How long will it take? If the answer turned out to be *the rest of your life,* would you quit? Or would you roll up your sleeves and keep working? As long as you're willing, that's how long.

Since a writer is someone who writes, the better question is not, "Have I got what it takes to be a writer?" but "Have I got what it takes *to write?*"

174 } THE SPACES BETWEEN WORDS: WHEN WE'RE NOT WRITING

And when you're not writing, then what are you? Then you're whatever else you happen to be doing.

You're a reader, a mother, a sales rep, a stockbroker, a lawyer, a daydreamer, a butterfly collector, a nuclear physicist, a lap swimmer, a jewel thief. But even when engaged in other activities, the writer is often still *writing:* She's still *thinking* in words, forming sentences, smoothing out lumps in a story line, devising a plot twist, sharpening a simile or metaphor. Not all writing has to take place in front of a computer or a yellow pad. Nor is all writing a conscious or deliberate act. Much of it happens when we're least aware of it, behind our backs.[61]

They tell us matter cannot be created or destroyed. We can't write what we haven't in some way experienced, directly or indirectly, in

---

61 I'm reminded of James Thurber, who said, "I never quite know when I'm not writing. Sometimes my wife comes up to me at a party and says, 'Damn it, Thurber, stop writing.' She usually catches me in the middle of a paragraph."

fact or in fancy. A writer who never leaves her word processor will eventually run out of things to say; the well will go dry. A writer isn't only *allowed* to do other things; doing them is *obligatory.*

Knowing when not to write is as much a part of the writer's regimen as applying the seat of your pants to the seat of the chair.

As for what else it takes to write, I refer you back to Matters of Soul.

Final Matters:
All Our Stories Are in Us

175} Q: WHAT IS A DISTRACTING DEVICE?

A student's story strikes me as witty and intelligent, though I'm distracted by the story's quirky structural conceit: a question-and-answer format that's more eclectic and provocative than efficient or amusing. I couldn't help thinking of the Ithaca chapter of *Ulysses,* which also uses the Q & A format, but with a purpose—to parody the catechisms forced upon him in childhood.

I'm not sure what organic purpose, if any, is served by the device in my student's story, nor am I sure who's asking and answering all these questions if not an author with a penchant for calling attention to himself. And since I have no idea who the narrator is *except* via this quirky device, I'm left grabbing at straws.

Such devices and gimmicks are quite popular in these post-modern times. Novels are riddled with footnotes (David Foster Wallace), photographs (W.G. Sebald), charts and chemical formulas—or they are tattooed, one word at a time, on the bodies of volunteers *(Skin Project,* Shelley Jackson). Collage, pastiche, metafiction, fragmentation; novels that can be read backwards or forwards, or in any order *(Hopscotch,* Julio Cortázar); novels with the letter *e* missing *(La Disparation,* by Georges Perec[62]); cyberpunk, hyper and "maximalist" texts.

For a recent example of a work in which the narrator calls constant attention to herself through gimmicks, pick up *Special Topics in Calamity Physics,* by Marisha Pessl. Among other things, Pessl tries to make a virtue of her protagonist-narrator Blue van Meer's having plowed through every book in her college literature canon, by naming each chapter after a different classic and hypertextually linking events of her story with works referenced. If that's not impressive enough, she throws in her own gouache drawings and peppers her narrative with other bibliographic references. All this is very droll until it turns annoying, as do some of Pessl's overwrought similes ("Her eyes were shockingly beautiful ... sudden sneezes in the dull silence of her face"). Given the author's youth (she published the book at twenty-seven) and her obvious gifts, such excesses are more than forgivable. And—as the reviewer for the *Guardian Unlimited* noted of the novel—"after page 311 it is unputdownable."

Devices can serve a purpose. They can reflect elements of a plot or milieu, or carry associations germane and organic to a story's theme(s). Or, they merely aid and abet an author's irresistible urge to show off.

I'm reminded again of James Joyce, who loved his literary gimmicks and who was said to suffer from "association mania." At a party in his Paris flat, the writer Frank O'Connor noticed a map of County Cork in an unusual frame that called more attention to itself than to the map it served. O'Connor asked his host,

"What is that?"

Joyce replied, "It's Cork."

---

62 Translated as *A Void.*

"I know it's Cork," said O'Connor. "But what's the frame made of?"
"Cork," said Joyce.

176} WHAT WRITERS DO

And what do we writers do, essentially? We sit alone in a room. We sit there with a purpose, but we sit alone. We sit with ideas and characters and scenes, alone. We sit with dreams of artistic glory and even of fame or, better still, fortune, but we dream alone. We sit with heads full of thoughts, trying to sort them out, to get them to add up to something that might, just might, mean something to others. We sit longing to share things that so far have been ours in solitude, to make something out of this miraculous disaster: life. We sit and stare out the window, we water plants, sharpen pencils, answer letters, pay bills; anything but write, because as soon as we turn to writing we know, with certainty, that we turn to it alone: No one else can write what we must write. And so, we sit, and sit. If we're lucky it goes well, and if not, not, but still we sit alone.

We sit alone in a room.

Breaking the Rules

177} ASTONISH ME: BREAKING ALL THE RULES

Earth is round and open, whole and beating in its early years. Middle of the night, the stars a bright smear against the blackboard. Sit in the secret centuries-long lull. A breath pulled so gradually still; the breath forgets. Clouds slowly shift their shapes. Winds run back and forth. Our planet in the slowest pink floyd

> intro. Melted tears run, then freeze. Stubborn ice blocks will not
> be niced down by the fat sun.

Pedagogically, writing like this puts me in a delicate position. It forces me to have to defend a piece of work which on its surface violates every single law or rule of fiction writing, rules meant to apply loosely to traditional narratives. Here, though, tradition is violated at every turn, with a "plot"—the story of man's evolution from fish to present-day upright pink creature—woven from a series of staccato glimpses of changing habits of excretion. There are no traditional characters, no characters whose personalities are evoked with any particularity, or whose emotions we invest in or whose plights we care about. There is no conflict, no resolution, no dialogue. The effect of the piece is cumulative, rather than energeic or profluent, with motifs accruing through repetition, sentence by sentence, with the hypnotic insistence of a metronome or a hypnotist's watch. The experience as a whole is boggling, and yet, somehow, for me, anyway, satisfying.

This is writing that disarms, then charms. Beginning with its naughty title ("Pee on Water") it has already disarmed this reader, or begun to. Pee on *Water?* An imperative? A description? The title of a painting (like "figure in landscape")? With these first three words already I'm induced—compelled—to play the game not by my own stodgy rules but by the author's. The first sentence takes the disarming process further, invoking both the world's "ancient past" and the reader—myself—in a juxtaposition that should make me wary, if not altogether hostile. But it doesn't. Too curious to stop or to let my defensive instincts gird me, I read on to find "my" grandparents evoked (along with their bones) and furthermore to learn that I have fallen in love. By now the narrative's second person "you" has become a sort of Everyman or Everyperson, carrying me back to that nostalgic time before there were such things as floors and feelings. One short paragraph into the story, and we are—I should say *I* was—hooked.

The delicate problem for me arises when I have to explain the difference between this piece of writing and writing that's mannered, pretentious, forced for effect, or willfully obscure. It's a hard difference to explain, since this story is indeed hard to follow at times, and arguably obscure. Except that here, each sentence feels authentic and earned, as does the idiosyncratic punctuation and aggressive use of fragments. The writing says to me, from the start: *This is my world, with my rules: Abandon all predigested notions of fiction ye who enter here.* So intent is this author on breaking form she even resists numbering her pages with numbers, using capital letters instead. Here too this *should* annoy and offend. Instead, it charmed, in part because it's so consistent with the work's theme, which is, after all, evolution. And shouldn't a story about evolution be—well, revolutionary?

It's the confidence with which the writer shirks the rules, the quality of conviction that, like an armature of steel giving support to a sculpture, holds up this work and others like it and makes them succeed. Behind each word is the author's wit and fancy as she flies her rhetorical kite fearlessly up into the stratosphere. By page 3 I was cheering her on, hoping she'd bring me to a satisfying conclusion (one definition of a good story being *ten to fifteen pages of interesting prose with a good ending).* She did (again: for *me).* It's worth invoking Schopenhauer here: "Talent hits a target no one else can hit; Genius hits a target no one else can see."

Given that, I ask myself: What of writers like Joyce, Woolf, Faulkner, and Beckett; what of works like *Mrs. Dalloway* and *The Sound and the Fury,* let alone *Moby-Dick, Ulysses,* or *Watt?* How would they have fared in MFA programs, or at the hands of pettifogging fussbudgets like me? I wonder and worry, and so should we all. Some of you who've read the passage quoted above may think it a complete waste of paper and me a lunatic; for you maybe it was and I am. But can we be entirely sure that its author won't be the next Virginia Woolf—or Shakespeare (who broke a few rules himself)? But then, without rules, what fun is any game? Rules give us something to bounce the ball against and, sometimes, to tear down with sledgehammers.

Writing fiction is an art, not a science. We honor its conventions and rules as much for the pleasure they give us when brilliantly obeyed as for the occasional thrill of seeing them as brilliantly subverted or destroyed. It pays now and then to remember Diaghilev's challenge to the French poet Jean Cocteau, when Cocteau asked what he wanted from a work of art. "Astonish me!"[63] was the great impresario's curt response.

In exchange for being astonished, I'll happily take back *all* of the advice I've dispensed in these pages.

The Truth of Imagination

178} FROM AN OLD NOTEBOOK

"Never try to be professional, keep it smutty, write with bodily fluids on sandpaper, and damn the men with clipboards in white suits, the literary bean-counters, the prose police."

How to reconcile these words of mine with becoming a *teacher* of fiction writing—and with the whole notion of teaching and learning to write? With this book?

Maybe Joseph Campbell's words can help, or at least provide an antithesis:

---

63 "Etonnez mois!"

The crude notion that energy and strength can be represented or rendered by abandoning and breaking structures is refuted by all that we know about the evolution and structure of life … the mere shattering of form is for human as well as for animal life a disaster.[64]

There's no one answer; both statements are true. Each of us must strike our own balance between Apollonian impulses (harmonious, measured, ordered) and Dionysian (wild, orgiastic, unbounded), and this balance must develop (and will most likely shift) over time. I don't want to throw a wet blanket on anyone's literary orgies; nor do I want to wear the clinical white suit and badge. But then there's that other impulse, the impulse to say *Here's what you need to do to succeed; here is what you must do to bridge the gap between private self-expression and public communication.*

However we do it, somehow we have to find ways to put our own visions into the heads of strangers.

179} FINAL WORDS OF ADVICE

Which leads me to this next, last, and possibly best bit of advice— not mine, but E.M. Forster's:

Only connect the prose and the passion, and both will be exalted, and human love will be seen at its height. Live in fragments no longer. Only connect, and the beast and the monk, robbed of the isolation that is life to either, will die.

---

64 From *Myths to Live By.*

Other Matters

As fiction writers, our job is to give experiences to our readers. And what you yourself don't have you can't give to others. Since we can't fully live the lives of all of our characters, we have to let our characters do it for us through the instrument of the imagination that allows us to inhabit those characters and their experiences as fully, as richly, as deeply as possible. *I am certain of nothing but the holiness of the heart's affections and the truth of imagination.* Surrender to that instrument, trust its truths and find the forms that fit them best, and you'll write good—and even great—fiction.

Q. DO YOU THINK WRITING WORKSHOPS ARE A GOOD IDEA?

A. I do—up to a point. That point comes when you can no longer stand participating in writers' workshops. There comes a time when you simply don't want to hear twelve or more more-or-less random opinions about your work-in-progress, when you realize that of those twelve sets of opinions maybe one is worth anything to you. At that point you should consider cultivating a private relationship with that person, and ditch the group.

But feedback is important. As I've said elsewhere, if you can find one or two good readers of your work, people who understand and value your intentions and who can be constructively honest, treasure their souls.

Q. WHAT ABOUT BOOKS ABOUT WRITING? ARE THERE ANY WORTH READING?

A. I hope this one was worth reading. They range from purely prescriptive (nuts and bolts) to purely inspirational and philosophical. I tend to prefer writing books that are more philosophical, mainly because they tend to be better written, and also because they avoid pat formulas or "recipes." A novel may be many things, a pot of soup isn't one of them.

In choosing writing books to read, I look first to the author's style. If the author can't impress me with the sound of her own voice, I'm not that sure I want to apply her wisdom to mine. And since I don't separate style from substance, I distrust any advice dispensed through a poor style. That's just how I'm built.

A "poorly written writing book" would seem to be oxymoronic, and yet there are many out there. *Most* writing books are poorly written.

A handful that aren't:

> *The Lonely Voice*, Frank O'Connor
>
> *Burning Down the House*, Charles Baxter
>
> *The Art of Fiction*, John Gardner
>
> *If You Want to Write*, Brenda Euland
>
> *The Practice of Writing*, David Lodge
>
> *Aspects of the Novel*, E.M. Forster
>
> *Mystery and Manners*, Flannery O'Connor
>
> *First Paragraphs, Painted Paragraphs, Invented Voices*, Donald Newlove
>
> *Bird by Bird: Some Instructions on the Writing Life*, Anne Lamott
>
> *Art & Reality: Ways of the Creative Process*, Joyce Cary

Also:

> Joseph Conrad's preface to "The Nigger and the Narcissus"
>
> The letters of Anton Chekhov

Index